AGATE

By the same author

Biography
Saint-Saëns and His Circle
Sacha Guitry, The Last Boulevardier
(In French: *Etonnant Sacha Guitry*)
The Duke of Wellington
Massenet
Rossini
The Astonishing Adventure of General Boulanger
The Ox on The Roof
Gounod
Lost Illusions: Paul Léautaud and His World
Erik Satie
Folies de Paris: The Rise and Fall of French Operetta
Offenbach
Maurice Chevalier: His Life
Jacques Tati: Frame By Frame

Anthology
Lord Chesterfield's Letters To His Son

Translation
Francis Poulenc: My Friends and Myself

AGATE

JAMES HARDING

Methuen . London

First published in Great Britain in 1986
by Methuen London Ltd.,
11 New Fetter Lane, London EC4P 4EE

Typeset and printed and bound in Great Britain
by Richard Clay (The Chaucer Press) Ltd
Bungay, Suffolk

ISBN 0 413 58090 3

To the memory of
George Felton Mathew
and
Herbert Van Thal

'I wish I were anything rather than an actor – *except a critic*: let me be unhappy rather than vile!'

W. C. Macready

CONTENTS

LIST OF ILLUSTRATIONS

between pages ooo and ooo

ACKNOWLEDGEMENTS

The late George Felton Mathew, Agate's oldest friend and literary executor, gave me a wealth of valuable information. He died at the age of eighty-seven while this book was being written, and the dedication expresses some of the gratitude I owe him. With his name I link that of my dear friend the late Bertie van Thal, who published Agate and knew him well. Mr Dennis van Thal has also been kind enough to give me the benefit of his reminiscences. I am, in addition, much indebted to Mr Joseph Azzopardi, a companion of Agate's last years.

Members of the Agate family who have given help in research include his niece Mrs Ann Evershed Harries, Mr W. A. Evershed, Major James Agate and Mrs Grace Irwin. Mrs Margaret Snow (née Aspland) was informative about the early years.

Mr Anthony Curtis of *The Financial Times* enabled me to consult the script of the BBC radio programme he wrote to mark the occasion of Agate's centenary, and was most helpful throughout. It is a pleasure to acknowledge, as well, the assistance of Mrs Jean Huckett, Alan Dent's step-niece. Others who have very civilly aided my researches are: my old friend Mr Oliver Morchard Bishop; Dr Levi Fox, The Shakespeare Birthplace Trust; Mrs E. Gotch, The Royal Literary Fund; Mr L. R. Hiscock; the poet Mr Kenneth Hopkins; Mr Bernard Jones; Mr David Lee, Radio Times Hulton Picture Library; Miss C. Lingard, City of Manchester Central Library; Mr Tony Peake and Miss Kathleen Nathan, London Management; Mrs Anne C. D. Piggott, Times Newspapers Ltd.; Messrs Rubinstein Callingham, Agate's solicitors; Mrs Eileen Singleton, The Society of Authors; and Mr Jeff Walden, BBC Written Archives.

As always, my sincere thanks go to Miss Winifred Marshall for her secretarial skills and to Mrs Stella Mayes-Reed for her photographic expertise.

FOREWORD

Critics are by no means popular figures, least of all in the theatre. The dramatist is affronted when a play which might have taken him years of work is dismissed by a hasty judgment timed to catch the early editions. The actor is hurt in a peculiarly cruel way by disobliging remarks about his face, his voice and his physique. Yet, as Johnson said, the drama's laws the drama's patrons give, and each member of the audience, however ill-informed, however unjust, is entitled to express an opinion, since the very act of public performance invites criticism. Agate himself was not unaware of this. Having once been imprudent enough to dramatise one of his own mediocre novels, he stepped before the curtain at the first night after what seemed to be a favourable reception. He was greeted with a humiliating storm of boos and noisy execration organised by enemies in the audience. It was, you may think, a just return such as would have pleased many actors, among them Laurence Olivier who on one occasion actually hit him.

It often happens that famous Londoners are provincial by birth. Such was the case with Agate, who must be accounted one of the liveliest and most readable drama critics of the century. For twenty-five years until his death in 1947 he wrote about plays for *The Sunday Times*, mixing each week a heady blend of wit and erudition spiced with a zest that never flagged. The belligerent Lancashireman did not settle in London until the age of forty-six, and he used to declare that, except for the years spent in growing up and learning his craft on *The Manchester Guardian*, his time had been wasted until then. He soon established himself as a London personality with his pugnacious look and bookmaker's garb of hard bowler hat and loud check overcoat – though few bookmakers ever wore a monocle. The domain he ruled over was small and limited to the theatres of Shaftesbury Avenue, the Savage Club, the old Café Royal and the Ivy restaurant, with occasional trips to Paris for the Comédie-Française and a brothel whose custom he shared with Marcel Proust.

He has been described as 'a philistine with the equipment of an intellectual'. His passion for golf, cricket and Hackney ponies was complemented by an encyclopaedic knowledge of Balzac, Zola and the nineteenth-century French theatre. At the end of a career remarkable for dogged industry he calculated that he had written over seven million words. 'I was asked tonight why I won't have truck with intellectuals after business hours,' he once said. 'But of course I won't. 1. I am not an intellectual. Two minutes' talk with Aldous Huxley, William Glock, or any of the *New Statesman* crowd would expose me utterly. 2. I am too tired after my day's work to man the intellectual palisade. 3. When my work is finished I want to eat, drink, smoke and relax. 4. I don't know very much, but what I do know I know better than anybody, and I don't want to argue about it. I know what I think about an actor or an actress, and I am not interested in what anybody else thinks. My mind is not a bed to be made and re-made.'

Drama critic to *The Sunday Times* and the BBC, book reviewer on *The Daily Express*, film critic in *The Tatler*, pseudonymous contributor to dozens of other papers, he was urged on by the demon of work. He felt unhappy if no deadline threatened, no editor was screaming at him over the telephone, no messenger boy was clamouring for copy. His relaxations were frenetic. Although he was one of the highest paid journalists of the time, his debts, he flattered himself, were Balzacian in scale. Extravagant in all things, he could deny himself nothing – the best champagne, the finest wine, dynamite-stick Havanas. He would hire a taxi just to cross the road, and then keep it waiting for him into the early hours of the morning while he played bridge at the Savage and took a masochistic pleasure in the thought of the meter ticking away pound after pound. Bailiffs, moneylenders and tax collectors lurked everywhere on his path. Nearly forty years after his death his doctor has not yet been paid and the Inland Revenue still waits patiently for its due.

Around him he gathered a circle of people who, though they might be failures in the worldly sense, were admitted as cronies purely on the ground of their wit or their charm. They included an ancient Jew of infinite malice to whom he was devoted, a former chorus boy once beloved of Oscar Wilde, sturdy ex-boxers and a host of working-class lads who adored him. He could play the nastiest of tricks, as Beverley Nichols found, and then, surprisingly, could do the nicest things. For he was a riotous mixture of egotism and thoughtfulness, bravado and humility, ostentation and reserve, meanness and generosity. In his will he even remembered his favourite rent boys.

A great character? Yes. A great journalist? Yes, and in the mould of George Augustus Sala. The quick eye and lightning reaction of the born journalist are evident in those nine irresistible *Ego* volumes of autobiography. True, he sometimes reviewed a book without reading it, or a play or a film without seeing it, but so do most journalists. A great critic? That was what he wanted to be known as, and to this end he zealously reprinted his newspaper articles in book form. His chief duty, he believed, was to record the great acting he had seen. He certainly exerted an authority which could persuade his readers to buy theatre seats, as was proved by his campaigns for *Journey's End* and Wolfit's Shakespeare seasons.

Vivid writing, trenchant expression and acute watchfulness make his record of the London stage from the nineteen-twenties to 1947 an indispensable source of reference. But was he, as obituaries claimed, the Hazlitt of his age? It is time to decide.

JH

Chapter One

MASTER JAMES

All my life I seem to have been 'putting myself forward', as my old nurse used to say.

James Agate

i
DRAPERY AND THE THEATRE

I inherited none of my extravagances from my father, who was a man of the simplest tastes, never spent a penny on himself, and never bought a new hat until my mother made him.

JAMES AGATE

The name Agate is a corruption of 'Heygate' and should be pronounced, not as if it were the precious stone, but with an open 'a'. The bearers of it had links with the Evershed family in Surrey who traced their ancestry back to the seventeenth century and who number among their descendants Lord Evershed, Master of The Rolls. William Evershed (1784–1865) took as his second wife Mary Dendy, born Agate and a first cousin to James of that name. This James (1792–1866) married an Elizabeth Evershed (1792–1854) and ran a prosperous linen drapery in Horsham. His two sons were brought up on the strictest Unitarian principles. The younger of them, Charles James Agate, born in 1832, showed promise for the drapery trade and was sent to London where he served a three year apprenticeship with a wholesale linen draper. In the warehouse he met a fellow apprentice called

Gustave Garcia, grandson of the musician who sang Almaviva in the first performance of *The Barber of Seville* and nephew to those dazzling prima donnas Pauline Viardot and Marie Malibran. The young man's uncle was, for good measure, Manuel Garcia II, who settled in London, became a well-known singing teacher, and lived so long that he was able to take part in a festival to mark his own centenary before he died at the age of 101.

Gustave was to be a lifelong friend of Charles James Agate. He represents that side of the industrious linen draper which cherished music and the theatre. The other side never allowed his love of art to interfere with the important business of selling cloth. When Charles Agate's father died he left his son ten thousand pounds which helped to establish the young man as a cotton manufacturer's agent in Manchester. The business flourished since he was as prudent in the office as he was at home. Household accounts were recorded to the last penny, and he always tried as a matter of principle to keep his annual outgoings below two thousand pounds. After his death it was discovered that this upright man had once been guilty of cheating for the only time he succeeded in achieving the magic figure of less than two thousand pounds was when he slyly erased his annual subscription to the Lancashire County Cricket Club and transferred it to the following year.

In the eighteen-seventies he met a young woman by the name of Miss Eulalie Young. She and her sister were descendants of the eighteenth-century actor Ned Shuter and of a famous Harlequin. The girls' mother rarely spoke of these glamorous antecedents, believing that a sensible education was more important for a well brought up young person than the dubious excitements of the theatre. Mrs Young had lived in France, spoke and wrote excellent French and German, and could make lace as fine as a spider's web. Having been widowed at an early age she gave piano lessons to earn money for her daughters' education and charged what was then the remarkably high fee of a guinea a time. When rich people complained of the extra shilling she would declare: 'You pay your specialist in guineas, so why not me?'

And she was right, for she had a reputation as the best piano teacher in the North of England.

She sent Eulalie to school in Paris and Heidelberg. Miss Young, after being thoroughly grounded by her mother in the art of playing the piano, went on to take lessons from a Madame Heinefetter who in her time had been a pupil of Chopin. This, of course, was to obtain a professional competence and certainly not to prepare her for a career in public. As soon as she was ripe for her début, Miss Young was smartly recalled to Manchester and work as a teacher of the piano. For all that she had been educated in Paris and studied, unknowingly, with the young Sarah Bernhardt whom she was later to know well, her duty lay in Manchester and not with improvident theatre folk and itinerant musicians. Yet her strong-minded mother was by no means a harsh or abstemious figure. When prosperity attended she would allow herself and her family a barrel of oysters and a Stilton cheese. If she restricted her daughter to twopence a week pocket money, on visits to the Continent she would gaily spend a hundred pounds or more. As she lay dying she refused all drugs to relieve pain except when she knew her daughter was to call. Only then would she accept morphia to help her put on a calm and smiling face. 'She cannot do her work if she sees me suffer,' she murmured to the nurse.

The daughter whose feelings she had so touchingly striven to spare became the fiancée of Mr Agate, an established businessman some ten years older than his future bride. After an engagement long enough to satisfy Victorian convention Miss Eulalie Julia Young turned into Mrs Charles James Agate. The couple set up house at Ivy Bank, Sedley Road, Pendleton, which in fact belongs to Salford, although residents in that genteel neighbourhood liked to feel they were a part of Manchester. On the 9 September, 1877, their first child entered the world. It was a boy whom they christened James Evershed, the second name being a gesture towards the Horsham cousins. In the following year appeared Charles Gustave, so named after his father's dear friend Garcia. Over the next ten years came Sydney, Edward and Harry Bertrand. The five sons were joined in 1882 by a daughter to be called

May. She had been born, said a verse written by Mr Agate and handed to Mrs Agate together with a large diamond ring on the day of her birth, 'as a blessing to her mother.' Being something of an afterthought to so many brothers, of whom James was fifteen years her senior, May often felt isolated. Later on, when asked if she were related to James Agate, she would reply: 'Distantly. He is the eldest of six and I am the youngest.'

Life at Ivy Bank was a contented round smoothly sustained by the number of servants deemed proper for a family of that class and period. There was a nurse called 'Old Jane' who stayed with the Youngs and then the Agates for half a century, having first, at the age of sixteen and pregnant, entered the service of Grandmother Young. She remained to tyrannise over both adults and children, and even Mrs Agate was a little afraid of her. When she died her place was taken by Lizzie Barson who ruled with a strict but loving kindness. Lizzie's dramatic readings from *Count Funnibos and Baron Stilkin* were the rage of the nursery. So impressed was the six-year-old James that he proposed marriage to her. She was touched but not as flattered as she might have been had she known that only one other woman was to receive such an offer from him.

His earliest memories were of lying in bed at the top of the house as the smell of his father's cigar drifted up the staircase. From below came the sound of his mother or his aunt playing Chopin, Schubert or some flamboyant piece by Weber. Mr Agate, who disdained the telephone and scorned to set foot in a motor car, would each morning take a carriage to the office and, each evening, would return at seven o'clock. Sometimes there was a dinner party when silver was unwrapped, glass was polished and the dining table bloomed with unaccustomed flowers at the direction of a waiter borrowed from Mr Agate's club. James's mother would look in at the nursery to kiss him goodnight, and he saw a beautiful woman dressed in a maroon silk gown flounced with ivory lace. She wore white flowers in her red-gold hair, and a gold chain and locket. Sometimes she let him into the secrets of her dressing table and allowed him to pour a few spots of scent on her handkerchief. It was a simple essence called White Rose which she preferred to modish perfumes like Opoponax and Ylang-Ylang. They were, she said, 'actressy'.

Despite the Nonconformist allegiance of the home, despite dreary Sunday visits to the Unitarian chapel where a myopic parson delivered exhortations in a fateful monotone, the atmosphere at Ivy Bank was relaxed and artistic. As the children grew up and one by one graduated to the adult dinner table they were intrigued to hear their father talk about the theatre. He was a connoisseur of acting and would speak with critical enthusiasm of the players he had seen in his youth. The memory of Barry Sullivan, Fechter, Charles Mathews and Samuel Phelps was furbished and kept alive by those conversations over the dessert. And Irving? While lacking the sense of tragedy, contended Mr Agate, he was the greatest English actor in melodrama and held more pathos in his little finger than Fechter had in his whole body.

From time to time the company was joined by Gustave Garcia. He had given up the linen trade, had studied singing in Milan and was now a teacher at the London Royal College of Music. The old man – 'old,' that is, to the children – impressed them with his tousled black mane and burnt-out eyes. Self-willed, temperamental, indiscreet, he hugged them at meetings and, while he kissed them, roughened their skin with a moustache that bristled horribly. 'My aunt used to say . . .' he would remark, and they quivered with excitement as they realised he spoke of la Malibran, for whom Alfred de Musset had written poetry, or of Viardot, whom he would always describe as 'ugly as a horse.' Then, in his lovely voice, he would sing Mozart and Lulli, or invest with a rare beauty Gounod's trifle 'Au Printemps'. When May was a girl and interested in singing she asked him why it was more difficult to sing an upward scale than a downward one. He pointed at a window-cleaner operating nearby. 'Is it not easier to fall off a ladder than to climb it?' he asked pityingly. 'Do not be so stupid.'

Although as a teacher he could be arrogant and crushing, his 'piopils', as he called them, loved him. For thirty years he spent each Christmas with the Agates and, as a seasonal treat, would sing them Mozart arias with the ornaments, still unpublished, which his aunt Malibran used. He joined the Agates on their summer holidays too. Often he brought rod and line with him to fish in the pond of the house they had taken.

'But,' James pointed out, 'there are no fish in the pond.'

'I don't want feesh,' retorted Garcia, 'I don't like feesh – I enjoy feeshing!'

So it was that round the dinner table of a strictly Unitarian household marooned in grim grey Manchester the talk was mostly of theatre and Italian opera. Given Mrs Agate's background it is not surprising that each child, when of an age, had to learn how to play a musical instrument. At seven o'clock every morning he or she would knock at their parents' bedroom door, give their name, and proceed downstairs for practice. Soon there arose from different rooms the cacophony of several pianos and fiddles all being played at the same time. Mr and Mrs Agate put up with a lot in their liberal wish to help their children acquire a means of self-expression. But, as Mr Agate often warned amid the squawks of an impromptu string quartet, music and the theatre were 'monkey tricks' to be reserved for private hobbies and not taken up as a profession. As for actors and actresses, he said with a humorous twinkle, they ought to be 'shut up in cages, like wild animals, and let out to perform.'

ii
W. G. GRACE AND BALZAC

> One of the boys has got ringworm, which only goes to show what a nice person Miss Duffield is. (Letter home from the schoolboy James.)

For James at the age of six the big event of the year was the seaside holiday. A yellow cab with red plush lining called at the door and took the family off to the railway station. The children skirmished for a window seat and feverishly counted the names of the stations as they flitted by, or speculated on the mysterious contents of the luncheon hamper. Then they arrived at their lodgings where hydrangeas flowered at the door and the bedroom window looked over to Puffin Island and the sea. Old fishermen from last year were sought out and questioned about shrimping prospects. Most important of all was the state of the tides, in other words the hours when cricket could be played on the beach.

For even at that early age James was a cricket fanatic. As soon as he could read, his permanent bedside book was a volume bound in yellow paper which appeared every Christmas during his childhood under the sonorous title of *John and James Lillywhite's Cricketer's Companion with which is incorporated Lillywhite's Guide to Cricketers*. The two Mr Lillywhites saw cricket not as a matter of county games but as an affair of public school and university, of the M.C.C. and of travelling clubs like the I Zingari, The Gentlemen of Yorkshire and the Uppingham Rovers. They told how Mr W. G. Grace, after receiving a testimonial and disappearing into the obscurity of county cricket, had played sixteen consecutive seasons and completed 415 innings in first-class matches, obtaining in all 20,842 runs and taking 1,349 wickets. Statistics are not the lightest of reading, but those sober columns of figures were heady stuff for a small boy entranced with the game. They suddenly came to life a year later when, at the age of seven, he was fooling around with bat and ball on the sands at Blackpool. A very tall man with a luxuriant black beard came up and paused to watch him. He said he would like to bowl, and James, defending the two walking sticks that served as wicket, hit him all over the place. Politely, he offered his small bat and enquired: 'Perhaps you, Sir, would like an innings?' The gentle giant took up his position and James bowled. The soft ball hit a pebble and whizzed over the sand. The big man saw too late that if, with his size and large belly, he tried to get down to the ball with the tiny bat, he would most probably rupture himself. So he stood back and let it fly on between the walking sticks. James had bowled out his opponent for a duck. Mr Agate, who was supposed to be fielding at square leg, put down his *Financial Times* and laughed. 'That was W.G. Grace,' he said.

On a day of cricket not even love nor hate, nor battle nor murder, could have distracted James until the sun went down behind the trees and shadowy figures crept out to draw stumps. Jessop was a hallowed name for him, Jessop whose heroic stand at a sodden wicket triumphed with 104 runs out of 139 in an hour and a quarter, Jessop who scored a century within forty minutes against the pride of Yorkshire bowlers. The golden age of Lancashire cricket was summed up for him in the names of A. N. Hornby, A. C. MacLaren, Mold and Tyldesly. His native county held its head high and feared only Yorkshire. Of course, he was open-minded enough to appreciate non-Lancashire men such as the elegant 'Ranji', the virtuoso Macartney and the pugnacious George Hirst. During summer holidays at Appletreewick, where a friendly farmer let the Agates have the use of a newly mown field, the boys played cricket all day long under the tolerant eye of their father, who, though getting on for sixty, solemnly donned formal pads and gloves each time. James kept the score. He did so in a manner which ensured that his own performance at the wicket ran no danger of being underestimated.

Holiday succeeded holiday and with them came walking tours which began in Rosthwaite at Derwentwater and led to the wearying conquest of Great Gable and Scafell Pike. Toiling along a road in the lakes one summer he heard a terrible snorting as of some dragonish monster. Leaping out of the way up a bank he saw a motor car pant round the corner at the alarming speed of twelve miles an hour. He, also, took in time to wheels, though in this case a bicycle, and as a young man claimed to have traversed every cycleable inch of Yorkshire, Derbyshire and Westmorland. How pungent was that cycling suit in Harris tweed! How exhilarating that last long run of the day at sweat pearled handle-bars knowing that a warm bath and a soft bed were near at hand! But a puncture unmanned him. He knew you did something with a bucket of water, 'solution' and sand paper. As for adjusting the back wheel, a hearty bash with a coal hammer would probably do the trick.

Yet the cricketer, the Dales walker and the bicyclist was becoming at the same time a bookworm and an aesthete. On the drawing-room table at home lay a copy of the newly published *Yellow Book* sparkling with Beardsley drawings. It appeared at around the time of his first pair of trousers, which, herring-boned cashmere, matched his natty black jacket. For ever after he associated the lavender coloured garments with that *Yellow Book* which his parents forbade the children to read. Naturally he ignored the embargo as soon as he could, and was puzzled to find, at the end, advertisements for the wholesome novels of Stanley Weyman and Conan Doyle. Already he preferred stronger meat. His Meredith phase was succeeded by a Kipling phase, and at one time there was even a Henry James phaselet. George Moore's *Confessions of a Young Man* intoxicated him with its glorious nonsense while making a Francophile of him. It was Moore's essay on *La Vieille Fille* which led him to Balzac. Out of curiosity he took up that bulky handbook by Cerfberr and Christophe which catalogues every detail and every character of the vast novel known collectively as *La Comédie Humaine.* Browsing through those closely printed pages he was transformed into a Balzacian even before he had read any of the novels.

From childhood and into his teens he devoured Balzac. Rastignac and Diane de Maufrigneuse were real people who haunted his imagination. He came to know every corner of the Paris which Balzac depicted in the eighteen-forties, and he could cite from memory each item of furniture in the shabby *pension* run by 'Madame Vauquer, née de Conflans'. He learned how Parisians in the early nineteenth-century should approach the wife of their patron, and the tone you adopted in speaking to a *rat de l'Opéra*, a money lender or a ballet dancer. The shape of the earrings worn by the Chevalier de Valois was engraved on his mind, and he knew by heart the jokes perpetrated by the irrepressible Bixiou. The gigantic bankruptcies and tortuous financial intrigues of Balzac's world inspired him with the desire, never fulfilled, to write a novel whose plot would outshine even the commercial exploits of César Birotteau and the speculations of père Goriot. More practically, the shifts employed by Maxime de Trailles to keep his creditors at bay were to give him useful tips for the conduct of his own adult life.

A little later he contracted the Rougon-Macquart rash from those sprawling volumes in which Emile Zola traces the natural and social history of a family under the Second Empire. There were, he decided, three men in Zola: the artist, the scientist and the social reformer. Of these three it was the artist that fascinated him most. He concluded, perceptively, that Zola's greatest asset was his tremendous power for sheer story telling. What could be more thrilling than the final scene in *La Bête Humaine* where a driverless train rushes to disaster with its freight of soldiers shouting: 'A Berlin! à Berlin! à Berlin!'? And what more moving, more pathetic, than the little phrase that ends *L'Assommoir:* 'Fais dodo, ma belle!'

As a child, as an adolescent, he explored by-ways that few children with his background might be expected to know. He passed from the sardonic wit of Barbey d'Aurevilly to the comedies of Marivaux and Beaumarchais, from the romantic breast-beating of Rousseau to the gaiety of Casanova. In Théophile Gautier and Jane Austen he found enchantment indifferently. Dickens supplied a portrait gallery into which he dipped each time with new enjoyment. Behind closed door, starting guiltily at each footfall outside, he pored over Foxe's *Book of Protestant Martyrs* and a shameful *Putanisme d'Amsterdam*.

Pale by comparison was Sir Walter Scott's *Old Mortality* which he was ordered to read as a holiday task. Scott could never rival the exotic delights of the French and other writers whom he had found out for himself. Sent to boarding-school at Giggleswick, that place which can never be mentioned without a smile, he quailed beneath the remote cruelty of a clergyman headmaster who set algebra exams of inhuman difficulty. His school reports, even so, were not unpleasing. He came first in English, Latin and History, and, towards the end of his stay at Giggleswick, maintained his place as first in French while sinking steadily downward in mathematics. His French master little knew how much his fluency owed to dubious publications like *Le Putanisme d'Amsterdam*.

There was plenty of cricket to be had at Giggleswick and quite a lot of theatricals. James played Harpagon in Molière's *L'Avare* and revelled in the lace and flounces he donned for the part. This love of clothes, of dressing up, was splendidly gratified at the 1887 Jubilee celebrations. An exhibition was opened in Manchester by the Prince and Princess of Wales. Since Mr Agate was one of the guarantors young James had a favoured position to observe the ceremony. He wore a kind of sailor's pea jacket with twelve gold buttons and a cap embroidered in gold letters that spelled out 'H.M.S. Invincible'. This was accompanied by a lanyard and heraldic devices representing anchors and jib-booms on the sleeves. Knickerbockers, cream socks and white kid gloves completed an ensemble which rivalled the outfit of the Prince himself in frock coat and top hat of unbelievable gloss It had been arranged that proceedings should open with the first verse of 'O God, Our Help in Ages Past.' Now the Princess of Wales, later Queen Alexandra, suffered from extreme deafness. Unaware that the one verse had been concluded she launched bravely into a solo rendering of the next. Whereupon James, who was sitting very close, saw and heard her consort dig her in the ribs and snap in a gutteral German accent: 'Shut up!'

After a few terms at Giggleswick Mr Agate decided that his eldest son was playing too much cricket and imbibing too little learning. He took him away and sent him to the Manchester Grammar School, where, under the tutelage of a formidable master, he made better progress. The tyrant sat before his class, chair tilted back, feet on desk, and stroked his walrus moustache with nicotine-stained fingers the while his beady eye struck terror into the hearts of boys. One day the High Master walked in. The class held their breath to see if their master's sway over them would be challenged. They were disappointed. Continuing to jangle his keys and scrape his moustache, he watched his superior cross the room and snarled: 'In future, when you honour me with a visit, be good enough to shut the door!'

iii
IRVING AND BERNHARDT

'. . . whatever Rachel and Duse could do Sarah did almost as well; that which she did supremely they could not attempt.'

JAMES AGATE

Now that he was back in Manchester as a day boy at the Grammar School he could enjoy more of the artistic pleasures which the city offered. There were many of them.

A large colony of Germans flourished at that time in Manchester. They had come there for business and had brought their culture with them, a culture which they understood by the word music. The founder of the Hallé Orchestra, the friend of Chopin, Liszt and Berlioz, was a German born with the name of Carl Halle. Sir Charles Hallé, as he became, was later the husband of the violinist Madame Norman-Neruda whose elegant playing for many years charmed Manchester and the world. In the eighteen-nineties the permanent conductor of the Hallé Orchestra was Hans Richter, intimate colleague of Wagner himself, veteran of Bayreuth and a pioneer of *The Ring* in England. The Royal Manchester College of Music was directed by the plump and genial Adolf Brodsky, sometime leader of the Hallé Orchestra and a close associate of Brahms and Tchaikovsky. The first violinists in the orchestra included Siegfried Jacoby, who taught Edward Agate to play the instrument. He was much given to tea, hot buttered toast and mordant wit. Once James was deputed to play the piano part in some dauntingly fast *concertante* and ended up in a state of exhaustion. 'Vell,' murmured Siegfried, 've finished together, und dat is something.'

In a typical week it was possible to see a new play by Galsworthy on Monday and to hear a concert by the Brodsky quartet on Tuesday. Wednesday might feature a Bernhardt matinée and Thursday a Hallé concert with Richter and Busoni. On Friday there was a private performance of Ibsen's *Ghosts*, then a banned play in England on account of its immorality. Much of this activity was due to German Jews who, while prospering in the textile business, knew that there were other things to be treasured besides calico and cotton, and were, moreover, ready to spend their own money generously on the arts.

James went to his first Hallé concert at the age of seven. He and his father sat on red plush seats in a yellow four-wheeler cab which took them to the Free Trade Hall. Places had been booked so that he could see Hallé at the piano, a view of his fingerwork being considered beneficial to James as an aspirant pianist himself. The boy thought Hallé a nice old gentleman but not so fiery an executant as Mrs Agate, the former pupil of Heinefetter. Many times afterward he was to hear Norman-Neruda play the Mendelssohn concerto, a thin gold bangle fluttering wildly up and down her bowing arm as she pounced and grappled with swirling runs. He saw that noble ruin Charles Santley in *The Messiah* giving forth the sound of a lion in *delirium tremens*, and Albani majestic in ruby velvet, and Edward Lloyd intoning 'Comfort Ye' more beautifully than he ever heard it sung afterwards. He remembered Hans Richter directing the first Manchester performance of Tchaikovsky's *Pathétique* Symphony, and, throughout the second movement, putting down his baton and letting the orchestra conduct itself. All the great pianists came to the Free Trade Hall – d'Albert, Busoni, Backhaus, Rosenthal, and the energetic Teresa Carreño who walloped through the B flat minor Tchaikovsky concerto with all the vigour of a blacksmith at the forge. Perhaps it was she who inspired the boy to compose a piano concerto. It is a *presto* seven bars long, one for each of his years, with a multitude of grace notes, arpeggios and repeated chords. At the bottom of the manuscript a childish hand has added:

> 'Publishersh to
> 'Her Most gracious Magesty the quen
> 'His most Gracious Magesty Prinse of Wales
> 'and to His Imperail Majessty Napoelan III
> 'Publishers
> 'Boozey & Co.
> 'London.'

All slow movements, decided James, were too long, and nothing later was to change his mind on the point. Beethoven especially was a grave offender and could easily have cut three minutes from the Allegretto of the Seventh Symphony. Recitative bored him horribly, as did pretty well everything Bach wrote. There were vast areas of Brahms which drove him into a deathly trance. He could not stand Schumann and loathed all the piano pieces, especially the one entitled *Grillen*. On the other hand he loved the tunes in Weber, Nicolai and Cherubini. Once every season a statuesque lady would bawl 'Ocean, thou mighty monster,' with a mouth that looked big enough to swallow as well as address it. And he adored the voluptuous meanderings of Strauss with, naturally, torrents of Wagner conducted by Richter in the proper German manner, all beer and 'baccy stains.

As for the drama, he had early experience of that, too. His first pantomime, and his first visit to the theatre, was *Bluebeard*. It had topical jokes about Gladstone and a leading lady whose ample contours were mobled in black silk. After the matinée he bored the adults by re-enacting the whole piece until bedtime. A little later came *Robinson Crusoe* with Vesta Tilley as the principal boy. Man Friday sang 'I want yer, Ma Honey', and Vesta trilled ditties about following in Father's footsteps, the Piccadilly Johnnie and the swaggering recruit. When she immortalised the joys of flirting at the seaside the audience joined in a chorus which attained a certain measure of poetry:

'From the sad sea waves back to business in the morning,
'From the sad sea waves to his fifteen bob a week,
'Into a cook shop he goes dashing,
'Who should bring his plate of 'hash' in,
'But the girl he had been mashing
'By the sad sea waves.'

Even the newspapers agreed with James that *Robinson Crusoe* had been a wonderful affair, for did they not print, in the theatre advertisements, at least twelve times over, the legend 'gorgeous pantomine' and 'enormous success'?

Since at school he had himself acted Shakespeare's Cardinal Wolsey, Molière's Harpagon and Corneille's Le Cid, he was anxious to see how matters were ordered on the professional stage. The first words of Shakespeare he heard in the theatre were those of Orlando in *As You Like It:* 'As I remember, Adam, it was upon this fashion . . .' Orlando was played by Frank Benson with Mrs Benson as Rosalind. His first experience of Shakespeare had excellent credentials. In the years that followed he was to hear Benson in *Coriolanus* saying: 'There is a world elsewhere', and, overcome, to burst into tears. He remembered Benson's entry in *King Lear* bearing Cordelia in his arms, Benson's gnarled walk across the stage as Hamlet, and Benson as Caliban hanging upside down from a palm tree. What had his father's world of cloth and factories and ledgers to offer him one half so precious?

When he saw Sir John Martin-Harvey he learned that a great actor was not necessarily dependent on great plays. For decades that handsome Romantic toured as the hero of *The Only Way*, a melodrama based on Dickens's *A Tale of Two Cities*. It was tosh, but it enabled him to create beautiful moments, among them the occasion when he spoke of his self-sacrifice: 'It is a far, far better thing that I do . . .' Hackneyed over the years, parodied by comedian after comedian, those words in Martin-Harvey's liquid voice never failed to move his audience. At the same time, he felt there were occasions when it was his moral duty to defy the box-office and to mount good plays. Thus one evening James cut short a Richter concert at the Free Trade Hall and rushed to glimpse him in the last act of *Hamlet*. It was spoken with ineffable beauty. There lingered about him a quality of feyness which served him well in another of his 'uncommercial' plays, *Pelléas and Mélisande*. Mrs Patrick Campbell put it into words when, about to go on as Mélisande to his Pelléas, she greeted his luminous presence with: 'You look like a great moth!'

His fellow-knight Sir Johnstone Forbes-Robertson came before James's view one October evening in the eighteen-nineties. He was already half way through his career and, like his colleague, often toured claptrap, which in his case was Jerome K. Jerome's *The Passing of The Third Floor Back*. James waited many hours outside the theatre to see his Hamlet. Though the eyes were sunken and the brow was trenched with lines, much of his striking beauty remained. His gestures had as pure a loveliness as his speaking of the verse, and his hands, more expressive than any James had seen on man or woman, added a richness of meaning to the lines. Yet although he acted with passionate care, he freely admitted that he did not like acting much and was relieved when it was all over. In spite of which he was generally accounted the most popular Hamlet since Irving.

Both he and Martin-Harvey served their apprenticeship at the Lyceum under the eye of Sir Henry Irving. Martin-Harvey often revived his old patron's *The Lyons Mail* and followed Irving's example by playing the dual role of Lesurques and Dubosc. At the fall of the curtain he would step forward and say: 'Everything I do in this famous old piece I learned from my great master. With every fibre of my being I ask you to believe that my performance is not a patch on his.' The young Agate could believe him, for he had himself seen Irving and was ever afterward to use 'the old man', to give him the nickname people spoke behind his back, as the standard for appraising all actors. Irving was in his early fifties when James first experienced the power this dominating personality exerted over the theatre. When people said that he was 'always Irving', James would agree if, by that, they meant that to every part he brought a touch of Mephistopheles. No-one else could make the faces that Irving displayed in his various roles: macabre, jaunty, diabolical, pathetic, saintly, regal. A sardonic humour peeped through everything he did, a hint of the eerie and the grotesque which was wholly and uniquely Irving. He suggested mystery and aloofness, arrogance with an odd hint of sweetness, and blandness underlain with malevolence. When, as Hamlet, he said: 'I will speak daggers to her, but use none,' James could see his eyes actually looking them.

Irving's voice and legs had their faults but James, like the rest of the audience, was mesmerised into forgetting them by the gestures, the faces, the deportment. Just after Irving made his entry in *The Bells*, and even before he had shaken the snow from his coat, he had gripped every heart and soul in the theatre. In his portrayal of the character Mathias he suggested unheard-of depths of pathos and torment. For years afterwards the unhappiness of that first act would come back to James in all its unforgettable emotion. After an evening of this great player his sleep would be disturbed by vivid pictures of Irving as Dante and his expression when he saw Ugolino starving in his tower, of Irving as Dubosc in *The Lyons Mail* with a face like a dirty hatchet, of Irving as Shylock the Sephardic Jew, stiff and noble. James was in the Manchester Gaiety Theatre the night after Irving died. His partner Ellen Terry had the lead in Barrie's *Alice Sit-By-The-Fire* that evening. Just before the end she spoke the lines: 'I had a beautiful husband once, black as the raven was his hair . . .' At which she broke down utterly. The curtain dropped in silence, everyone filed quietly out of the theatre, and they left her to her sorrow.

The greatness of Irving was, for James, parallelled in a different way by Sarah Bernhardt. He saw her for the first time in Manchester round about eighteen-ninety when he was thirteen or so. How small yet how important he felt, as he jostled grown-ups in the queue! The sunset of a warm September evening changed gradually from blood-red to mauve, and a single star began to shine. The poster on the wall of the theatre showed a delicate woman posing wistfully against a background of white camellias and silver stars. Once inside the dingy theatre he waited a long time, his blood throbbing with expectancy. The curtain rose on *La Tosca* and an opening scene of exquisite tenderness. Later there was *La Dame aux Camélias*, that venerable tear-jerker which Sarah transformed with her genius in the same way as Irving did *The Lyons Mail* and Martin–Harvey *The Only Way*. In her role as the dying courtesan Marguerite she looked up at her lover Armand and said: 'Tu ne sais pas? Nichette se marie . . .' The happiness she put into the lingering syllables – 'Ni-chette se ma-rr-ie!' cut James's heart to ribbons.

On her visits to Manchester Sarah performed the repertory which she toured all over the world. In *Pelléas et Mélisande*, the French original which Martin-Harvey and Mrs Patrick Campbell did in English, Sarah acted Pelléas. There was a scene where Mélisande sits at a window in the tower combing her long hair. From off-stage came the sound of Pelléas hailing her: 'Holà! Holà! Ho!' The voice that spoke those words, thought James, was the sweetest and the most child-like he had ever heard. Mélisande asks who is there, and the reply comes: 'Moi, moi et moi.' The subtle repetition of that banal pronoun flooded his mind with happiness. Sarah was getting on for fifty then. Her eye was not so bright, her step perhaps not so firm as it once had been, but on stage the effect of youthfulness, of awed innocence, was overwhelming. By contrast her delivery of the famous alexandrine in the classical tragedy *Phèdre* –

'C'est Vénus toute entière a sa proie attachée' –

stormed the audience with a fine frenzy of self-loathing. And when, in Victor Hugo's melodrama *Ruy Blas*, she spoke the line,

'Elle avait un petit diadème en dentelle d'argent',

the caressing tone and the crystal diction had the music of lyres and flutes.

The newspapers talked much about the coffin she slept in at night, of her lovers, of her pet cheetah and of her extravagant private life – talk which, it must be admitted, was encouraged by Sarah the publicist. But Sarah the artist was a different matter. In that domain she kept a supremacy which compelled recognition. Once, at the Midland Hotel in Manchester, James saw her return from a performance of *Pelléas et Mélisande*. As she walked through the winter garden all chatter ceased. Hard-headed cotton manufacturers took off their hats. Businessmen, open-mouthed, paused in their conversation. Everyone stood.

He had, then, while still only a boy in Manchester, witnessed some of the finest acting the nineteenth century could offer. In a paraphrase of Dr Johnson he was to maintain that 'if anybody thinks Irving was the greatest English actor of modern times and does not say so, he lies. If he does not think so, he is mad.' As for Sarah, half sylph, half rainbow, she had created visions so strangely troubling that they evoked in him a state not far from anguish. Much later he realised that the ache of *Tristan and Isolde* and the glory of *Antony and Cleopatra* had all been anticipated for him on the

September night in Manchester when he first came under the spell of Sarah Bernhardt. 'Her acting on that evening,' he said, 'unveiled for me the ecstasy of the body and the torture of the mind.'

Chapter Two

COTTON MERCHANT AND CRITIC

'Here then are the reasons why I love my country [Lancashire]. We invented the word 'jannock', which means the square deal and no nonsense. We do not beat about the bush. We wrap up nothing. We do not care a tin hoot for anybody. We don't mind liking you, and we don't mind if you don't like us. We inhale tripe, and exhale fish and chips. We wear hard little hats on our hard little heads. We are as common as dirt. We are the salt of the earth, and you can do what you like with the sugar.'

James Agate

i
HORSES

'Perhaps it may fairly be said of me that no dramatic critic has ever showed better ponies, and conversely that no exhibitor of ponies has written better dramatic criticism.'

JAMES AGATE

At the age of eighteen he left Manchester Grammar School. The Speech Day of 1896 took place, as usual, in the Free Trade Hall. Here, on an earlier occasion, he had heard Joseph Chamberlain, Lord Mayor of Birmingham, government minister, deliver an important speech. In the course of it he said: 'Will the young gentleman sitting on the fifth ventilator on my right kindly get down?' That young gentleman was James.

At his last Speech Day he also won distinction of a kind.

He mounted the steps and, as part of the ceremony, recited Don Diègue's speech from Corneille's *Le Cid* which begins:

'O rage! O désespoir! O vieillesse ennemie!
N'ai-je donc tant vécu que pour cette infamie!'

Unfortunately, like Sarah on her 1879 visit to London and with another famous tirade, he began on too high a note and left himself with nothing in reserve for the climax. This, combined with his perfervid delivery, raised unkind laughter. When it was over he confessed to his father that, as an actor, he feared he was not much good. 'I agree with you, my boy,' said Mr Agate genially. 'Not worth a damn! And never will be!'

The shades of business were closing in. From school he went to Mr Agate's cotton mill in the Lancashire town of Nelson. There he learned how to weave cloth so efficiently that he could run four looms at the same time, although he never mastered refinements such as 'tackling' and 'overlooking.' Another useful art he picked up amid the hellish clatter of machinery was that of lip-reading, something which later came in very handy when attempting to decipher the speech of inaudible actors. Much of the time, also, he furtively read Archer's translations of Ibsen which he concealed in the weft-tin.

At Nelson, mixing with the factory hands and listening to their talk, he contracted a mild form of socialism. This he quickly shed when, in 1897, he left the mill and joined his father's office in Manchester. In the years to come he sold millions of yards of calico, velveteen, sateen and flannelette. From Manchester went shirtings to Calcutta and draperies to Buenos Aires. Samples were brandished, deals agreed, contracts signed. You did not, he realized, need to know much about cloth – what you needed to know was the customer you sold it to, his thoughts and his psychology. One of the most successful Manchester dealers at the time was a German Jew totally ignorant of calico but extremely knowledgeable about the South Americans to whom he sold vast quantities of the stuff. Outwardly James lived in a world of Acceptance at Sight, Draft at Thirty Days and Bills of

Lading seen through a mist of C.I.F. and F.O.B. Yet while his lips mechanically dictated 'our best offer 10,000 No. 17 shirtings at 11/9d. Aug–November equally, cannot improve or leave over', his mind was filled with Lucien de Rubempré, with Rastignac and with Félix Gaudissart, who, though a commercial traveller, had a Balzacian glamour which the Manchester Cotton Exchange failed to provide.

Toiler in the vineyards of Philistia as he probably reckoned himself to be, the calico he despised earned him up to four hundreds pounds a year, a sum which then represented over thirty times the purchasing power it has today. His expenses were small. As a young bachelor he lived at home in the solid comfort of his father's house. There was plenty of money left over to buy good seats at the theatre, tickets for concerts, books, magazines, clothes and dinners in fashionable restaurants. After less than a year he put by enough to go on his first trip to Paris, the city he had read so much of and dreamed about so often. With him travelled Fritz Dehn, a Hamburg Jew whose maternal uncle was Bismarck's doctor. Fritz worked as apprentice to a Manchester shipping firm and in time became a very successful businessman there. He had charm, wit and a lightness of touch quite different from the other serious young Hamburg lads who came to make a living in Manchester. Unchanged by triumph or disaster, he weathered commercial slumps with gaiety and *panache*. He was to become James's closest friend, and James stood as best man at his wedding and as god-father to his firstborn son Paul, subsequently a talented writer and critic. During the 1914–18 war, for obvious reasons, he changed his name from Fritz to Fred, despite James's outraged objections. This was the only difference they ever had in over half a century of friendship.

Once in Paris the two young men hurried to the Café Anglais, a Balzacian stronghold that James had always wanted to visit. Here was a place renowned in Balzac's day, a monument that breathed the atmosphere of the *Comédie Humaine*. They dined alone, in sombre grandeur, except for two emphatic English ladies demanding tea and toast. When they left an old waiter closed the doors in melancholy fashion.

Next day they understood why, because the Café Anglais had shut for ever and had entertained its last customers.

The main reason for James's trip was to see the actress Réjane, who, unlike Sarah Bernhardt, never came to Manchester. As a child bred in the theatre from her earliest years she had been praised by the writer Barbey d'Aurevilly, an incident which made her a piece of history even in 1897. Yet there was nothing fusty about her *jolie-laide* appearance, the wide-awake little face with its hint of mockery and its refusal to be shocked. Perhaps not at her best in tragedy – she lacked the needful serenity and repose – she had blazing temperament and a hoarse voice that challenged and provoked. She was, above all, a Parisienne with generations of *gaminerie* behind her. An August heat-wave blazed over the city when James saw her, and perhaps, made languid by the weather and the smallness of the audience, she just walked through her part. At the end of the second act his Lancashire bluntness could not be repressed. He sent her a note backstage: 'This is impermissible,' it read. 'I am a young man who has come all the way from England to see the best actress in the world, and you are not acting.' In the next act she stirred herself to give a magnificent performance. At the final curtain she came forward and dropped a little bow to James who sat all on his own in the front row.

Then it was back to Manchester and cloth and dusty ledgers. He kept going, though, and to such effect that in 1902 he became a partner at a salary that varied between two and four thousand pounds a year. He was twenty-five then and had acquired expensive tastes, not the least of them being harness horses. It is quite possible to throw away as much money on showing Hackneys as it is on betting at racecourses. Eagerly he drank in the lore of the show-ring and made himself an expert on the Hackney's stamina, its conformation and its turn of speed. He came to love the high-stepping little creatures and the moment when, before entering the arena, they were stripped of their rugs and emerged a miracle of sheen. The show-Hackney in its prime was, he thought, a dream of poise and pose, majesty and courage. The beat of its hoofs fell on his ear more sweetly than the music of any concerto. He did not grudge the outlay on leather and livery that enabled him to cheer his stout-hearted *First Edition* as it competed with a giant of a horse to win the Southport Championship. Round they went, the big horse stepping out majestically, the smaller one outshining him with fussy self-importance. When *First Edition* in a flurry of spume and white socks had done ten laps to his rival's nine, the judge gave him best. It was a glorious moment, and one only to be equalled when James saw himself in a photograph printed by *The Live-Stock Journal* with the caption: 'Live-stock Men of Mark, No. 35. Mr James Agate.'

At Crewe sales he mixed with copers, jobbers and auctioneers, loving the talk of deals and the slang he heard in Northern accents all round him. It was at Crewe that, infuriated by a bid of thirty-five guineas for a horse that had cost him eighty guineas some weeks previously, he swore he would buy the next animal that appeared. This was 'Vivianette', soundness to be doubted, conformation poor, and he got her for a silly price of twenty-six and a half guineas. Her points were not ideal, but she had a wealth of intelligence and courage. Twelve hours' slog over the Derbyshire hills left her fresh as when she had started. She could trot forty or fifty miles in a day without problems. Outside village inns she waited while her master refreshed himself, and then, when she judged he had enough, would tap discreetly at the snuggery window. He doted on the bright bay and her fourteen hands' worth of pluck and staying power. She was succeeded by many others with a litany of gracious names; the colt 'Rose Knight', the gelding 'Smokeless Diamond', the mare 'Black Tulip', the stallion 'Vortex', and 'Ego' and 'Cassilis Sonnet', 'Volpone' and the rest. If he fancied an animal he was ready to buy at any price. And that was the price he usually paid.

What was the lure of the show ring that he found it irresistible? He admired a show harness horse, he said, in the way he admired an Irving or a Talma. To praise a horse that runs faster than his rival was like praising an actor because he gabbled quicker than another. A show horse in the ring was an actor whose performance could be judged. Each harness class had its mystery, and every clue that helped to solve it was publicly on view. The spectacular exhibition of the horse's merits gave it an excitement which was unique.

Harness horses were but one of the things that exercised his critical spirit. For he now knew that nature intended him not to be a creator but to be an appraiser of other artists' work. In his early twenties he wrote a play called *The After Years* which he soon realized was melodrama of the most bombastic type. Later in life he was to perpetrate another play and three novels which are of small import. To be a critic, on the other hand, was to be a discoverer. Criticism was the joy of making discoveries and the pleasure of sharing them with your readers. It meant placing and defining a book, a poem, a symphony, a cricketer, a Hackney horse, a picture. It inspired the righting of old wrongs and the starting of old thrills at the mention of a long dead mummer. It concerned argument and arbitration among present-day supremacies and evaluating their divers 'points', to use a term from the show ring. Most of all, for Agate himself, it involved a sentimental wish to perpetuate the transient glory of an actor or actress who for an hour upon the stage had moved or astonished him. And the critical faculty had been with him as long as he could remember, as far back as when, an infant of five or six, he had surveyed one of his mother's visitors and declared: 'I like you all but your boots, Miss Pickering.'

ii
MANCHESTER GUARDIAN

> 'A professional is a man who can do his job when he doesn't feel like it; an amateur is one who can't when he does feel like it.'
>
> JAMES AGATE

When Agate was a boy his mother said to him: 'Jimmie, I want you to make me a promise. I want you to promise me you won't smoke or drink until you're twenty-one.' He made the promise and kept it. On his twenty-first birthday, the 9 September, 1898, he was in London for business. He went to the old Salisbury Hotel where Mr and Mrs Agate had spent part of their honeymoon. Here he smoked his first cigarette and drank his first whisky and soda. He enjoyed them vastly.

At the same time as the smoking and drinking promise was mooted, his father remarked: 'I'm going to ask you to make me a much more difficult promise – to have nothing to do with sex until you're twenty-five.' The promise was duly made. There is no evidence that he did not keep it if we except an incident when the nineteen-year-old boy, suffering from tonsillitis, was horrified to see his young night-nurse jump into bed with him and stay there all night. Next morning, in priggish outrage, he implored the doctor to send her away.

How, then, did he occupy his leisure hours until the fatal age of twenty-five was reached? He used jokingly to instance his cricket playing, his football, his strenuous walking tours of the Lake District, his bicycling trips up and down the Dales, his showing of Hackneys. More seriously, he was now a dedicated theatregoer. He saw everything that Manchester had to offer and most, on frequent trips there, of what London could provide in the way of good playgoing. In January, 1906, he wrote a letter on some theatrical subject to the Manchester *Daily Dispatch*. The editor printed it and asked for more. As a result it was agreed that he should contribute a weekly drama criticism for the rest of the year. Agate, by his own account, suggested that at Christmas the editor pay him what he thought his articles were worth. The *Daily Dispatch* owed a great deal of its prosperity to the racing coverage it provided, and when its new drama critic presented his credentials at the theatre, resplendent in his loud check overcoat and horsey clothes, the box-officer manager treated him with a deference born of the impression that he was the newspaper's racing tipster 'Carlton'.

Whenever he attended the theatre Agate carried in his pocket an article already written as insurance against nerves or drying up. However fine a writer you may be, however graceful a stylist, unless you can put together anything up to a thousand words in an hour or so ready for the press, you will never be a drama critic. You must report the play as news, you must criticise, and you must put something unique of yourself into it. You either have the gift or you haven't. Bernard Shaw had it. Henry James, most obviously, did not. From this apprenticeship dates the obsession with misprints that dogged Agate for the rest of his career. He noticed that if he made a reference to Sarah Bernhardt it would invariably appear next morning as Sarah Dewhurst or some such travesty. So he developed the habit of staying at the newspaper until two, three or even four o'clock in the morning to read his proofs over and over again. Only his robust constitution enabled him to be in his office five hours later ready for another day of selling cloth.

The Christmas Eve of 1906 duly materialised and with it the last of Agate's forty-six articles. Several versions exist of the way in which his connection with the *Daily Dispatch* ended. Neville Cardus, a Mancunian who knew him well in those days, says that he used the word 'hypergelast', which he borrowed from Meredith, in a notice of a French farce. It means someone who laughs excessively. The editor did not laugh at all and, according to Cardus, demanded his resignation. As Agate told the story, he asked the editor to honour their original bargain. A cheque for seven guineas arrived with an accompanying note to say that five had been contemplated, but that, owing to the 'superior quality' of the work, the figure had been increased. So he had poured out the best of his blood and brains for a trifle! In his fury he gave the cheque as a Christmas present to the cabman who had regularly driven him to the theatre. At other times he said he had gone round to his tailor and treated himself to a winter overcoat. Either version is equally believable. What does beggar credulity is the financial arrangement. Would Agate, however much the tyro journalist, have agreed such a contract, given his ten years' experience in the hard-selling cloth trade?

No record survives of these 'prentice articles for which the *Daily Dispatch* paid some twelve pence each. Agate's own press-cuttings book was abandoned during his early London years when, for a reason unknown but easily guessed at, he was obliged to quit his lodging with extreme speed; and the newspaper files in the British Library for this period have large gaps caused by German air raids. The articles served, however, a very useful purpose since they had been noticed with interest at *The Manchester Guardian*, and soon afterwards he was asked to join that paper as a junior drama critic. He assuredly did not earn a great deal more there because the editor C. P. Scott paid wretched fees. Such was the prestige of the journal, which was then enjoying a golden age, that keen young writers who worked for it valued an occasional word of praise from the laconic, authoritative Scott more highly than a rise of fifty pounds. Although he delegated expertly and gave his full confidence to the men who wrote it, especially in the sphere of the arts which he did not know so well as politics or international affairs, he read every word in every edition. Certain words and phrases were banned, among them 'commence', perhaps on account of its genteelism. Things did not 'commence' in *The Manchester Guardian*, they 'began'. Neville Cardus once used the phrase 'from thence' and received a courteous rebuke from Scott. He dared to argue that Fielding had used it in *Tom Jones*, and so had Smollett. 'Did they?' replied Scott. 'Neither Mr Smollett nor Mr Fielding would have used it twice in my newspaper.'

Scott's Puritanism vetoed words like 'sex'. He did not like 'basically'. He detested puns. A sub-editor who worked many years for the paper once gave to an item about the cinema being threatened by the growth of the radio a headline which read: 'Tragedy in reel life'. Scott immediately sent a memorandum: 'Is this intended as a pun? It looks perilously like one.' The sub-editor was so distressed that he thought of resigning. But Scott had a sense of humour, reserved, very wry. After much argument by his advertising manager he was persuaded to have the name of the paper displayed outside the office in neon lights. 'Very well,' he agreed, 'but only on the condition that it does not twinkle.' One scandalous anecdote alone is told of him. On the occasion of Pavlova's visit to Manchester she was shown around the newspaper offices and danced a tarantella on his desk. The fiery ballerina was interrupted by the entrance of Scott himself, who surveyed the scene with bristling beard and popping eye. Pavlova jumped down, threw her arms round his neck, and shouted: 'O, you *sweet* old man. I *lov* your white 'airs!'

The 'All-Father', as his employees called him, was high priest of a temple where the worshippers looked up to fine writing as a sort of Holy Grail. The Chief Reporter was a tall, witty, elegant man called Haslam Mills who later went into advertising as a star copywriter with the old London Press Exchange. He insisted on, and was given, a room with a view of the church of St Martin-in-the-Fields in Trafalgar Square so that he could, each evening, draw inspiration from the flocks of starlings gathering round the spire. This helped him to immortalise the claims of manufacturers of armchairs, pots and pans in copy which is esteemed by romantically minded advertising men. In his *Manchester Guardian* days he was no less dedicated. Neville Cardus was summoned to his office one Friday and told, an accolade this, that he had been chosen to review an appearance by Little Tich at the Manchester Hippodrome on Monday. He would be allowed to sign the notice with his initials. 'I don't want you to have any social engagements on Saturday or Sunday,' stated Mills. 'I want you to be alone. Tomorrow, Saturday, if it is a fine day, I want you to go for a walk. Go to the fields of Cheshire. Go alone, Cardus, and meditate upon Little Tich.'

Agate came to know Mills well, although he was more concerned with acting as third string to C. E. Montague and Allan Monkhouse. Montague, the senior drama critic, set a high standard of honesty and integrity in his reporting, and his volume *Dramatic Values* was Agate's permanent bedside book. He was a shy, kindly man who wrote standing up like Victor Hugo at what seemed like a writing-pulpit. Deeply absorbed in his own writing, he said little about the work of his younger colleague, let him go ahead and make his own mistakes, and apologised profoundly on the rare occasions when lack of space forced him to cut an article. An appearance of Bernhardt in Manchester might draw from him an apologetic note: Mr Agate wrote so charmingly about the theatre of Molière, but would he just for once allow Montague to attend the performance, and would he mind, as a special favour, accepting seats that night for *Are You A Mason?* which he understood was a topping little farce? Next morning, under the initials C.E.M., there would appear an article so full of graceful wit and learning that Agate blushed to think of what his own stammering effort would have been like. When the 1914–18 War began Montague was too old for the army. He dyed his white hair and enlisted. 'Montague,' said a friend, 'is the only man whose hair, through courage, turned black in a night!'

His second in command was Allan Monkhouse, author of many clever plays and novels whose insuccess failed to blight a sweet and youthful nature. In old age he remained boyish and quoted joyfully 'There's sap in't yet!' when Agate enquired after his health. Though he knew London and Paris he preferred to live in Disley and to compose immaculate journalism for the newspaper he loved. The velvet glove, though, concealed a claw. Of Bernard Shaw he once wrote: 'He is a wonderful person who can be everything but human, and even that sometimes . . .'

Manchester Guardian reporters were the envy of all Northern newspaper men. They began at £4 a week and progressed by infrequent rises of five shillings or so. Their real reward lay in writing for a paper that was liberal, civilised and cultured. The leader writer was a Balliol man with the Lancastrian name of Herbert Sidebotham. He did not limit himself to politics but, in the Scott tradition, was ready to write about anything. When the music critic was unable to attend the first Manchester performance of *Der Rosenkavalier*, Sidebotham went at short notice and produced a magnificent review. Though he might take an hour to find his first sentence, once he had it on paper the rest of the article wrote itself. He knew everything and forgot everything. The tall, clumsy, barging frame concealed a mind of purity and precision.

Soon after Agate joined the *Manchester Guardian* a young lion from Oxford called George Mair was recruited to help on the drama side. Any feeling of rivalry was soon swept away by Mair's good fellowship. He had a buoyant zest for life, an insatiable curiosity and an endless capacity to absorb facts. Once he went on a six-week holiday and returned with a *History of Literature for Schools* which began with the Venerable Bede and ended at James Joyce. He had written it without consulting a single book, and on checking found that only six dates were wrong. Always keen to wring every experience dry, he was not familiar with the meaning of the word 'No'. Into his short life of thirty-nine years he packed more than most men would into an existence of eighty. Even at the *Manchester Guardian*, that shrine of meticulousness, his fastidious temperament evoked admiration. 'Man,' whispered a Scottish reporter, 'he once telephoned a semi-colon from Moscow.'

Yet another colleague, briefly, was Ernest Newman, who wrote on music before moving to the *Birmingham Post*. His clear, vigorous style pleased Scott, who had sometimes been a little uneasy with the lyrical moods of Samuel Langford whom Newman succeeded. This style drew on a treasure of wide erudition. Born with the name William Roberts, Newman had spent fourteen years as a bank clerk in Liverpool, where he devoted his evenings to studying music, philosophy and languages. After immersing himself in Rationalism and other 'progressive' ideas he felt that he was 'a new man in earnest', and thenceforward wrote under the sobriquet he made famous. He was almost entirely self-taught and had equipped himself with a formidable range of knowledge that extended from Schopenhauer to the niceties of Finnish grammar. Yet for all his intellectual *hauteur* he dearly loved the sensual delights of wine, good food, witty conversation and, above all, a fragrant cigar. He adored gambling and was a knowledgeable critic of boxing. 'Performing fleas!' he would snap disgustedly in his flat Liverpool accent when two contestants failed to make the blood run. He had much in common with Agate, and a decade or so later the two men were to share adjoining columns in *The Sunday Times*.

Over the next seven years Agate was a happy man. He worked for a newspaper where he could begin a music-hall review with the phrase 'Et in Arcadia . . .', aware that no illiterate sub-editor would strike it out and that it would, on the contrary, be passed with an approving smile. He still carried with him to each first night an article written in advance should he be found wanting at the crucial moment, but he never had to use it. Every Tuesday the best part of a column bearing the initials 'J.E.A.' was to be found next to those signed by the illustrious 'C.E.M.' and 'A.M.'. As time went on Montague wearied with age and Monkhouse fell ill, so that by the arrival of the 1914–18 War most of the drama criticism devolved on 'J.E.A.' assisted by George Mair.

There were three 'legitimate' theatres in Manchester then, the Royal, the Princes and the Gaiety. On their stages, at one time or another, all that was best in contemporary drama could be seen and heard, from the polished comedy of Sir George Alexander to the tragedy of Duse, from the classicism of Forbes-Robertson to the Ibsenite fire of Mrs Patrick Campbell. Agate soon learned that what an artist intends is very different from what the critic or the play-goer thinks he intends. Benson once gave a performance as Richard III which drew forth an ecstatic appreciation from Montague. The critic detected all manner of symbolism and a masterly presentation of Richard as an artist. Why, though, had Benson left out the famous words: 'I cannot do it; yet I'll hammer it out'? Presumably the cut was essential to his reading of the part? Determined to settle the matter, Agate forced his way into Benson's dressing-room and was received with the actor's usual courtesy. Why had he left out those vital words? He didn't, said Benson mildly, think they mattered. Agate referred to Montague's praise for his interpretation of Richard as an artist. All this was quite new to him, responded Benson, and he'd never had the slightest intention of suggesting it. And how, Agate persisted, had he hit on the moving gesture which Montague praised so highly as summing up the whole interpretation? 'That is a brilliant thought on the part of your friend,' said Benson. 'But I confess the idea never entered my head. To me it has just seemed that to rise on my elbow would be theatrically effective.'

Mrs Patrick Campbell burst upon the provincial darkness

in Pinero's *The Second Mrs Tanqueray* as a star who could shine in her own right beside French and Italian luminaries. Turning her head to reveal the sweep of throat and chin, or flooding her voice with a certain intonation, she sounded a characteristic note of restless importunity, of pleading for more than life could hold. Agate had an acute ear for inflections. When he heard George Alexander deliver the line 'Your conduct is despicable' with the accent on the second syllable of the epithet, he rebuked him in his notice for ignoring the rule about throwing the accent back. At a later performance he heard Alexander say: 'Your conduct is . . . *dastardly*.'

The Gaiety Theatre had just been taken over by Miss Horniman. This pioneer of repertory derived her fortune from the Hornimans Tea company founded by her grandfather and was known to all as 'Hornibags'. In the Midland Hotel where she held court wearing sage-coloured brocade and a corsage covered with green dragons, she startled the habitués by openly smoking cigarettes. She was forgiven by intellectuals because she introduced Manchester to what was called the play of ideas. Money from tea financed productions of Euripides, Shaw, Galsworthy, Masefield and Verhaeren. For a time it looked as if, thanks to her patronage, a Manchester school of dramatists was to emerge with Allan Monkhouse and Stanley Houghton, author of *Hindle Wakes*, as its gifted leaders. The *Manchester Guardian* dutifully supported her, though Agate was not alone in finding an air of gloomy strenuousness about this high-thinking venture. But the Gaiety Theatre could laugh at itself – and at Agate. Lewis Casson produced a one-act play by Allan Monkhouse called *Nothing Like Leather* and dedicated it to Agate, who appears as a critic under the barely disguised name of 'Topaz'. Miss Horniman actually played herself, and with a satirical enjoyment that surprised her respectful company. Agate coached the actor playing 'Topaz', who made frequent reference to Sarah Bernhardt, and lent him, for extra realism, one of his own flamboyant overcoats which were notorious throughout greater Manchester and in places where they show Hackneys and play cricket.

Agate was also a pioneer in his way, and, through his acquaintanceship with the actor Courtenay Thorpe, arranged the first Manchester performance of Ibsen's *Ghosts*. No-one has heard of Thorpe these days, although Bernard Shaw speaks very well of him in his drama criticisms. Many people thought him the ghostliest Ghost ever to appear in *Hamlet*, his mien suggesting the infinite spaces, his voice coming from a world unknown to man. The effect of eeriness was enhanced by the glove he always wore to conceal the stump of a hand mutilated in a shooting accident. When Agate saw him play Prince Hal in *King Henry IV, Part II*, it was the first time he had witnessed real tears being shed on stage. This impressed him, and he said so in a favourable notice. The result was an invitation from Thorpe to supper at the Midland Hotel. He arrived and found awaiting him a tall, gaunt figure that looked as if it had been rejuvenated by some alchemist's brew. Was he twenty-four years old or eighty? He always seemed either one or the other, nothing in between, and the casual onlooker would probably have thought him twenty-four. His elaborate make-up, crowned with an auburn wig, presented a strange beauty, glassy and unalive. 'That work of art, Thorpe, haunts me,' said Ellen Terry once to Bernard Shaw.

Underwritten by the German merchants who were Agate's customers, the production of *Ghosts* succeeded in convincing a number of people that Ibsen was not really the disgusting subversive he was claimed to be. It also inaugurated a friendship with Thorpe that taught Agate a lot about acting. He was an extremely good actor, and at three o'clock one morning, while they were discussing his interpretation of the line,

> '. . . the undiscover'd country from whose bourn
> 'No traveller returns . . .',

he produced an expression of such ghastliness that Agate was reduced almost to a jelly with fear.

Despite his artistry Thorpe often found himself without engagements and between times ran a flourishing antique shop which made him more money than his acting. His little house was decorated with ornate mirrors and rich tapestries. A very grand piano of ebony and gold stood silent in a corner, and the bedroom, like that of a ruined *belle marquise*, contained a bed of scarlet lacquer with hangings to match. For hours through the night the rococo Thorpe discoursed in choice accents about acting and the people he'd known. He spoke of Sarah Bernhardt in the box of a New York theatre forced to watch some fashionable actress slog through *La Dame aux Camélias*, and of the actress bowing to her at the final curtain and of Sarah applauding graciously while muttering under her breath 'Cochonne! Cochonne!' He recalled his old friend Ellen Terry at a supper party in that house. At the end, swathed in mufflers, imprisoned behind a large pair of spectacles, she prepared to enter the cab ordered for her. 'Boost me in, Courtenay!' she trilled. 'So,' said the cabbie, 'the lady as I have the honour of driving is Miss Ellen Terry. I ain't seen yer, Mum, since you was at the Lyceum in *The Amber Heart* – 'eighty-seven I think it was.' 'There now, Courtenay,' she gurgled, turning to her host, 'I told you I hadn't altered.'

Thorpe had studied under Irving and known Lily Langtry. He took Agate to see Mrs Langtry, and Agate told her he had always thought her the most beautiful woman he ever saw. She offered him a photograph and asked Thorpe whether she should write anything beside her name. Piqued at not being given a photograph himself, he hissed: 'You might add "matchless for the complexion"'.

An aura of the macabre hung about Thorpe, and this made him peculiarly effective in death-scenes. His own dissolution was managed with impeccable style. Agate telephoned him to find how he was. 'Dying', replied a sepulchral voice. A few days later the process was complete. He bequeathed to Agate an ivory walking stick which the latter admired. It had something of its deceased owner's strangeness, and Agate rather fancied it might walk about the house on its own. One day it vanished.

Through Courtenay Agate was able to meet Mrs Madge Kendal. In the high Victorian summer she was the star of triangular dramas which enabled her to display an overwhelming technique. Her husband, who appeared with her, had little talent but was swept along on the raging current of her own brilliance. When she died in 1935 Bernard Shaw saluted her as more accomplished than any other actress of the day, even though Ibsen's plays and his own had killed dead the type of piece in which she appeared. Thereafter she became a public monument as Dame Madge Kendal. That she ruled her audience in private life as she did on the stage is proved by Shaw's complaint that when they met he, of all people, could never get a word in edgeways.

Agate thought that she, and no man, was the legitimate successor to Irving. Her comedy was enchanting precisely because it had a sense of guilt that the proprieties were about to be infringed. In the old Victorian plays which she and her husband put on she could summon up when required the utmost of pathos or the maximum of fun. She concluded the epilogue to *As You Like It* with a half-intoned 'farewell' that seemed to come from an immense distance, an exhalation from the grave. She was a fine comedienne and a fine tragic actress – the third greatest, Agate decided, after Bernhardt and Réjane.

Mr Kendal was not much of an actor, but Dame Madge worshipped him. As a great favour she invited Agate to see her husband's collection of Sicilian pottery. Some of the items were monstrously improper, but since Mr Kendal had collected them his adoring wife saw nothing objectionable about them. 'Wonderful glaze, don't you think, Mr Agate?' she observed, stroking one particularly obscene animal.

This indulgence did not extend to the actors she employed. A twelve-year-old girl engaged to play a village child was adorned by her mother with a chaplet of flowers. Mrs Kendal tore them off two minutes before she made her entry and raged: 'Do you think you're going on my stage looking like the village harlot?' Two minutes later, on stage, her mothering of the child was so pathetic that both the audience and some of the cast were in tears. At rehearsal she could be terrifying. She once asked a manager to bring a kitchen chair and to place it in the middle of the stage. The company was summoned to gather round while she knelt down and said: 'Oh Lord, we pray Thee out of Thy infinite mercy that Thou will cause some notion of the rudiments of acting to be vouchsafed to this company for Jesus Christ's sake, Amen.' She got up and dusted her knees. '*Well, now we'll see what that will do!*' she snapped.

iii
A VISIT FROM MADAME SARAH

> 'Take Bernhardt for all in all, it is, in my humble opinion, rank nonsense to pretend that the world has ever looked upon her like.'
>
> JAMES AGATE

As a journalist Agate quickly mastered the tricks of the trade. Sent to review an obscure Lessing melodrama given in German, a tongue he knew little of, he saved himself with a quotation from Christopher Sly in *The Taming of the Shrew*: ''Tis a very excellent piece of work, madam lady; would 'twere done!' and used as his theme the difficulty a foreigner has in evaluating a performance by actors speaking an unknown language. Ballet and corybantics of any sort were among his blind spots, and when faced with Maud Allan dancing her 'Vision of Salome' he wriggled out of the difficulty by quoting a bejewelled passage from the French Decadent writer Huysmans. How often he blessed the wide reading of his youth which never failed to provide a reliable safety net!

No man is on oath, said Dr Johnson, when he writes a lapidary inscription. Neither is any journalist when he writes his piece. In the battle to capture a reader's attention and to hold it, Agate learned, it is necessary sometimes to gild the truth and even to geld it. Whether or not he had anything he really wanted to say, at a given time Agate was obliged to produce a certain number of words to fill a certain amount of space. Everything that happens to the journalist or to any of his friends is valued as 'copy'. If his wife leaves him, if he suffers a heart attack, if his dearest child is attacked by some hellish disease, if his roof falls in, if he is smashed up in a car accident, he is delighted because he now has the raw material which, processed by his quick-silver mind, will serve to fill his twelve column inches. He may be forgiven his flamboyant language because he deals in the sensations of the day, and what was exciting on Wednesday is forgotten on Thursday. In any case, when you have a secret or a juicy piece of gossip to pass on, you naturally make it as vivid as you can. The journalist lives for the hour and survives one deadline after another in a perpetual state of excitement and turmoil. As Agate discovered later in his career, whether you write for a newspaper adorned with pictures of naked women or one that allows itself sentences with subordinate clauses, the tension and the pressures remain the same.

It must be remembered that while he was building his reputation on *The Manchester Guardian* he was also a full-time cotton merchant. He had, it is true, the luxury of a weekly deadline – other reviewers, obliged to deliver a verdict at midnight on five days out of seven, would regard this as child's play – but even so he worried endlessly about it. He was not, to begin with, a ready writer, and he agonised over his reviews, never satisfied with them, tearing them up and starting all over again until there was positively not another minute left before the printer set the machines in motion. On press days he waited anxiously for proofs, checking and re-checking, striking out an epithet and replacing it with another, clarifying, re-shaping, and sometimes redrafting the whole of an article. All this had to be fitted in with his business career, and there were moments when the burdens of his double life created grinding stress.

Even as a boy he had been what neurologists describe as a *migraineur*. At the age of seven, while digging castles in the sand at Llanfairfechan, he had looked up to see that half the bathing vans and all of Penmaenmawr Mountain had suddenly melted. As he grew older the attacks of migraine increased. They exploded at the worst possible moments: when he was making a speech, or reading a proof, or judging at a horse-show. A small fleck would dance across his vision.

It whizzed round and round to grow into a massive disc that blotted out sight and flamed into something like the glittering filament of an electric light bulb. Or it would give him the sensation of trying to look through a cracked and dirty window pane at a world of which he could see only half. Snowstorms raged and fluttered, fireworks exploded in vicious colours, faces dissolved as in a Francis Bacon drawing. Then came headaches that chipped away at his skull like a remorseless ice-pick.

One cause of this foul affliction is stress. Another can be rich food and drink taken irregularly. Both these elements were present in Agate's life and continued to plague him increasingly for the rest of his years. His father, a repository of humdrum wisdom, could have warned him of this, but Mr Agate had gone to his grave in 1909. Neither would the shrewd old man have been very pleased at the careers some of his other children were taking up. While Harry, Gustave and Sydney had embarked in orthodox directions like surveying, architecture and the law, Edward, who had always been something of an odd fish, was playing the viola in Mr Thomas Beecham's orchestra. Worst of all, Mr Agate's cherished daughter May was acting on the stage. 'I *won't* stay at home and label jam-pots!' she declared, and she bullied her mother into letting her study in Paris under Sarah Bernhardt. She was to write, in time, the best technical and artistic account of Sarah that exists either in French or in English.

Sarah's birthday in 1912 marked the fiftieth anniversary of her début at the Comédie–Francaise. It was celebrated in London with a 'British National Tribute' signed by 100,000 admirers, and in Manchester by a ceremonial visit to the Agate family residence. What should they give her to eat? 'I suppose the poor body eats like everyone else,' said the old Agate nurse, 'her stomach will be none the worse for a good warming.' Who should hand her out of her carriage? The gardener, who had performed this duty for Mrs Agate over many years, was chosen for the task. On the 23 October, with the first chill of autumn, came Madame Sarah Bernhardt, a mantle of misty grey like the breasts of sea-birds draping her figure. James, chattering French, took her in to lunch.

Although she observed that 'critics know nothing', she was ready to concede that this young writer was 'très intelligent.'

Her hosts were nervous of talking theatre with this infinitely dignified lady, though towards the end of her visit she spoke of actors and acting. Seated by the fire in Mrs Agate's drawing-room she told stories in a manner as fresh and radiant as that of a twenty-year-old girl. She detested the cold, and recalled how on her first tour of Scotland the servants persistently ignored her requests for a fire. Finally, exasperated, she rushed out on the landing and screamed 'Fire! Fire!!' at the top of her resounding voice. Within two minutes the hotel was cleared.

After a time she fell to talking about the stage. Henry Irving, she said, was a great artist but, given his oddities and queer technique, a bad actor. Forbes-Robertson was a jewel. She was generous about 'ce bon Coquelin' and Réjane. James daringly mentioned Réjane's tragic gifts. 'No,' replied Sarah with icy politeness, Réjane had 'a vulgar voice'.

Like many an actor, though, Sarah was disappointing when she referred to her own roles. She could not tell them much about her Pelléas, her Phèdre, her Joan of Arc, her Marguerite in *La Dame aux Camélias*. She preferred to relate her little stories, to remember how, on tour in cold climates, she was ready to burn whole suites of furniture and cheerfully pay for them rather than shiver. 'Mahogany doesn't burn well,' she mused pensively.

Time flew and the hour of the theatre arrived. The gardener helped her into her carriage and she made an affectionate remark to Mrs Agate. Then she drove off up the street and looked back with grave amusement in her eyes at the young folk who gathered to watch her departure. From the carriage window a bunch of flowers waved.

iv
'LE CAPITAINE AGATHE'

'Now one bale of hay is very much like another, and I have since computed that the number of trucks I loaded and despatched during those four years would, if placed end to end, reach from London to Manchester and back again to Rugby.'

JAMES AGATE

Under the articles of Agate's partnership in the firm he was authorised to draw advances on account of profits. This was a useful arrangement for a man who loved luxury and kept a Hackney stud which gulped up money wholesale. It was also a dangerous one, as he discovered at the outbreak of war in 1914: up to the 4 August, he was dismayed to find, he had drawn something like £4,000 on account of his share of profits. That year, alas, his share was no more than £96.

Ever since 1905 he had slithered on the edge of, and occasionally tumbled into, the depths of insolvency. A debt begins as a small thing, a minor inconvenience. Accommodation, only temporary of course, is sought, and were it not for something called interest the debt would soon be paid off. But other needs arise: a livery bill falls due, a forage account has to be paid, and the debt begins to expand and feed on interest until, like a voracious animal, it has more than doubled the size it was at birth. Agate's initial alarm gave way to a perverse enjoyment of, even pride in, his growing debt. He drew from it the exquisite pleasure that sucking an aching tooth can sometimes give. He added to it with ruinous delight by indulging not only in horses but also in women. Chorus girls from the Manchester theatres were expensive, and so were the champagne breakfasts and clothes and flowers and 'presents' he lavished upon them. From the arms of women he fled to the arms of money-lenders, and although he eventually deserted the former he was never free of the latter until he died.

In May 1915, he was walking down St Martin's Lane when he heard the band of the Irish Guards playing in

Trafalgar Square. He was both an impulsive and a sentimental man whose emotions were easily aroused. A quarter of an hour later he marched into the War Office and enlisted as a Captain in the Army Service Corps. A patriot? Yes, but also a shrewd Northerner who chose the A.S.C. because he was thirty-eight years old and out of condition for anything more strenuous, and because supplying the Army from the rear struck him as safer than doing so from anywhere else.

For six months Captain James Evershed Agate trained under canvas on Salisbury Plain. Off-duty he toured the vaulted abbeys and cathedrals of Salisbury, Bath and Winchester. History books came to life in traceried windows and in stone knights gravely slumbering. Somewhere, he lied straightfaced, he had seen the legend: 'Hengist and Horsa, Haberdashers', over an ancient shop front. In the evenings, when all was still except for snatches of soldiers' songs drifting on the air, he smoked a sixpenny cigar and listened to the regimental sergeant-major twanging a mandolin, and from further down the lines the inevitable, the omnipresent 'Keep The Home Fires Burning'.

At last they were off, although for months Captain Agate travelled no further than the drearier purlieus of Le Havre and Boulogne. Here he mucked out stables and groomed the mounts of transport drivers. Although he loved horses this was not his idea of fighting a war, and he applied to be sent further up the line. 'Do you know anything about hay?' enquired the commandant. Startled, but never without an answer, Captain Agate replied that he knew a great deal about it and still owed hundreds of pounds for the upkeep of a dozen horses before the war. Could he speak French? Fluently, he said. So he was posted to Arles in Provence where he spent the war requisitioning forage to be sent to the British Army in Salonika. As he boasted thereafter, he held the record of being the British officer farthest from gunfire.

The practical bent of his nature quickly solved the administrative problem that faced him. He remembered the accounting system used in Fritz Dehn's Manchester company which made it possible to tell, at any given hour or date, what the turnover was, had been and was likely to be. He maintained his hay statistics in the same way and was especially proud of his profit and loss account. It reduced to clarity and order a situation where British soldiers had to check hay delivered to Spanish balers by Provençal farm hands in a babel of misunderstanding. The system was eventually recognized by the War Office and made the subject of an official handbook. Each month Captain Agate spent more than four hundred thousand francs on hay, and each month his accounts were correct to the last centime. He liked to pretend that throughout the Bouches-du-Rhône a synonym for keen buying and strict economy was 'Le Capitaine Agathe', as the natives called him.

Having settled the small matter of hay Captain Agate turned his curious eye on the town of Arles. He admired a Greek theatre, a palace built by a Roman Emperor, an amphitheatre of Coliseum proportions, and the burial ground of Alyscamps where slept the mighty dead. Far livelier, drenched in the odour of garlic and *pastis*, was the Café Malarte on a Saturday morning. Next day, in the place du Forum, you could hire a shepherd or a labourer from among the teeming mass of red-sashed Spaniards, gesticulating Italians, Arabs and the occasional Serb and Frenchman. The Parisian tongue was here a dead language: to carry on a conversation you needed a bit of ordinary French, a touch of Spanish, a phrase or two taken from Italian opera and a garnish of Provençal.

For the rest of the week the quiet village square trembled in a noonday haze. At one end stood a bronze figure of the poet Mistral watching eight carriages surmounted by eight giant parasols and attached to eight bony nags. On the evidence of the shops the population of Arles seemed to live by cutting each other's hair, selling each other cups of coffee, and sending each other garish picture-postcards. Among the statuettes of Joan of Arc and beautiful, too beautiful Arlésiennes, were displayed bottles of perfume with innocent names unknown to Paris: 'Rosée de Jasmin', 'Etoile de Napoléon' and the simple 'Coeur de Jeannette'.

This was the county of Alphonse Daudet, who wrote, among much else, the *Lettres de Mon Moulin*, those scenes of

Provençal life, funny and moving by turn, which also contain the tragedy of *L'Arlésienne* afterwards made into a play with Bizet's poignant music. Agate walked along the rue Daudet and came upon the dusty little windmill, more like an overgrown pepper box, where the writer escaped the fevers of Paris. The Rhône flowed blue in the distance, and blue were the hills with their hot scrub and gnarled almond trees. From the mill he followed a path to an untidy-looking château, its drive now covered in grass, its gate overgrown with creeping foliage. It was here, in fact, that Daudet composed his 'letters' and dated them, by an innocent fiction, as coming from the mill.

The landscape held no secrets. The vivid sunshine lit everything up with piercing dazzle and created shadows of unforgiving black. At day's end the sun set abruptly and, without pausing for twilight, the countryside vanished into impenetrable night. Agate soon tired of endless heat and found himself longing for the wetness of the Lake District and the sooty showers that fell on Manchester. He welcomed the distractions offered by his batman Jenkins. 'See that house on the hill, guvner?' said Jenkins once. 'It belongs to a French officer. He's at the front.' 'What's that got to do with it?' enquired Agate. 'His missus lives there. *I'm her maîtresse!*' came the answer. One day, as they went out on a mission together, the temperature reached a hundred degrees in the shade. Jenkins asked what Captain Agate would like for dinner. Knowing that Jenkins had a talent for scrounging, Agate ordered roast chicken and suet pudding. His batman did not let him down and both items were served. Agate noticed that Jenkins was sweating profusely, and, feeling that discipline might be relaxed since they were alone, suggested he take his tunic off. 'It's against the rules, Sir.' 'Rules be blowed. Take it off!' 'Impossible, Sir. I ain't got no shirt on.' 'Why, Jenkins, have you no shirt on?' 'Beg pardon, Sir, but I used it to boil the pudding!'

Christmas Day, 1916, was another occasion of high temperatures and sizzling heat. With his C.O., Major Devas Jones, and a couple of other officers, Agate drove to Vaucluse and lunched at a hotel there. It was so hot that they ate their

Christmas dinner out of doors and took off their tunics. The hotel perched on a small hill, and on another hill nearby stood a farmhouse. They watched a French soldier burdened with gear struggling up to the farmhouse. Once he reached the door he waved cheerily to them and then reappeared at the bedroom window clasping his large wife. 'Bon appétit, Messieurs!' he shouted. They wished him the same. Whereupon, tactfully neglecting to pull down the blind, he ravished his lady.

The other entertainment in Arles was provided by touring companies which regularly played the stuffy little theatre. They brought with them ancient boulevard comedies and once fashionable dramas of adultery which years ago had been the latest thing in Paris. Not very often there came a real star. Then talk would be heard of 'les artistes' about to visit Arles. 'Quels artistes?' enquired Agate. 'On ne sait pas trop,' he was told. 'A ce qu'on dit, des Parisiens.' A ramshackle phaeton dating back to the days of the Empire creaked into the sunlit square. It stopped, and from it descended a lady who threw back a long blue veil to reveal the features of Réjane. Réjane! She who was the essence of *chic* in the theatre, and, off-stage, the last word in frumpishness! But there was no mistaking the buoyant walk, the careless manner.

That night she appeared in *Madame Sans-Gêne* before an audience of Arlésiens determined not to be impressed by Parisian froth. Agate was, though, and he marvelled again at the superb insolence with which she personified the *sans-gêne* of Sardou's bouncing character. He sent her flowers with the compliments of the British Army and an invitation to dinner. Since, she replied, she had a son in the French Army she deemed it not improper to sup with an English officer. At table he revealed that his note was not the first time he had addressed her, and he spoke of the occasion twenty years ago in Paris when he had sent a message backstage.

'Are you the English boy who wrote to me one evening when I wasn't giving a performance?' she asked. 'Yes.' 'You taught me a lesson that has lasted all my life. You made me realize that there may be somebody in any theatre at any time to whom you are opening a new door, a new gateway to beauty. You put into my heart that no artist is ever entitled to give a bad performance.*

Réjane's visit provided him with copy for his next despatch to *The Manchester Guardian*. He had an arrangement to supply, in the shape of open letters to Allan Monkhouse, articles about his war experiences. Thus he contrived to keep his hand in and, at the same time, modestly to augment the small army pay which was all he had to live on. Of journalism inspired by the 1914–1918 war Agate's is not at all the most sensational – but neither is it the least amusing. His adventures safely behind the lines are small beer, and nothing much happens in the sleepy town where he buys, bales and distributes hay, yet the telling is all: it has wit, sympathy and observation. In 1917 he collected up these articles to make his first book, *L. of C. (Lines of Communication)*. For a good journalist, he demonstrates, nothing is too small to serve as a subject, and no experience is wasted, however trifling.

In that same year he made the acquaintance of a pretty young Frenchwoman called Edmée. She lived in Salon and was the daughter of a rich land-owner, a man with a considerable reputation thereabouts. Edmée had pretty little features and a delicate walk she inherited from her mother. What is more, there was money in the background. Agate had many debts, and naturally an idea began to form in his mind. Despite the heavy chaperonage which convention imposed, he managed to see a great deal of her. When he felt in the mood, or wanted something very badly, he could exercise much charm, and there is no doubt that Edmée's family came to think well of him. True, he was forty years old and she only half his age, but this presented no barrier, indeed was an argument in his favour, since, according to French bourgeois custom a husband as old as he would have

* Three versions of this incident exist, one in *L. of C.*, one in *Ego*, and the third in a conversation Agate had thirty years later with Dilys Powell and her husband Leonard Russell. The tale of dinner with Réjane was added in the course of the latter. Embroidery? At least the circumstantial detail is convincing – e.g. Réjane's mention of her son, and the French idiom, literally translated, of her last sentence.

sown his wild oats, be ready to settle down, and have a store of worldly wisdom enough to protect and guide his young charge. Among the many other things they did not know about Edmée's betrothed was that, far from having finished with his wild oats, he was to go on sowing them in ever increasing quantities for the rest of his life.

'Le Capitaine Agathe' pleased them with his fluent command of their language and with his discerning love of French culture. Was he not a cotton merchant in civilian life, a partner in the firm and a man likely to prosper when the war had ended? Perhaps it was this argument which most influenced Edmée's father, and a marriage was arranged. Certain formalities, though, had to be discharged, since Edmée belonged to the Roman Catholic faith and Agate was a Unitarian. A solemn dispensation had to be obtained before Mother Church would allow her daughter to wed a heretic, and a visit was paid to the local priest. He, having bent down to rummage in a low drawer of his desk, straightened up again bearing a document which he handed over as unconcernedly as if it had been a dog licence. Several pounds' worth of francs changed hands and the happy couple were enabled to unite without fear of eternal damnation.

In between whiles Agate took his fiancée to England, presumably to show her around his family. They went on a theatre trip to that long-running musical show *Chu Chin Chow*. 'You English are an odd race,' observed Edmée wonderingly. 'You make a joke of war, and take this seriously!'

Back in Salon the mayor, Monsieur Fabre, conducted the marriage ceremony and gave the usual address about married bliss and the duty to procreate lots of little Frenchmen and Frenchwomen. All Agate could remember about it was Monsieur Fabre's compulsive habit of stroking his beard as though to reassure himself that it was still there.

The marriage was never consummated and soon crumbled into divorce. Agate explained it away by saying that no-one could expect a Provençal to endure the fogs of England, whereas he for his part couldn't stand the monotonous sunshine of the Bouches-du-Rhône. It is true that Edmée refused to settle in Agate's home country and that he, quite reasonably, did not see how he could earn his living in France. But another more compelling factor played its part: Agate had by now realized that he was bisexual and that, impossible though it always is to establish the exact proportions, his inclination toward men was greater than his leaning in the direction of women. After his experiences with Manchester chorus girls and a Provençal wife he was to find, in Paris and London, that his own sex was much more accessible and much more congenial.

Chapter Three

THE ASSAULT ON LONDON

James Agate to Lilian Braithwaite: My dear Lilian, I have long wanted to tell you that in my opinion you are the second most beautiful woman in London.

Lilian Braithwaite to James Agate: Thank you so much. I shall cherish that, coming from our second-best dramatic critic.

---

i
AN ENGLISH BARON DE CHARLUS

'. . . the peculiar tragedy of the homosexual, which is that of the tight-rope walker preserving his balance by prodigies of skill and poise and knowing that the rope may snap at any moment.'

JAMES AGATE

The rue de l'Arcade in Paris has its source near the Gare Saint-Lazare. Thence it bustles on its way across the rue des Mathurins and gains in fashionable tone until it expires by the smart neighbourhood of the Madeleine. From about 1917 and for some years afterward there stood, at Number 11, a building somewhat obscure in nature. You might have taken it for a small hotel. During the wartime black-out, when zeppelins throbbed overhead and skeletal aeroplanes chattered unseen, shafts of light escaped from the windows and bespoke a flourishing business envied by other tradesmen in the locality.

A staircase led up to a door, and beyond it was a sort of hall. People sometimes entered and asked for a room. No, they were told, the place was full and nothing was available. The hall opened into a cramped lobby, very hot, with chairs, a sofa, and carpets obviously antique and valuable which contrasted oddly with the rest of the cheap furnishings. On the walls hung coloured pictures of women cut out of illustrated magazines. A young man sat there who might have been a slaughterhouse worker, thick-shouldered, his hands bruised and massive. He chatted with a chauffeur whose white teeth when he smiled shone brightly against an olive complexion. Next to them a pom-pom hatted sailor-boy played cards with a soldier in uniform. A burly youth who looked like a navvy came in from the street wearing a handsome gold watch chain. The others looked up, winked knowingly at the chain and teased him, enviously.

Behind the reception desk sat a man in his late thirties. His fair hair was sparse, his lips were thin and his eyes, cold and fish-like, shone with an icy blue. He was deep in a book about genealogy which lay open before him. On a shelf, next to directories and timetables, stood a French translation of Ruskin's *Sesame and Lilies*. A bell rang. 'There's Number 7 again,' he said. 'Go and see what they want. And Maurice! What are you hanging about for? You know they're waiting for you in 23.' The young men came and went. 'Who are you here for?' one of them asked the chauffeur. 'Pretty Pamela,' giggled the other.

The bell tinkled in Room Number 3 and a frock-coated, top-hatted gentleman came out. He could have been a Senator, a Deputy, a business magnate. The proprietor escorted him deferentially out into the street, where the gentleman pulled his hat further down over his eyes and turned up his collar before flitting away. A tall bearded man entered. The proprietor greeted him. 'Ah, Monsieur Eugène!' he said, giving him the name by which he was known in that place. He introduced him to one of the young men. 'He's a milkman, but he's also one of the most dangerous thugs in Belleville.' The visitor looked bored. 'And he's done time for theft and burglary,' added the proprietor, anxious to please. 'What's more, when he was in the army he killed his sergeant!' This recommendation failed to enthuse the client either. 'I tell you who I have here,' went on the proprietor gesturing towards another of the young men. 'A slaughter-house worker. He kills oxen. Would you care to try him?' A gleam of interest showed in Monsieur Eugène's eye. There was a chink of metal as the proprietor hauled out a coil of chains, and, bearing the heavy load in both hands, he took Monsieur Eugène and the ox-killer up to one of the rooms.

'You'd never think he was a real Baron,' said one of the young men. The proprietor returned to his desk and his book on genealogy. An ugly priest in black robes came down the stairs from one of the rooms above. He was joking with a soldier who accompanied him. 'What do you expect?' he chuckled, finger raised. 'I'm not a good girl.' The priest, delighted with his little joke, forgot to settle up and made for the door. The proprietor rattled a box on his desk and, with sharp wit, called out in his Breton accent: 'Don't forget the collection plate, Your Reverence!' The priest apologized and slipped in his coins.

Readers of *À La Recherche du Temps Perdu* will have recognized Number 11, rue de l'Arcade, as the famous establishment described in the last volume of the novel. The proprietor, 'Jupien', was in real life Albert Le Cuziat, and whereas the fictional 'Baron de Charlus' is supposed to have set him up there, it was actually Marcel Proust who helped him get started. Albert as a youth had been extremely handsome, and when he left his native Brittany he went into service as a footman with aristocratic families where his good looks and athletic body won the favour of Princes, Dukes and Counts who shared the tastes of the Baron de Charlus. His life as a servant of the great inspired him with a passion for genealogy, and in time he acquired a phenomenal erudition on the subject of armorial bearings and etiquette. Proust found him an inexhaustible authority on precedence and consulted him often for documentation of his novel. If a Duchess invited a general and a bishop to dinner, who should have the place of honour? The Bishop, he was told instantly, took precedence and must sit on the right of the Duchess. No-one could challenge Albert on the fine shades of difference that separated a premier Duke from a royal Princess, or a

Papal Count from a Napoleonic Baron. Albert was a living *Almanach de Gotha*.

When his looks began to fade and his hair started vanishing, Albert left the service of the aristocracy and took over a bath-house for gentlemen. Soon afterwards he bought a lease on the Hôtel Marigny at 11, rue de l'Arcade, for which Proust gave him family furniture that had been in store for years and was superfluous to his own bachelor apartments. This accounts for the superior items which graced the anteroom. It explains also Proust's translation of *Sesame and Lilies* which reposed next to genealogical works on the scholarly Albert's shelves.

Agate made his first visit to the Hôtel Marigny either towards the end of his stay in France or soon after the Armistice of 1918. For reasons of professional secrecy, and also because he had a sense of humour, Albert referred to his clients by nicknames – 'Jean the Pole', 'the Grand Duke', 'God's Gift on a Rainy Day' (a notably generous customer) – and it would be amusing to know what he called his bluff English patron who turned out to be a thick-set, middle class version of the Baron de Charlus. The 'Temple of Impurity', to give it Albert's own camp description, thrilled Agate with a constant and always varied supply of simple, honest working-class lads. And, like all simple, honest working-class lads throughout the ages, they were pleased for a consideration to beat, whip, chain and generally rough up all the gentlemen who cared to present themselves. Penetration was charged as an extra.

As one day he was making his choice among the talent set before him, Agate heard a fluttering at the door. He looked up and saw a thin middle-aged customer pass through the ante-room. The man had a pallid face, large eyes and a black moustache. He vanished upstairs, followed at his coat-tails by an acolyte bearing a cage of white rats. The customer was Marcel Proust who often came to the Hôtel Marigny and who relied on Albert to cater for his recondite pleasures. These must surely have been among the most elaborate to be staged even under the roof of the Hôtel Marigny, for Proust could not achieve relief until he had seen the rats stabbed with hatpins and beaten to death by young men.*

Although Agate was never able to finish a novel by Proust – in later life he gave up the attempt as beyond his power – the incident of the rats fascinated him. In congenial company he loved to tell the tale with macabre relish, pointing up each detail but not always, depending on who was present, revealing the purpose that had brought him to the hotel. While the incident gave him the sort of anecdote he seized on and enjoyed retailing, it also acted as a palliative to any guilt he might have felt about his own adventures. If a great writer like Proust allowed himself such indulgence, who was to deny a mere critic his little escapades? Moreover, what he asked for was regarded as banality itself in the exotic domain ruled by Albert.

His needs were simple and easily fulfilled by the well-equipped resources and the obliging staff of the Hôtel Marigny; some brief titillating conversation about the underworld, perhaps, and then a little fellatio, after which maybe an episode of sodomy, although his increasingly corpulent frame made overmuch exertion impracticable. Often he would choose to sprawl back in a chair while his partner, sitting opposite and twiddling excessively agile toes, produced the desired effect by, as it were, remote control. He also had a fetish that involved feet. The lad he chose would be instructed to wear, night and day, until their meeting, the oldest and dirtiest pair of socks available. When they met Agate would go down on hands and knees to sniff the ripe odours exhaling from the objects of his fetish until, in a state of growing rapture, he arrived at a climax. In addition to this his genital obsession required lovers to urinate into a goblet which, after adding a measure of whisky, he quaffed at a gulp.

* Agate mistook one detail and described the creatures as mice, but otherwise his account was correct. Despite the hot denials of Céleste Albaret, Proust's loyal housekeeper, the facts have been established beyond any doubt. My old friend Marcel Jouhandeau, who died recently at the age of 91 after a gorgeously misspent life, was another satisfied customer of Albert Le Cuziat. In *La Vie comme une fête* (Pauvert, 1977, pp 139–140) he records for posterity further details of Proust's *ébats charnels*.

On one level it may be argued that, preoccupied much of the time with beautiful poetry and great acting and exalted literature, he felt the need on occasion to plunge into the gutter as an escape from excessive refinement. His friend Ernest Newman, for example, found relaxation watching boxers pound each other into pulp as a change from scrutinising the endless harmonic subtleties of *Tristan and Isolde*. But Agate's *nostalgie de la boue* was an altogether darker and more convoluted thing. There is nothing in his background to explain it: no domineering mother, no ineffectual father, in short none of the totem figures psychologists pounce upon. His childhood had been disappointingly happy and obstinately serene, cushioned as it was by the generous affection of both parents distributed equally among a large and lively family.

Perhaps something had happened in his youth to encourage a latent Baudelairean distrust and fear of women. He was at his best in the company of men, playing cricket, frequenting clubs and judging horses at shows. He needed men around him, and not those airy creatures whom Dr Johnson once described as 'un-idea'd women'. Within this man who looked like a farmer, dressed like a bookmaker, spoke gruffly and acted heartily, there was an unquiet spirit that craved, not the soft ways of women, but the harsh and exciting contact of raw masculinity. And it was so much quicker and easier to get what he wanted at the Hôtel Marigny than to waste all the time and thought needed for the successful pursuit of women.

The Hôtel Marigny was only one of the houses he visited regularly while in France. There were others, and he soon acquired an intimate knowledge of every square and every street where promising encounters were to be made. In spite of his discretion, English friends gossiped about his adventures. One of them, it came to his ears, said that when he was in Paris he always made a bee-line for the nearest brothel. Was not such a remark actionable? he asked a barrister of his acquaintance. 'You, my dear sir, may or may not succeed,' he was told. 'The bee will certainly get heavy damages!'

ii
KIPPERS AND CHARTREUSE

'. . . swallowed a sandwich and off to *Service*, a foolish play about a bankrupt stores which amused everybody very much except me. But then I once kept a bankrupt stores, and know how much more interesting it is than this sentimentalised, fairy-godmother version of it!'

JAMES AGATE

In 1918, a bachelor again, he returned to civilian life and started looking about for a job. His pre-war business partnership had come to an end since the mill for which he acted was sold in the cotton boom that followed the Armistice. It reached the sensational price of three hundred thousand pounds. None of that money was legally due to him, but the managing director, a friend of many years, made him a generous gift of two thousand. This, together with his small army gratuity, he used to finance what he described as 'the assault on London'. For, like Balzac's hero Eugène de Rastignac, he shook his fist at the capital and declared metaphorically: 'À nous deux, maintenant!'

The dramatic gesture arose in part from the bitter thought that he had thrown away half his life. He was forty-one years old in 1918, and, with the exception of the war period, the eighteen years needed to be born and educated, and the articles he wrote for *The Manchester Guardian*, he felt he had been wasting his time. Yet, romantic though his challenge to London might have been, the man from Lancashire chose a commonplace way of making it: he decided to set himself up in a shop. Had not the prudent Samuel Richardson composed his masterpieces in the back room of a flourishing print business?

The premises he bought were in the South Lambeth Road. The shop was of the type which *Dalton's Weekly* in its arcane style would have described as 'conf., tob., s.a.v.' Here he proposed to dispense confectionery, tobacco, cigarettes and stationery, with, as a useful sideline, a choice of groceries. At first the novelty of the thing delighted him. The goodwill he had bought included the name 'Warren's Stores', so he commissioned an artist to paint him a weatherproof picture of Mr and Mrs Rabbit and their family of bunnies trooping back to the warren. Then he hung it up outside and admired the effect from the pavement across the street. The phlegmatic inhabitants of Lambeth took not the slightest notice. His brother Harry at that time lived in the flat above and on Sundays helped out behind the counter. It was Harry's idea to place in the window, at night when the shop was closed, a small toy theatre illuminated with twinkling lights and scenes and captions that were changed each week. Together they stood and watched to see how this charming idea would strike their prospective customers. Again, the passers-by came and went, unseeing, unappreciative.

Inside the shop were displayed armies of ink bottles in blue and violet, sticks of red and green sealing wax, pink fields of blotting paper and snowy expanses of writing pads. There were mountains of violently coloured cigarette packets and tins of tobacco in more sober livery. Beside them stood dropsical bottles of sweets, oblongs of chocolate and bags of marzipan. The grocery section contained massive sides of bacon which lay raw and unappealing on a slab. What Agate had not realised was that in hot weather the two unsaleable hocks of a side melt remorselessly into four.

He did little better with the cigarettes and newspapers he attempted to sell his customers. Among the legions of competing brands which filled his shelves he could never remember where to find the variety required, and by the time he had located it the prospective buyer had tired of waiting and gone elsewhere. It was the same with newspapers. Quite a long time passed before he realised the immutable truth that a customer who wants a copy of *The Daily Mirror* will not, if your supplies have run out, be content with *The Daily Telegraph*, even when offered free of charge. He consoled himself with the thought that when, inevitably, the time came for him to sell matches in the gutter, they would at least be all of one kind.

So most of the time he retired upstairs from the alarums and excursions in the shop below and put together a book of that title. It was to be his fourth publication. The first, as we have seen, was *L. of C.* which he based on his wartime experiences in France. Then had come, in 1918, *Buzz, Buzz! Essays of The Theatre* by 'Captain James E. Agate'. ('*Polonius.* The actors are come hither, my lord. *Hamlet.* Buzz, Buzz!') These were chiefly reprints of articles written for *The Manchester Guardian* and contained tributes to Sarah Bernhardt, Réjane, Forbes-Robertson and Mrs Patrick Campbell, not forgetting music hall idols such as Vesta Tilley and Fred Emney, together with reflections on the art of the actor. One day at St Pancras station he saw Thomas Beecham carrying a book under his arm. 'Good morning, my dear fellow,' said Beecham to his fellow Lancashireman. 'I've just bought one of your books. It's called *Buzz* . . . I forget the rest of the title!'

In the same year as *Buzz, Buzz*! he published his first novel entitled *Responsibility*. As yet unused to the ways of literature, he did not know what he should ask on account of royalties. Anxious to find some standard of comparison he interrogated the commissionaire of a fashionable restaurant on what he earned. 'Four pounds a week, Sir, reg'lar,' came the answer. Since the book had taken him two years of steady work to write, he decided to specify a half of what the commissionaire would have made in that period, namely two hundred pounds. He was offered fifty. 'You see,' remarked his genial publisher, 'the commissionaire fulfils a useful function.' The typing bill came to over twenty-one pounds. The cost of author's corrections was twenty-five, (he followed Balzac's example and rewrote his novel on the proofs), and his agent charged a fee of two pounds fifty pence. This left him with a net profit of fifteen shillings, or seventy-five pence, which would not be enough to keep even a hermit of circumscribed needs for two years. In fact, his publisher had been generous: the royalties actually earned fell short of the amount advanced, and, not for the last time, the publisher of an Agate book lost money.

Responsibility tells the story of a North countryman who spends his childhood in Lancashire, goes to a boarding school very much like Giggleswick, is taken into the family cotton business, sells uncounted yards of the stuff, becomes a fanatic admirer of Balzac, joins up for the war, leaves the cotton firm and writes a novel. It is, in short, autobiography, down to the anecdote where the hero gives to his cabman the derisory fee he receives for writing drama criticism in a provincial newspaper. There are even whole paragraphs written in 'Balzacian' French to describe a Northern town – the pastiche is rather good, though shamelessly stolen from a youthful letter Agate's brother Edward once wrote to him. Like, however, the long digressions on whatever takes the author's fancy, they are, though acceptable as essays, out of place in a novel and clog the pace of the narrative. The author also falls back on the device of many inexperienced writers which consists in featuring long letters exchanged between the main characters. And he proves once and for all that he is not a born novelist when he refers to an old cashier in the cotton firm as being 'too typical of old cashiers to need describing.' Dickens would have taken the old cashier and, in a couple of phrases, would have made him unforgettable.

One review of *Responsibility* gave Agate inordinate pleasure. Carefully preserved in his most cherished scrap book, it spoke of him as 'Aldebaran among our pasty twinklers', and, though deploring the novel's 'second-rate metaphysics', hailed him as a new and important addition to literature. The critic who spoke thus was Humbert Wolfe, now but dimly remembered as a Georgian poet, though in the nineteen-twenties a name of importance. Another review, even more favourable and innocent of the slightest adverse comment, happened to describe the author as: 'In appearance jovial, red-faced and inclined to stoutness, he is essentially *homme du monde*, and the possessor of a biting wit, which is the dread of his friends and the delight of his enemies. He has an inexhaustible fund of Lancashire stories of a distinctly Rabelaisian turn.' It was a dream of a review, the sort of thing every author longs for. So it should have been, since Agate himself wrote it anonymously.

Alarums and Excursions, the book which he compiled in his room over the shop, is another collection of free-lance journalism and essays. Among them is 'Sarah Bernhardt. A Postscript', although this was by no means his last word on the great actress who had enthralled his youth. The subjects range from *The Beggar's Opera* to the music-hall expertise of George Carney, from music in Shakespeare to the plays of John Drinkwater. The style is brisk, sometimes prickly, and only an occasional outdated idiom or topical allusion reminds you that it was written over sixty years ago. He revels, as always, in startling you from time to time with an outlandish word, like a music-hall chairman rapping his gavel to call attention: an essay entitled 'Hippocampelephantocamelos' turns out to be a piece on the function of the red nose in melodrama.

In *Alarums and Excursions* there is a review of Arnold Bennett's *The Author's Craft*. Agate much admired Bennett for his personality, his artistry and above all for his approach to life. Bennett was a compulsive worker who often started the day by writing five hundred words before breakfast. His habits were orderly, and his manuscripts, written in a neat clear hand, contain at regular intervals in the left-hand margin a meticulous word-count. Early in his career Bennett resolved to write potboilers, but workmanlike potboilers, until the time when his talent and his income were ready for 'the big book'. Like any tradesman, he knew the value of the goods he was delivering, and he was careful to distinguish between his popular rubbish and his masterpieces *The Old Wives' Tale* and *Riceyman Steps*. A diligent routine enabled him to write, when required and to a strict deadline, a play, a magazine serial, a novel, a film script, an opera libretto, a book review, a 'self-help' manual, a short story or a newspaper article. The only genre he does not seem to have attempted is poetry. The imaginative faculty, however, cannot always work to order, and whereas the grocer can cheerfully supply all the varieties of cheese, meat and eggs his customer needs, the creative artist who emulates his versatility is bound to pay a heavy price. In Bennett's case the incessant demands he made upon his imagination brought terrible headaches and psychosomatic illnesses which helped to shorten his life.

There was a lesson in this for Agate, who, while praising and even following his hero's example of unremitting hard work, preferred to ignore the physical penalty it could exact. Twelve years later the publication of Bennett's *Journals* inspired him to write his own autobiography. He had known Bennett and eagerly looked, as anyone would, to see if his own name was in the index. Then he turned to the appropriate page and read: 'A man named Agate joined us.'

Agate made Bennett's acquaintance in 1920 and asked for advice on his literary career. He presented himself at Bennett's home on the 22 March, and in a journal entry for that day which was not published until after Agate's death, Bennett noted his impressions. 'J.E. Agate came early for tea in order to get counsel. He is a man of forty or so, rather coarse-looking and therefore rather coarse in some things. Fattish. Has reputation for sexual perversity. Married a beautiful French girl (twenty-three or so), who has now evidently left him, after about a year or less of marriage. He was a dramatic critic of the *Manchester Guardian* for ten years. A.S.C. during war. Principal job; partner in some cotton trade concern. Has just sold out for (he says) £5,000 and decided to come to London to make a living. Wants to be in publishing, with sideshows as a novelist and dramatic critic. Has published two war books and a novel. All good. Some fine things in the novel. Made £100 out of it, and £120 out of the war books together.

'Writes with difficulty. Knows a deuce of a lot about French dramatic literature. Seems to understand acting. Has certain sensibilities. Yet his taste capricious and unreliable. Has various conventional prejudices against institutions. The man has points and refinements; but he is fundamentally unintelligent . . . He wouldn't go. Stopped one hundred minutes and was dreadfully boring.'

There are obvious factual discrepancies here. Bennett was an acute observer, and his remark 'he says' *à propos* of the £5,000 Agate claimed to have sold out for indicates a correct scepticism. He also took on trust the amounts said to have been made from the novel and 'war books', figures which Agate must have inflated perhaps to keep his self-respect in the presence of a best-selling author. Otherwise the summing-up is perceptive. It shows that Agate was already known in certain quarters of London, at least for the nature of his private life, and it accurately picks on his good points and his bad. But 'unintelligent'? 'Dreadfully boring'? Might this not have been the reaction of one North countryman on the make when confronted with another?

Agate made sure that Bennett did not forget him, though the latter often shrank from his boisterous personality. The stammer which afflicted Bennett sometimes made him shy, and when two guests in particular were expected he always asked his trusty friend Frank Swinnerton to be on hand as his protector. One was Osbert Sitwell, whose conversation was lively and often upsetting, and the other was Agate, who, said Swinnerton, 'could be noisy and aggressive'.

During this early London period while he kept, half-heartedly, the shop in the South Lambeth Road, Agate lived at a variety of addresses. He started off with an apartment in Pimlico at Warwick Street. Then followed, in no particular order that he could recall, Hogarth Road in Earl's Court; Great Ormond Street, Portsdown Road, Maida Vale; and Ladbroke Gardens. Partly this was due to his congenital restlessness and partly to the need, which often became urgent, to escape his creditors. For the shop was losing money at a vertiginous rate, and his attempts at stock-taking, when he remembered to make them, were disastrous. In June he would suddenly come across a large bundle of unsold calendars for the year before, and in August his disbelieving eye would light upon box after box of mouldering Christmas puddings.

For a time he came to rest at 55 Doughty Street, where he supped on kippers and green Chartreuse and entertained visitors with supplies of beer wheedled out of a nearby pub which foolishly allowed him credit. Over the mantelpiece hung a picture of Beadsman, a famous nineteenth-century Derby winner. Beside it were displayed a De Wyndt landscape of harvesters and a view of Richmond that might have been drawn by Hablot K. Browne, Dickens's illustrator. On a shelf below stood the silver cups and trophies his Hackneys had won. A signed photograph of Lily Langtry had for its neighbour a picture of Sarah Bernhardt in an all-enveloping mantle, and nearby was Réjane toying with a jewelled chain and looking infinitely modish. Ellen Terry and Forbes-Robertson were there, and so was Henry Irving in a snapshot taken on the golf links at Cromer, he in a broad-brimmed hat and baggy trousers and looking for once less than Mephistophelian. An image of Vesta Tilley, celebrating perhaps the relief of Mafeking, completed this little portrait gallery. Everywhere, of course, there were pictures of his horses: Talke Princess, in her harness as she lived; her first foal Axholme Venus; Rusper Maryan, the three-year-old filly who gained him first prize at the London Hackney Show of 1913; and many another elegant high-stepping animal the sight of whom caused his heart to beat faster.

On the other side of Doughty Street Charles Dickens had lived in a house, now piously restored by the Dickens Fellowship, where he wrote much of *The Pickwick Papers*, one of the few novels Agate had ever read right through. Agate's neighbours included Paul Robeson, the actress Elsa Lanchester and her husband Charles Laughton, and the daughter of that once very popular but now quite ignored writer E. V. Lucas. At Number 55 two massive white boxer dogs, chained but ever threatening to go for the throat of the unwary caller, served as Agate's first line of defence against creditors. As a reinforcement he employed the first in a long series of what he called 'personal attendants', an amiable bruiser by name Freddy Webster, once of the Coldstream Guards and later to end up as chucker-out at a cinema down Lambeth way. He had a punch in either hand that could smash through a barrack-room door, and he knew how to handle duns and bailiffs foolish enough to lurk on the doorstep. Confident in Freddy's protection, the master of the house gave his friends tea and condensed milk – champagne was to come later – poured from a chipped mug. 'He might have had all Hazlitt and Balzac at the end of his pen,' remembered a guest, 'but what he had on the end of his nose was pure Tony Weller.'

iii
THE SUNDAY TIMES

'Of course, Jimmy will die naturally – in his sleep at a first night.'

ALAN DENT

The first night of a play in the Twenties was an occasion of some glitter. London was smaller then, less cosmopolitan, and the audience, usually described in the illustrated papers as 'brilliant', mostly knew each other well. Always in the front row sat Gordon Selfridge, the richest shop keeper of his day. Near him was Louis Sterling, the gramophone magnate who had made so much money that he started giving it away, although to his annoyance the golden tide kept rolling in as fast as he pushed it out again. His fellow millionaire, Solly Joel, another regular, glared imposingly from a box. In the stalls not far away sat James White, a former navvy with a brick-red face who made his millions out of gigantic property deals, selling – or was it buying? – Covent Garden in a five-minute telephone call. He, like everyone else in stalls and circle, wore evening dress, the men in glistening white shirt fronts, the women sparkling with jewels in an atmosphere heavy with scent.

A seat at the end of the fourth row of the stalls was invariably occupied by Golding Bright, most prominent of theatrical agents and authors' representatives. Almost assuredly it was he who had sold the play to the management, had acted for the author and had negotiated for the cast. When the curtain rose he crossed his hands, sheathed with kid gloves to prevent himself biting his nails, and dropped off into a gentle sleep. He had done all he could, and his future percentage depended on the whim of the audience.

Somewhere in the audience there was bound to be the shining face of Edward Marsh, Churchill's private secretary, generous patron of the arts, and a man of inexhaustible enthusiasm for the stage. 'Eddie's a terrible fellow,' grumbled Arnold Bennett. 'He enjoys everything.' Another familiar personage was Mrs Eliza Aria who wrote for the paper called

Truth. She had been a close friend of Henry Irving and so became Agate's. At a luncheon party in her honour someone began to tell anecdotes about Irving. 'Do go on, dear,' said Eliza. 'You know, of course, that in all that concerns dear Henry I am supposed to be a past mistress!' The headdress she wore at first nights seemed to be made out of the wings of enormous bees. During the interval of some especially dire play this monstrous bonnet once appeared over Agate's shoulder and a voice all in one breath enquired: 'Dear Mr Agate, how are you liking the play I am sitting next to the author's mother?' Mrs Aria died in a theatre at the very moment when the curtain rose on the première of *Grand Hotel.* How, thought Agate, she would have liked to pretend that she died as a result of that piece.

After the fashionable ladies and gentlemen had taken their seats a furtive trickle of drama critics emerged from the bar and found their solitary places, for in those days they were only given one free ticket each. *The Evening News* was represented by Jack Bergel, a Balliol man who with the effortless superiority of his kind could write equally well on bridge or ski-ing, on aeronautics or Morris dancing. The stately figure of A. B. Walkley personified the authority of *The Times.* He was a small man who wore a Gallic pointed beard and remained aloof in his seat during the interval while others fought to get into the bar. The genial W. A. Darlington wrote for *The Daily Telegraph*, and *The Morning Post*, not yet amalgamated with it, was the responsibility of a cherubic S. R. Littlewood who often crept in late. A breath of the past came with H. Chance Newton, 'Carados' of *The Referee*, who had acted under Samuel Phelps back in the eighteen-sixties and who composed warmly eulogious articles in which his subjects were automatically described as 'old and esteemed friends'. The gaunt silhouette of Hannen Swaffer was clothed in an ancient dinner jacket unlike those worn by anyone else. Around his neck he swathed a high black stock, and upon his shirt-front lay an ever-increasing deposit of cigarette ash. He and his colleagues were joined, from 1921 onwards, by a burly gentleman who, urgent, ominous, bustled in with monocle dangling, spectacles pushed up over his forehead, ventripotent waistcoat jutting forth like the prow of a banana boat. 'Better late than never!' he would rasp, collapsing into his seat and startling the other occupants of the row with a seismic shock that reverberated along the line. Mr James Agate, drama critic of *The Saturday Review*, had at last arrived.

In the autumn of that year he had heard that the post was likely to become vacant. At a dinner to C.P. Scott, editor of *The Manchester Guardian*, he asked his neighbour, a drama critic, for an introduction to Filson Young who then ran *The Saturday Review*. His request was turned down, so he introduced himself. Young was not an easy man. According to his mood he would greet a visitor with exquisite kindness or with black indifference. 'Cutting yer froat may get yer into the presence o' Gawd a'mighty,' an office boy once told Agate when Young was in a sullen fit, 'but it won't get yer ter see ahr Editor.' Music was the only pursuit which gave him consistent pleasure, and he wrote about it with charm, although towards the end of his life even this activity had palled on him: at the age of sixty he taught himself to fly an aeroplane.

Young had heard of Agate's work on *The Manchester Guardian* and asked him if he would do a sample article. 'No!' replied Agate firmly.

'Why not?'

'Because out of sheer nerves I should put into it every damned silly thing of which I'm capable.'

'What do you suggest, then?'

'I will become your drama critic now, and you can sack me the moment I am not the best drama critic in England bar Montague.'

'Right. Let me have your first article the day after tomorrow.'

The article was delivered next day. 'That's the stuff!' said Young, and he printed it in the issue of 24 September, 1921.

Throughout the months that followed Agate contributed a weekly article. As a talker, as a raconteur, he was spontaneous and witty without effort. As a writer he was slow, uncertain and laborious. It took him three days to write his *Saturday Review* article, and he rewrote it as many as six or seven times. The manuscript ended up as a maze of crossings-out and nervous scribblings, of desperate revisions and pressing second thoughts. He would go to bed reasonably satisfied with what he had done. In the middle of the night fresh ideas would strike him, new phrases would present themselves, and he would get up and slave at his desk again until dawn.

Filson Young retired and was succeeded by his assistant Gerald Barry, a fresh-faced, fair-haired youth of Scandinavian appearance. In the nineteen-thirties Barry left *The Saturday Review* and, within six days, had founded *The Week-end Review*. What is more, he persuaded the leading names of the decade to write for him, among them Chesterton, Galsworthy, J.B. Priestley, Aldous Huxley and Compton Mackenzie. But the magazine was too good, and after three years of brilliance it was absorbed into *The New Statesman*. Barry went on to edit *The News Chronicle* and became Sir Gerald as a result of organising the Festival of Britain in 1951. He often called on Agate in Doughty Street, and some years later he wrote: 'When I first knew him (which was when he first invaded London, seeking fame and tempting fortune) he looked to my inexperienced eye more like a successful coachman than a would-be drama critic . . . The coffee, poisonous at any time, would be doubly undrinkable on Tuesdays, for that was the day on which his theatre article had to be finished, and this meant ardours and endurances prolonged throughout the day and on into the small hours, labouring portentously to produce twelve hundred words of sparkling spontaneity while the coffee congealed, turned green.'

These articles which caused their author so much toil and anguish were remarked by another and much grander newspaper office. In June, 1923, a letter from *The Sunday Times* plumped on the door mat of 55 Doughty Street. It contained an invitation from the editor, Leonard Rees, to call on him. 'This is the most important letter I ever received in my life,' Agate wrote afterwards, 'for as a result of it I entered into what I must call my life-work. I am conscious of no absurdity in saying this; the point is not the size of the work but how much a man puts into it. If a man is no more than an inventor of mousetraps and gives a hundred per cent of himself to inventing them he is doing his life's work, and a Napoleon cannot do more.'

The Sunday Times was very strong on distinguished critics. The lordly Sir Edmund Gosse dominated the book page and each Sunday he pontificated with Olympian urbanity. In his time he had written that small classic *Father and Son*, a subtle account of his childhood, and, as the occupant of various undemanding posts in the Civil Service, had in his spare moments acquired a formidable literary reputation. He translated and wrote about Ibsen, he produced an important study of John Donne, and he published biographies of many dead authors. At his house near Regent's park he conducted a *salon* to which an invitation was regarded as an honour, especially by young and personable writers in whom he was interested. His friendship with André Gide, a frequent correspondent, typified his wide Gallic acquaintance, and he was a Commander of the Légion d'Honneur. He had been very close with Swinburne, was the friend of Thomas Hardy and Henry James, and, given also his association with the nobility through his librarian's post at the House of Lords, was apt to overawe newspapermen. It was unfortunate that his polished and worldly style concealed a lamentable inaccuracy and slapdash attitude to facts which, in the eighteen-nineties, made him the object of a vicious but justified attack by a fellow scholar. That unfortunate incident was, however, forgotten in the nineteen-twenties except by his enemies, and he now shed an uninterrupted lustre on the pages of *The Sunday Times*. What most people did not know, and what has only been confirmed in recent years, is that this eminent bellettrist had, like his new colleague, Mr James Agate, a penchant for young masculinity.

Music criticism was the fief of Ernest Newman, Agate's old acquaintance from Manchester days. No-one ever saw him at *The Sunday Times* office except in 1944 when he turned up to be presented with a gold watch for long service. He lived remotely at Tadworth in Surrey where his wife protected him from unwelcome telephone calls. A large garden hut contained his vast library of books and scores and records, and there he wrote his weekly articles in a neat clerkly hand.

These manuscripts were sacred, and once his proofs had been passed none dared to tamper with them.

Agate's experience was sadly different. 'These Sunday papers will cut your stuff to hell!' Filson Young had warned him when he accepted the *Sunday Times* offer to become their drama critic. 'The only thing to do is to send them yards and yards of it and not care a damn what happens.'

He spoke truly. In the early months Agate worked on good terms with the editor Leonard Rees, a small and peppery man in his sixties who had devoted some twenty years to building up *The Sunday Times*. Success came to Rees late in life, and he also had an inferiority complex, perhaps as a result of associating with men like Gosse and Newman. He could give them jobs and decide their salaries but he could not hope to equal them intellectually, and although he was proud of the distinction they gave his paper he nonetheless experienced a sense of frustration. Being, too, very short of stature, he tended to strut like a bantam and to look on the world through defiant eyes. He was a man of rigid conventional morality, and it may be that, after a while, enough details of Agate's private life had reached his ears to shock his notions of proper conduct. He screwed his monocle in his eye and began to examine his critic's drama reviews with bristling attention. Changes were made. The phrase 'a light woman' became 'a woman unstable by nature'. The day after this appeared Agate played golf with Rees, a game at which he was tactful enough to win whenever he could. 'I wish you would tell me what's the matter with my driving,' said Rees after missing a tee shot several times. 'I'm afraid, Sir, it's unstable by nature,' said Agate. Rees put up his monocle and replied steadily: 'I thought you were very good yesterday.'

When first proofs came in Rees would take a pen, scribble delete signs haphazardly all over the page and knock out whole paragraphs regardless of meaning. Like any professional journalist, Agate did not mind his articles being cut so long as it was done intelligently, but the Rees approach made him sick with rage. On Saturday mornings he took to hanging around the St Clement's Press where *The Sunday Times* was printed and himself cutting the material to the required length. Once this was done and final approval given he would leave at four o'clock and wait for the first edition, only to discover that once again the piece had been reduced to an almost unrecognizable shred. The Rees technique left sentences hanging in the air and unexplained phrases which had no connection with what had gone before. The unhappy critic therefore wrote paragraphs which began 'Notwithstanding the foregoing' to make sure that the foregoing was retained. He sat up late into the night arranging his review so that if the odd sentences were deleted it would still make sense, and then would revise it so that all the even sentences, if taken out, would not harm the meaning either. None of these ingenious attempts prevailed. Despite violent protests Rees continued to cut savagely. 'Damn it, man,' he replied to Agate's arguments, 'I could cut the Lord's Prayer.'

Agate battled on and consoled himself with hopes of the old fellow's retirement. He could have resigned, but he had found his niche in life and was determined not to give it up easily. For a long time he kept on his desk a tray which he labelled 'Rows with Rees'. After five years of war he hovered on the edge of a nervous breakdown. And then, when hostilities were at their most venomous, he would find a note from Rees: 'A line to congratulate you on today's article, which I think tip-top – thoughtful, sound, sympathetic, and with style. I couldn't have cut a word, and you finish with your flavour unexhausted.'

Chapter Four

LONDON CAPITULATES

'Have made an arrangement with a doctor friend whereby every week I send him two of my review books against two of his free samples. This week while he is absorbing two nauseating novels I am imbibing Incretone, a preventive of senile decay, and Agocholine, "the most active cholagogue obtainable", whose function is drainage of the biliary tract. Next week he gets two dollops of fragrant bilge against cures for gout and gravel.'

James Agate

i
LEO AND EDWARD AND JOCK

'After forty-five only two things matter – to be amused if you've got money, and amusing if you haven't.'

LEO PAVIA

A regular salary as drama critic of *The Sunday Times*, though not munificent, encouraged him to dig deeper the abyss of debt which permanently engulfed him. The stable of Hackney ponies grew, horseflesh was bought at warmly contested auctions, new harness and sadlery were acquired. Resplendent in bowler hat, orange check overcoat and yellow gloves, he diffused in his wake an aroma of cigars and champagne as he proudly took his place one year as a judge at the Newmarket Hackney show. Other sporting hobbies absorbed him. At the age of thirty-three he had started on golf. Having one day played a cricket match at Chapel-en-le-Frith and scored ninety-eight not out, he went to the local golf course and met his brother Gustave coming in after a round. He told him about his near-century at the cricket match and Gustave said to him: 'Well, have a go at this.' His brother teed up a ball and James hit it 250 yards down the fairway. 'This is a daft game – too easy!' said the novice.

After that he never touched a cricket bat again. Determined to make himself as accomplished a golfer as his brother, within eleven months he reduced his handicap to two. From then on he revelled in the boozy companionship of the club-house and the glory of making a successful long low brassie shot. He could rarely see a glistening new set of golf clubs in a shop without entering and buying up the lot. His panoply of mashies and niblicks became in time the most elaborate to appear on links anywhere in the Home Counties or in Lancashire. The plus fours he sported were of the smartest cut, his cap was immaculate, his jersey knitted to luxurious perfection. Professionals were always the best-dressed people on the course, and yet it irked him that he was never taken for one. Why was it that, however cunningly he stage-managed his performance on the course, people always knew he was an amateur? He put the question to a young professional with whom he sometimes played. The reason, he was told, had something to do with the old theory that grooms get to look like their horses but owners never succeed in looking like anything but owners. 'You can tell a mug anywhere, Sir,' added the young man thoughtfully.

Away from the golf course he attracted to himself a coterie of friends, pensioners and camp-followers whose only qualification for joining his circle was physical beauty or wit. One evening in 1923 he was standing at the bar of a saloon in the Duke of York's pub next to the Victoria Palace. He heard, crackling above the bar-room chat, a loud voice which remarked: 'Originality is the thief of time.' The epigram delighted him, for it summed up what oft he'd thought but ne'er so well expressed, especially when plagiarising an old article to make do for a new one urgently required. He looked in the direction of the voice and, through the smoke and din, perceived a man with a bullet-shaped head cropped close and a dome-shaped forehead. The man was very short-sighted and screwed up his eyes so that he looked like one of those india-rubber dolls able to change its expression at will. He wore a shabby suit and was very untidy. Agate bought him a drink and was enchanted by a flood of venomous wit.

Such was Leo Pavia, 'a Jewish Dr Johnson' as Agate described him and destined to be a lifelong friend. He came of vaguely Hispano–Jewish descent and had been a child prodigy. Bernard Shaw wrote of his début as a pianist in 1890 at the St James's Hall: 'He went at the *Waldstein* sonata like a young avalanche, *fortissimo sempre crescendo e prestissimo sempre accelerando,* keeping his feet cleverly over the straightforward bits, staggering gamely through the syncopated passages, going head-over-heels up and down the flights of octaves, and finishing, flushed but unbeaten, after a record-breaking neck-or-nothing "reading" that would have made Rubinstein gasp and Mme Schumann faint. When he got up to make his muscular bow, straight from his shoulder, how could an audience whose battles had been won on the playing fields of Eton refrain their applause?'

Leo (no-one ever called him Isidore) then studied in Vienna with the tyrannical Leschetizky whose famous 'method' drove him to despair and crippled his fingers. His fellow pupils at the time included Mark Hambourg, Harold Bauer and Artur Schnabel. They later achieved fame, but not Leo, who, a refined and sensitive musician, was overcome with nerves the moment he attempted to play in public. He composed music, a violin sonata for example, of a rich lyrical texture in the manner of Richard Strauss, which was never played or published. In the early nineteen hundreds he had been the official German translator of Oscar Wilde's plays and knew all about the four-act version of *The Importance of Being Earnest* which was cut to three by George Alexander. The original third act, he revealed, included a scene where Algernon was arrested and told he would be taken to Pentonville. 'Never,' runs Algernon's speech. 'If Society thought that I was familiar with so remote a suburb it would decline to know me.'

His favourite authors were the Marquis de Sade and Krafft-Ebbing, to whom he added Johnson, Dickens, Jane

Austen, Thackeray, Goethe, Schiller and Ibsen. Their works he had read and committed to heart, and he was a walking dictionary on Restoration comedy. He could even quote at word-perfect length from the widely unread novels of Samuel Richardson. His genius, however, was strictly unmarketable. He reminded Agate of a comment made by a character in a Henry James story: 'There was something a failure was, a failure in the market, that a success somehow wasn't.'

During the 1914–18 war he served as a clerk in the Royal Flying Corps and astonished the airmen of Lydd with his non-stop talk and his performance at the canteen piano. Thereafter he drifted around London, his headquarters, when he could not persuade a friend to put him up, a little room in Notting Hill Gate with a few sticks of shabby furniture and curtains that rotted where they hung. Somebody once complained to him about the difficulty of keeping a roof over one's head in these hard times. 'For forty years,' replied Leo, 'I've found it a struggle to keep myself under other people's roofs!'

At the Café Royal, where Agate took him to dinner, Leo saw a total stranger at the next table proposing to leave a leg of chicken. 'I disapprove of waste,' he snarled, leaning over to stick his fork in the leg and transfer it to his own plate. He drank the drains of other people's teacups and put the butt-ends of Agate's cigars into his pipe. Although his piano playing had an exquisite cantabile, in everything else he showed arrant clumsiness and could not pick up an object without short-sightedly knocking over two others. He coughed, sniffed and sneezed from October to March in an aroma of stale Vapex and acrid pipe-smoke. Yet the feast of malice flowed from a generous soul which often befriended young men in trouble. An acquaintance who saw him walking down the Bayswater Road with a new protégé observed: 'Look, here come Wormwood and Scrubs!'

However exasperating Leo's preposterous behaviour, Agate was always disarmed by some unexpected gesture which softened his wrath. It might be some little present, a hat-brush, for instance, with the date 1845 dyed into the bristles, which Rossini gave to Leo's grandmother. Or it might be a witticism at dinner where a violin and piano discoursed Palm Court music – Leo summoned the head-waiter and said: 'Kindly ask them to play the Ninth Symphony.' Or it might have been in the bar afterwards, when Leo complained: 'The worst of this place is that they let in too many Christians.' He remarked of a well-known Baron de Charlus type: 'I hear he is writing an autobiographical novel called *Lui et Lui*.' His raucous tone often caused embarrassment. Drinking in a pub with Agate Leo noticed a very ugly prostitute with a muscular sailor in tow and whispered: 'Is that the face that sank a thousand ships?'Since his whisper was the loudest in London, they drank up and left immediately.

This relic of the nineties had accompanied rehearsals in Vienna under Mahler and driven the bad-tempered composer into a fit of rage. He had seen Johann Strauss conduct in the theatre and could remember the forceful pianist Teresa Carreño, who nearly murdered her three husbands and who played so loudly that people in the street could hear her perfectly without needing to buy a ticket for the recital. A grand hostess once invited Agate to a society dinner. He took Leo with him on the promise that, if he behaved himself, he would be allowed to play the piano afterwards. At the dinner table Leo's face got redder and redder with the things he suppressed. The conversation turned to Cora Pearl and Lady X said Agate must be wrong in supposing that the famous courtesan, a woman of infamous character, ever appeared on the stage. Leo erupted. 'Lady X,' he shouted, 'I hold no brief for Mr Agate's critical opinions. They are his. But on matters of fact Mr Agate is invariably accurate. Cora Pearl *did* appear on the French stage. She appeared at the Bouffes Parisiens in June, 1867, in Offenbach's *Orphée aux Enfers*. I know because my aunt, who was also a harlot in Paris, was in the chorus!' Here he became really excited. 'That is to say, my aunt was not a harlot – she was kept sometimes by one man, sometimes by two. In the end she married . . . *But*, Lady X,' he roared, thumping the table, 'I will not allow you to say that my aunt was a harlot!'

Leo could always be relied on to say the wrong thing, and where other people would blush with shame he, discomfited, would redden with pride. He never did an unkind thing nor said a kind one. On a trip to Blackpool he watched the pleasure-steamers through a pair of opera-glasses which had been a present from Meyerbeer to his grandmother. 'These glasses saw Malibran and Pasta and Tamberlik,' he said. 'The leather still smells of 1830.' A professional wit whose barbs were meant to sting and did, he suffered from moods of profound melancholy. On his sixtieth birthday he celebrated by staying indoors and reading the Book of Job.

Another character from the same mould was Agate's brother Edward. While James, Gustave, Harry and Sydney were all doing well in their various professions, and while May had become a well-known actress, Edward stubbornly remained the odd man out. He was the most gifted musically of the six Agate children and had joined Thomas Beecham's orchestra as a viola player. Together with Beecham he arranged the first performances of Delius in Manchester and himself composed music. His *Sechs Lieder* were described by Josef Holbrooke as having originality and as being the work of 'great genius'. Ernest Newman called his harmony 'modern of the moderns'. But he, with the perversity of a Leo, went out of his way to annoy those who sought to help him. Thanks to his sister May he was commissioned by Sarah Bernhardt to write some music as an accompaniment for one of her recitations. Madame Sarah patiently rehearsed what he had written and did not utter a single criticism. With kindness, with tact, she told him she was *désolée*, but the programme had been changed and she would be unable to use his beautiful work. She paid him a handsome fee, and, at a lavish luncheon, assigned a place of honour to 'mon petit Edouard'. He enjoyed the luncheon much more than he would have relished the ordeal of performance.

Edward stumbled through life determined to be his own man. He was invited for a large payment to collaborate on a film about Cyrano de Bergerac yet refused out of respect to the original, to Rostand and to himself. He never compromised and never turned his gifts to commercial advantage. For months he would occupy himself in translating the works of Klopstock without caring if they ever found a publisher.

His annual income did not rise much above fifty pounds. As twilight fell on his wretched little room in Clapham he would sit by an empty grate, and, wearing overcoat, gloves and socks as he had no money for coal, would read the sermons of John Donne. Since there were no pennies for the meter either, he would pore by the light of a candle over Burton's *Anatomy of Melancholy*. Here and there he borrowed sums of half a crown or five shillings and repaid them in the form of quotations from his learned browsing.

Whenever a little money came in he spent it on drink, for in middle life he had become an alcoholic. The bulk of his tiny income derived from translations of opera libretti, the most widely performed of them being Offenbach's *Tales of Hoffmann* and Massenet's *Manon*. He knew Russian, German and Italian as well and did polished renderings of operas by Glinka, Borodin, Moussorgsky. He found that running over Spanish irregular verbs was an infallible cure for insomnia. Alas, his knowledge of Spanish yielded him precisely ten shillings and sixpence, which was the fee he received for translating some stupid aria.

The tang of eccentricity in Agate's retinue was set off by a flavour of the young and the personable. On the 1 September, 1926, Freddy Webster put his head round the door and announced that a young man had called to see him. Agate, wallowing in bed like an angry beached whale, put his nose over the blanket and told him to go away. The air was thick with last night's tobacco smoke, and on his bedside table, which held an unfinished whisky and soda, a remedy for flatulence and a dirty pipe, lay the morning's letters. He knew they would contain polite requests for the settlement of debts and less polite reminders from moneylenders. With a groan he closed his eyes and turned over. Freddy looked in and said the young man had gone, leaving behind him a bundle of handwritten essays and the following note:

Alan H. Dent

aspires to be a dramatic critic, hopes you will look at this
his book, and will call again at 11 A.M. tomorrow morning.
I should add perhaps that I have run away from home – Scotland.

Next morning Dent called again. Agate muttered something about coming back in three weeks' time and went to ground under the blanket. During those three weeks he glanced at the material that had been left behind. It was, he decided, alternately naïf and overwritten, but quite as good as anything being printed in the weekend reviews.

The aspiring Scot passed the three weeks tramping from London to Egdon Heath and the Hardy country. On the way he slept under hedges and begged for his food. He had been born twenty-one years ago in Ayrshire, despite which, his parents hailing from the North of England, at school he was dubbed 'a dirty Englishman'. Although bred up in a small town forty miles south of Glasgow, he had from childhood been infatuated with the theatre. His mother died while he was yet an infant, and his beloved father, a Micawberish figure who ran a chain of tobacco shops, would often take him to the music hall in Glasgow where he saw Marie Lloyd, Harry Lauder and Little Tich. He always thought Little Tich the funniest stage comedian he ever saw. At one matinée starring Sarah Bernhardt the child fell asleep, something his father often teased him about. In after years he never dared tell Agate this.

By the age of eight Alan was swimming in Shakespeare and listening with awe to his father's reminiscences of Irving and Ellen Terry. He was already taking piano lessons, and the lilt of *The Count of Luxembourg* had a magic that never faded throughout the years. All his life he cherished an unrequited affection for the piano, which he played, especially Chopin, like Wilde's Algernon, not accurately, 'anyone can play accurately', but 'with wonderful expression'. In 1914 he saw his first *Peter Pan* in which the cheeky little boy playing Slightly was Master Noël Coward.

Against his will he enrolled to study medicine at Glasgow University. His father escorted him to the city and showed him round the paintings and sculptures in Kelvingrove Gallery. 'I dare say you'll spend about as much time here as over there,' he said, pointing through a window at the University. He was, as always, right, this sympathetic father who often scribbled the draft of a sonnet on the back of an account he had just drawn up. Dent senior was a keen musician – he would 'have a go' at anything, cello, viola, flute, flageolet – and more deeply acquainted with the best poetry and literature than anyone outside the literary profession. Rose-growing, stone carving, photography, bee-keeping and journalism all in turn attracted this rare spirit. In business, his son remembered, 'he could be both careful and extravagant, hard-working and nonchalant, as the mood took him . . .' When, eventually, Agate met him, he observed: 'You'll have guessed that my son inherits his genius from me!'

Promptly, when the three weeks had elapsed, Alan Dent appeared once more in Doughty Street. 'You've got to see 'im!' pleaded Freddy. Agate needed no urging for he had dipped into the essays and scented talent. He gave the boy two pounds and ordered him to go away and write an account of his tramp to Casterbridge. Dent returned four days later with a fifteen-thousand word essay which, under orders, he ungraciously boiled down to four. It was amateurish in part, but not, Agate reflected, as amateurish as the stuff he himself had been writing at that age. He sent the essay to Gerald Barry, who printed it in the next edition of *The Saturday Review*. Agate's lady secretary was discharged and Dent taken on in her place. 'Jock,' Freddy told Dent, 'you're engaged!' And from then on the bright-eyed Ayrshire Scot was known as 'Jock'.

Dressed like a peasant, large-maned, of a studied dignity which conferred honour upon those he addressed, Jock served as an inspired secretary for the next fourteen years or so. If the longhand in which he took down his employer's dictation was maddeningly hesitant and tended to inhibit Agate's unquenchable flow, he had gifts which went far beyond the merely secretarial. To check a quotation he would devotedly scan the collected works of Walter Savage Landor, and he always seemed to have by him the poem of Clare or Praed which Agate urgently needed for a vital reference. On the other hand he inclined to moon, was given to bouts of romantic dreaminess, and at hectic weekends would amble off to the country and leave the telephone ringing frantically in an empty room. It is true that his employer expected a great deal for a salary of fifty shillings a week, even then only just enough to allow of a cheap room near the Gray's Inn Road. Jock knew, though, that he was indispensable: he could, with fluent ease, write articles uncannily reproducing his master's tone of voice, and when Agate was too busy elsewhere, or when the demands of editors grew too importunate, he acted as an exceedingly talented 'ghost'. After his first year he rightly felt his talent needed more recognition, and he demanded a rise of ten shillings a week. It was granted with the utmost reluctance.

Besides on occasion writing Agate's articles for him, and paying household bills when there was money, and engaging or sacking valets, chauffeurs and houseboys, Jock also wrote half of his employer's next novel. In September, 1927, Arthur Waugh, father of Evelyn and chairman of the old publishing firm Chapman and Hall, commissioned a work of fiction from Agate. Now Chapman and Hall had been Dickens's publishers, and *The Pickwick Papers* were written a few yards away from the Agate headquarters in Doughty Street. Even more compelling was the cheque for a hundred pounds on account of royalties. But how was Agate to find the time needed for writing a full-length novel? He bethought himself of Jock. His novel would concern a young Scot arriving in London to find the streets paved with everything but gold. This hero, called Gemel, would meet a well-known music critic – to have made him a critic of the drama would perhaps have been overdoing things – who, an older man exhausted by a heavy work routine, would make use of the younger talent to further his own career. Jock was to draw his own self-portrait as Gemel and Agate was to do the same with the critic, Rubicon. The secretary, now a collaborator, found himself bundled off to his native land, where, in necessary solitude, he had orders to produce the requisite number of words.

He came back some time later with an untidy manuscript which they together expanded to some eighty-thousand words. The result, called *Gemel in London*, was a sprawling book, amusing in places and lightened with wry humour, but proving once again that Agate was not a novelist. The portrait he draws of himself makes vivid reading and shows a deal of shrewd self-knowledge. This, together with the picture of a young gay who is sharp on advancement and a grotesque mummified old actor obviously based on Courtenay Thorpe, makes up the only successful attempt at characterisation in the novel. The rest is material for a dozen or so essays. Arnold Bennett paid *Gemel in London* the compliment of devoting to it a long review in one of his famous *Evening Standard* articles. He was unusually tender. While he deplored the old-fashioned narrative manner, the poor characterisation and the lack of plot, he admitted to having been diverted by it. *Gemel in London*, however, was little more than 'a wayward lark' – a 'good lark', perhaps, but not a novel, and not the work of a story-teller. Other reviewers, less kind, spoke of 'elephantine archness' and remarked that 'nobody so clever succeeded in producing a book so stupid'.

Since Agate's contract stipulated that his name alone should appear on the title page, he contrived a graceful dedication which read:

To
ALAN DENT
the onlie begetter
of
and collaborator
in
much that ensues

Sales of the novel reached a figure of three thousand and then stopped dead. Agate, as novelist, decided to do likewise. A year or so before Alan Dent joined him he had published his second novel, *Blessed Are The Rich*. The young hero, a Mancunian, read Balzac and worked reluctantly in a business office. During the 1914–18 war he served in France and, surprise of surprises, fell in love with a girl from Provence. On demobilisation he ran an unsuccessful shop in London and threw it up for journalism. Like *Responsibility*, the book gives an account of Agate's own life and differs from it only in that the central character writes a best-seller and makes a lot of money. It was received, with its irrelevant episodes and musings, as tepidly as his other novels.

All would have been well had he left his fiction to go quietly out of print. In one of the rashest acts he ever committed, he and a collaborator dramatised *Blessed Are The Rich* and, worse still, persuaded Manchester friends to contribute several thousand pounds towards its staging. The first night took place at the Vaudeville Theatre in 1928 with a cast headed by the engaging Mary Clare. The curtain fell on a very indifferent comedy and there was a certain amount of encouraging applause – enough, in fact, to tempt the incautious author out front. The applause was a trap. As soon as Agate appeared before the curtain a hurricane of boos, whistles and loud calls of 'Rubbish!' poured about his bewildered head. Never had he been so taken aback, and never in his life had he been so humiliated. For once the master of repartee was stunned into silence before this onslaught. An eye-witness reports that the affair had been organised with care and precision, starting with the deceptively warm clapping and ending in the sudden torrent of invective from all parts of the house. *Blessed Are The Rich* limped on for thirteen performances, although at the last night both pit and gallery were full of people attracted by the notoriety of the event and, it is clear, by a feeling of *Schadenfreude*. The actors, authors, playwrights and other enemies who had suffered in the past from Agate's barbs congratulated themselves on having obtained a satisfying vengeance.

ii
JOURNEY'S END

'Bought an exquisite black mare from Albert Throup, and named her Black Tulip. My interest in her now exceeds everything. *Totally* indifferent to golf, plays, films, books, music.'

JAMES AGATE

Towards the end of 1926 the house at 55 Doughty Street took on an embattled air. The blinds were lowered, the door was locked, the telephone rang unanswered, and Freddy Webster manned defensive positions while his master went to ground in a flurry of writs. The bailiffs got through, however, and an invitation to Bloomsbury County Court was not to be denied.

What most impressed the drama critic's eye was the realism of the setting, as if it had been designed for a Galsworthy play. Two little desks, each with its Testament, stood on each side of the Registrar's throne. In the well of the court gathered a mob of baleful creditors fingering notebooks and documents. At a quarter past ten appeared a venerable personage with snow-white hair resembling Cyril Maude, an actor who specialised in elderly gentlemen. Agate took him for the Registrar and mentally applauded. Five minutes later, when the Registrar himself made his solemn entrance, he realised that this had only been the Clerk. He thought of those Lyceum audiences in the eighties who, at performances of *The Corsican Brothers*, always mistook the then unknown A. W. Pinero for Irving, and he knew he had made the same error. Even when judgment was given against him and he was ordered to clear the debt by monthly payments strictly observed, the impression of theatre lingered. He went out into the foggy street and heard the jolly tune of a hurdy-gurdy. The instrument, large and many-piped, stood on a four-wheeled chassis and was flanked by a miniature drum and cymbals. The strains of a Johann Strauss waltz died away and he persuaded the operators to let him turn the handle. After cranking out a march he'd often heard but never identified at the circus, he paused, arm-weary but refreshed, and with a flourish deposited in the cap displayed on the pavement a sum equal to one of the monthly payments he had just been commanded to make.

The next appearance in court was for the hearing of a libel action he had brought against *The Manchester Guardian*. A very disobliging reference in the paper which once employed him was the cause of this impulsive decision; he won a farthing in damages and had to pay his own costs. Another financial crisis blew up, and kind friends made him loans, though not enough. It was, he reflected, 'like taking a man who cannot swim out of twenty-four feet of water and throwing him back into twelve. Money-lenders, of course, take a man out of twelve feet of water and throw him into twenty-four.'

As always at times of financial stringency, he made new arrangements which only served to enlarge both his indebtedness and his dependence on money-lenders. His decision to move out of 55 Doughty Street was sensible because the place cost a lot of money to keep up. Where his reasoning went awry with a queer Balzacian logic was in choosing an even more expensive residence, a roomy flat in the Victorian grandeur of Palace Court near Hyde Park. Here, stimulated by an atmosphere of splendour, he gave better parties than he could afford. Probably through his friends in the Hackney Horse Society – colonels in high places who divided their allegiance between the turf and members of the Royal family – he made the acquaintance of Princess Marie-Louise. He invited her to a performance of Coward's *Bitter Sweet* and then to supper at Palace Court. That morning his 'man' fell ill. Urgent telephone calls produced various offers of butlers who reinforced the hired help from Gunter's, the catering firm. The Princess was escorted out of a hired Daimler by an unknown wearing white kid gloves. Total strangers relieved the party of their coats and ushered them into a sumptuous supper. All went smoothly and the host was preening himself on his staff work when the Princess observed: 'Really, Mr Agate, I had no idea that dramatic critics did themselves so well. Gunter's man, of course, I know. But *two* butlers!'

At this Royal party the discussion turned also on more sordid matters. Was it possible for bailiffs to effect an entrance after sunset? Into later negotiations with his landlord Agate proudly dropped the name of his guest. The landlord replied: 'Your Royal guest's assumption that you could not be disturbed after sun-down by the gentlemen referred to was correct, but with the approach of Spring you will no doubt appreciate the danger of fewer hours of immunity . . .' His tenant fully recognized that danger, and before the year was out he had discreetly moved to a much smaller flat in Kensington Gardens Square.

His hope of financial salvation rose again at talk of making the novel *Responsibility* into a film. The suggestion came from Edgar Wallace, novelist, playwright, journalist, and a man whose luminous vitality sparked off innumerable schemes and projects. Sustained chiefly by a constant flow of very sweet tea and by cigarettes smoked through the longest holder anyone ever saw, he was capable of dictating a complete novel over the weekend. His journalism was flamboyant, as exciting as his novels and plays and quite as free of the limitations imposed by factual truth. He was a Buffalo Bill of letters who supplied millions with sensational entertainment – and still does, for many of his books remain in print. He gave and he lent with a princely hand. Though he owned an enormous house in Portland Place he also kept up a suite at the Carlton Hotel. Agate dined with him there on a meal consisting entirely of drumsticks, the result of one-knew-not-what holocaust of chickens, for Edgar, Napoleonic even at table, had decreed that all other parts of the fowl be banished.

'I want to say that the more of your stuff I read the more I realise how firmly you write, and how honestly,' Wallace told Agate. 'I think you ought to be spared musical comedies and revues. I despise you only because you have given up writing plays (as far as one can gather). A failure is terribly hurtful to one's proper vanity, but the effect should be very stimulating.' After six months' havering his American associates decided against the novel. At this point Edgar's kindness revealed itself. 'I've been through the same hoop as you have been . . . *I* know what it is to be short of 'ready' and what I'd like to do with you is this. I'd like to pay you £100 for the option of filming your next book,' he wrote. Both he and Agate knew that this was a way of giving him money. It was also a typical gesture by a warm-hearted man.

The hundred pounds soon ran out in paying debts and settling the costs of the summonses and warrants that piled up ignored on Agate's desk. In emergencies he sought help from friends who often cashed large cheques to pay off the broker's man sitting in his flat, chatting agreeably and sipping a glass of beer. One of these friends who stood surety for him at a money-lender's was George Bishop, an amiable man who later wrote theatre notes for *The Daily Telegraph*. He had started his career in a solicitor's office handling tax matters, and later had become an official Assessor and Collector of Taxes, experience which gave him an informed sympathy with Agate's problems. In his spare time he had taken part in amateur dramatics with the young Edith Evans and written for a high-minded journal called *Christian Commonwealth*. The paper asked him to contribute theatre notices, and so, as has happened with others, he drifted uncomplainingly into a career which led him to *The Era, The Observer* and *The Sunday Times*. He earned a reputation as a 'safe' critic, a middle-of-the-road man who could be relied on to produce, without fuss or fireworks, a just and balanced review.

Bishop met Agate for the first time during the interval of a play and delighted him when he revealed that he had enjoyed *Responsibility*, even bought his own copy. After the play they walked out of the theatre together and Bishop quoted a passage from Dickens.

'That's from *David Copperfield*, isn't it?' said Agate.

'Yes, the last paragraph. It's this play in a nutshell,' replied Bishop.

'Exactly. May I use it in my notice?'

'Well, I'm writing one myself . . .'

'My dear Bishop, I've just joined *The Sunday Times* and your quotation is just what I'm looking for.'

Bishop good-naturedly answered that *David Copperfield* was public property, but that if he wanted the quotation so much he was welcome to it. From then onwards they were friends. When they met at first nights and Bishop produced an apt quotation, Agate would give him sixpence as a fee for picking his brains.

For years Bishop worked in hectic association with him on *The Sunday Times*, often finding himself with only a few inches to review two or three new productions. Sometimes at a first interval Agate could stand no more of 'this rubbish' and would leave him to write the notice. His colleague, Bishop soon found, was the most exasperating person he'd ever known: charming and generous at one moment, then ungracious and rude at the next, and always, inevitably, late for every appointment. Mrs Bishop, who had been a journalist herself, took to Agate, and, despite a certain austerity inherited from her Quaker forebears, adored him. He, for his part, valued her exceedingly and treasured her advice. On visits to the Bishop home he would bring extravagant presents for her daughter, a huge doll's house, for example, carried by a perspiring taxi-driver, and vast bunches of flowers for one of the rare women whom he liked.

It was George Bishop who helped him bring about a critical achievement that gave him much pride. In 1928 the Stage Society put on a matinee of a new play entitled *Journey's End* by an unknown writer called R. C. Sherriff. Agate, expecting an afternoon of intellectual flummery, was persuaded to accompany Bishop. At five o'clock he emerged full of enthusiasm. In the foyer they met three of London's leading theatre managers and stormed at them to put on the play in a commercial house. No, came the reply, it was too good for the general public. That evening Agate was due to broadcast one of the fortnightly theatre talks which the BBC had recently commissioned from him. He telephoned Alan Dent, ordered him to tear up the manuscript he was typing, and replaced it with an ecstatic notice of 'a marvellous play'. This it was not, being simply a fine and very sincere example of craftsmanship. But, as he later observed, in a world where everyone talks at the top of his voice any way, you need to shout loudly about something worthwhile. A fortnight later, on hearing that a manager had actually bought the play for production, he exploded another bombshell with ironic advice to cancel *Journey's End* because the public was utterly unworthy of such a play. The trick worked, abusive letters from outraged listeners flowed in, and theatregoers were stung into buying seats. 'Nobody can boost a bad play,' Agate said afterwards, 'and this play was good enough to run when once it had got a start. And in the theatre the start is ninety-nine hundredths of the battle. Without the thousands of wireless listeners who bombarded the box-office before the Press got busy, this play must have failed.' Whenever, and this was often, people accused him of over-statement, he would quote the episode of *Journey's End* as proving the uses of deliberate and cunning exaggeration.

iii
EXPRESS AND ADMIRABLE

'*James Agate* How many words have I done now, and what time is it?
Jock Eight hundred and it's one o'clock.
J.A. Look here, Jock, be a darling and . . .
Jock (suddenly wildly Scotch) A ken what's comin'. Be a darlin' and feenish the bluidy thing! All right then, since it's nearin' Christmas. Get up and get yer face washed and attend to yer visitor!'

His appointment as drama critic to the BBC made his voice as familiar as his writings. It was deep and precise, with a touch of asthmatic breathiness that made it distinctive. When he grew passionate a slight and not unattractive stutter characterised his delivery. The passion was not always confined to Agate. The management of an important theatre sought to prevent him and the BBC from broadcasting notices of their productions and issued press passes exclusively 'to meet the convenience of legitimate journalism'. Other theatre managers gallantly disagreed, *The Times* wrote a leader supporting him, and the husky tones continued to go out unchecked every fortnight on the air waves.

He also, at this time, conceived the idea of becoming a film critic. For *The Saturday Review*, in 1921, he had already written what he believed to be the first critical piece about Charlie Chaplin. Seven years later, when the cinema was talking as well as moving, he decided to specialise in the medium. How was he to set about it? Would not proof of ability be required? He was writing drama criticism then for a magazine called *Eve*, and, as an amusing experiment, slyly suggested that for one week he exchange duties with the lady who usually contributed the film notice. This was done, and, bearing his review of a new Emil Jannings film, he applied to *The Tatler* where he had heard of a vacancy. On the strength of this he was engaged. A friend who heard of the appointment said: 'You'll have to do a lot of research, won't you?' 'My dear boy,' replied the new film critic, 'I could write a thousand words on anything under the sun.'

It must be admitted that, over the next twenty years, he often did write for *The Tatler* on anything under the sun except films. His first article appeared on the 26 September, 1928, and argued that film criticism at this stage could not be other than 'the unsystematical impression of the moment'. This was because in other arts with a long pedigree such as literature, music and painting, there existed centuries of masterpieces by which new work could be judged. The cinema was only a few decades old, and had, moreover, been in the hands of film manufacturers rather than film artists. He remembered the first film he ever saw, 'a delicious, flickering, wild and woolly absurdity,' and decided that, far from being a credible imitation of life, some of the best pictures had been 'the delirious projection of something absurdly unlike life.' From this he adduced two rules. 'Rule 1 – all pictures must be about exciting things. Rule 2 – the spectator must know what those exciting things are about. Does the reader think I have forgotten pictorial values? Not at all. But I put plain meaning first.'

Writing with more freedom than the centuries-old art of theatre allowed him, he launched blithely on a journey without maps. The film industry charmed him with its sense of the *gigantesque*. In Brixton he marvelled at the new Regal where you passed a running fountain and a basin crammed with gold-fish on your way up marble stairs into an auditorium modelled on the plan of an Italian garden. Stars twinkled in the ceiling and fronds waved exotically. Tea lounges abounded. The Trocadero at Elephant and Castle had an even more Babylonian aspect. A giant cinema organ mounted on a lift and turn-table rose mystically from the depths to play music for piccolo, piano and every sort of instrument except the organ. In the Forum at Fulham, alliterative as who should say the Byzantium at Billingsgate, lush red carpeting stretched into pink-lit infinity. As for the actors and actresses on the screen they were, to eyes that had witnessed Irving and Bernhardt, as nothing compared with all this magnificence. 'If I behold a young woman striped like a zebra, wearing a pill-box of wild ass's skin over one eye, and being hypochondriacally tragic about nothing in particular, why then it must obviously be Joan Crawford. Or if I see a young woman composed entirely of Turkish-delight, then I guess that it must be either Constance Bennett or Jean Harlow, though again I have to look at the programme to know which. The reason is that film players as a class move across the screen without making any more impression on me than I presume a mannequin does on a female shopper.' This was the lighter side of Agate the film critic, and he was to find ample material for persiflage. As we shall see later, though, he could also be serious and respectful of a young medium which, despite itself, produced on occasion work that impressed as well as entertained him.

What with his articles for *The Tatler, The Sunday Times*, the BBC and a mass of free-lance writing he threw off in between, he has already achieved an output of formidable size. It is a melancholy thought for the journalist that the work to which he has given so much care will survive no longer than a day, at most a week, and that it will disappear almost as soon as it has lived the span of a may-fly. He naturally seeks a more permanent memorial to what he has written, and he finds it within the covers of a book. Agate lived at a time when the essay was still a recognized literary form. By then the legacy of Addison and Steele had declined into a whimsical trifle known as a 'middle' or a 'turnover' which encouraged newspaper-readers to follow on to the next page. It was a vastly popular item and widely read. Authors such as Robert Lynd and A. A. Milne composed thousands of elegant little pieces with titles like On Getting Up in The Morning, On The Art of Drinking Tea, and On the Hum of Insects. Hilaire Belloc took the process to its logical end with an offering entitled 'On Nothing'. Once an essayist had gathered enough examples to make a book, he put them together and issued them in a volume which usually sold quite well. One of the most prolific authors of this sort was E. V. Lucas. He published twenty-six collections of essays which were not only reprinted but reprinted over and over again. In addition to his eleven novels, seven anthologies and an authoritative biography of Charles Lamb, he brought out twelve travel books. Of these, *A Traveller in Paris* first appeared in 1909 and ran into more than twenty editions. It was still available, with small revisions such as 'taxi-driver' for 'coachman', in the late nineteen-seventies.

Agate was intrigued by Lucas, who, like him, worked as if tortured by some ruthless demon. With nothing to live for except writing, Lucas became the chairman of Methuen, whose prosperity was aided by his own very successful publications. Nowadays they people the shelves of second-hand bookshops in lonely rows, although among them are many pages which, for their polished ingenuity, deserve re-reading. He is neglected possibly because, as he admitted to his daughter, he concentrated on the surface of things. This was deliberate, for he did not relish what lay beneath. His voluminous writing, his membership of a dozen London clubs, his work at Methuen, failed to keep his mind off the darker side. His language, in private life, was often obscene, and his humour of the blackest. A friend once complained to him that while his garden suffered from drought the only water available trickled off the slope of a nearby cemetery and, annoyingly, drained into his cellar. 'You have one consolation,' said Lucas. 'Though your garden may wither, your wine will have plenty of body in it.' The jest was to be expected of a man who, on his trips to Paris, enjoyed spending solitary hours wandering round the Morgue.

He was asked who he would like to write his *Sunday Times* obituary when death came. 'James Agate', he replied. Although Agate was astonished at hearing this, he realized that they understood each other. Both men had a morbid interest in death, and both were uneasily aware of the murk that festered under the surface of life. Agate agreed with Frank Swinnerton's description of Lucas as 'a grimly unhappy man' who 'knew so much, was so unshockable', and who had 'unprinted knowledge of life, books and human beings'.

Expand this, thought Agate, to *unprintable* knowledge and you approach that 'combination of Montaigne and Rabelais' which was how Jock summed him up. The serenity Lucas adopted as a writer was, wrote Agate, 'a mask hiding the torment of a man knowing as much about hell as any of Maupassant's characters, or even Maupassant himself.'

Still he went on writing, up at half-past seven each day to work on his current piece of urbanity and then arriving in his office at Methuen for an afternoon of accepting or rejecting other people's manuscripts, and still he went on reprinting his essays in the well-known bijou format with titles stamped in crisp gold letters. Agate could not but envy, in the friendliest way, the big sales Lucas achieved with such apparent ease. When he tried himself the result was always disappointing. Between 1923 and 1930 Agate published in hardback, apart from the titles already mentioned, fifteen books, of which all except one contained essays first printed in magazines. None of them sold many copies. He did not have the Lucas knack of touching lightly on the quotidian in a style that appealed to a middle class none too keen about French literature, the theatre or the music hall.* It is, however, ironical that while the once-popular Lucas is forgotten, at least one type of reader finds Agate's books invaluable: for anyone concerned with the history of the London theatre between the two wars his frequent annual surveys made up of notices he wrote at the time are an essential reference.

The only one of his publications during this period not to involve the contemporary theatre is his book on Rachel, the great French actress, which came out in 1928. *Rachel* is a brief work and happens to be, as he said justifiably, his best book. He wrote it in a fortnight and was paid fifty pounds. Within some ninety pages he restores the subject vividly to life, and more important, explains convincingly just why she deserves her place as the greatest of all tragic actresses. She was moved by three springs of action which were, says Agate, 'pride of race and family, love of fame and money, love of

* Although, under a pseudonym, Lucas did write sketches for the comedian, Harry Tate, whom he admired.

love. Rachel was first a great Jewess, second a great actress, and third a great lover.' Although she was ill-educated and could not write a sentence without misspelling it, although she knew nothing of the classic plays in which she acted apart from her own cues and speeches, and although she was grasping and avaricious, her career, which began when she was thirteen and ended with her death at the age of thirty-six, brought her a reputation which has never been eclipsed. The other characters in the drama of her life are sketched with brio: her grubby father, her scrofulous lover the millionaire Véron, and the generous Adolphe Crémieux who helped her in the early days and was coldly dropped when he was no longer of use. Her smile was like 'the plating on a coffin', and her strong will smashed every obstacle. This book alone proves that Agate really knew his French nineteenth-century theatre. He can quote, superbly à-propos, a verse from Hugo's little-known and unperformed play *Cromwell*, and he moves easily in the world of Dumas, Vigny and Musset. One of his neatest phrases in a book full of considered delights is his judgment on the prolific Eugène Scribe as one 'who poured upon the French stage hundreds of comedies, vaudevilles and plays about top hats and umbrellas'. The whole of Scribe is in that sentence.

Despite a warm review from Arnold Bennett in *The Evening Standard* – he called it an 'excited and exciting biography' and 'beyond question the best life in English' of the subject – *Rachel* failed to sell. The general public did not care for the lives of dead French actresses, however scandalous the details. A little later, though, came an opportunity for its author to reach that bigger public which never saw the columns of *The Sunday Times* and *The Tatler*. In the summer of 1931 he heard from his friend Reginald Pound, then feature editor of *The Daily Express*, that the post of book-reviewer was likely to become vacant. Pound advised him to keep in touch. 'For a fortnight Reggie took no meal alone except breakfast!' Agate recalled. 'About a quarter to twelve one evening at the Club of which we were both members Reggie said, "Can you come over and see Beverley Baxter [then the editor]?" I said I could and would. I was shown into Baxter's office soon after midnight and came out at half-past twelve the official book reviewer to the D.E.' At the end of his first year he totted up the books that had come his way:

Books received 840
Read and reviewed 174
Glanced at and recommended 63

At least 500 of them, he concluded, could be pronounced worthless at sight.

The three million readers of *The Daily Express* had never heard of Rachel or Sarah Bernhardt or Balzac, and neither were they much drawn to Hackney ponies. Agate's job, as he saw it, was to interest them in books by interesting them in the reviewer, whose jokes, gossip and larger-than-life personality dominated a page in Britain's largest-circulation daily. There were those who deplored his flamboyant manner. Others, like *The Bookseller*, claimed that however much purists might dislike the treatment, it at least made *Express* readers as familiar with books as they were with fashions and dog-racing, and stimulated them to regard books as a medium of thought and debate. A troop of Agatian elves, big-eared, wide-mouthed, bald-headed, frolicked around the page to signal that Thursday had come and that the weekly dish of provocation seasoned with exuberance was ready to be sampled.

Agate knew that the first rule of popular journalism was to avoid names with which readers were not already familiar. Leonardo da Vinci might just scrape in, but Lope de Vega not. Once he spoke about the death of the musician Landon Ronald and was cut because readers 'aren't interested in conductors, except the dance-band variety'. His review of Arnold Bennett's *Journals* was thrown aside to make way for a list of winners in the Irish Derby Sweep. Four days after Bennett's funeral Beverley Baxter had told the staff: 'Gentlemen, please understand that so far as the D. E. is concerned Arnold Bennett is dead.' Cunning was necessary. How was Agate to squeeze Virginia Woolf's name in to the paper? Since his readers were cinema fans he began with a reference to the film called *The Barretts of Wimpole Street*. This led to Elizabeth Barrett, to her dog 'Flush', and eventually to Virginia Woolf's 'biography' of the dog. The paragraph went in without a murmur.

Beverley Baxter was succeeded by Arthur Christiansen, an editor of genius who propelled the *Daily Express* to yet greater heights. So far as history was concerned he probably did not know the difference between the Edict of Nantes and the Diet of Worms, and in the arts he could not have listed the complete operas of Verdi or the plays of Ibsen. In geography he was doubtless innocent of whether the Volga runs into the Caspian Sea or the Sea of Azov, and one could safely assume that the reasons for the Battle of Salamis were hidden from him. Thus he had the comprehensive ignorance which is the sign of a great editor, but also the vital quality of intuition. Although he lacked specialist knowledge he had an intuitive sense of rightness. Which is why Agate would receive from time to time a polite note such as this: 'Do you think, dear James, you could get some book to take the place of Boswell's *Johnson*?' Only rarely was he hoodwinked. When *Anthony Adverse* appeared, an immensely long American novel of a type still fashionable, Agate had not even had time for a brief skim. He heard that George Bishop's wife Meg was one of the few people to have read it right through. Would Meg be a dear and write an *Express* review of it for him? She was a dear and obliged. A week later he sent her a letter from Christiansen telling him it was the finest thing he had written for the paper. He did not, though, enclose the fee he received.

Agate's encounters with Lord Beaverbrook, the owner of *The Daily Express*, were generally characterised by staccato questions from the deity of Arlington House. How old was he? Was he strong? Why, if he had asthma (from which Beaverbrook also suffered), did he smoke? and then suddenly: 'You are a charming writer!' At dinner with his employer and Brendan Bracken, Agate decided that Beaverbrook contained seven personalities within him: businessman, idealist, daemonist, dictator, realist, fanatic, and imp of undiluted mischief. The brain was like a blow-lamp which went straight to the point and missed everything else. Agate had an uncomfortable experience of this over his review of a Sinclair

Lewis novel which, badly overworked at the time, he had asked Jock to ghost for him. He had not, needless to say, read it. The telephone rang and a familiar bark echoed down the line: 'Good day to yah. I want you to tell me why you think so much of this novel by Sinclair Lewis. Come to lunch.' This was one of the few appointments for which he dared not be late, and he spent a difficult hour extemporising a discussion about a book he'd never glanced at. With great charm and still greater adroitness he managed to satisfy the Lord that he really did think well of the novel.

Other mishaps were more serious. He never refused a commission and often had to make one man's brain do the work of two, or even three, since under the pseudonym of 'George Warrington', a name taken from Thackeray's *Pendennis*, he wrote drama criticism for *Country Life*, and as 'Richard Prentis' contributed theatre notes to *John o' London's Weekly*. A further and more compelling reason for *noms de plume* was that the Inland Revenue, while only too aware of James Agate, was less inclined to pursue Mr Warrington or Mr Prentis, and the pseudonymous author was able to pocket his fees unharassed by the tax collector. Ralph Richardson once observed to Jock: 'I've found a critic who's better than your Jimmy Agate. He writes in *Country Life* and his name is George Warrington.' Jock smiled blandly.

For a time, a very short time, this opinion was shared by Beverley Nichols. Now if Gladstone, Asquith and Curzon had once been Presidents of the Oxford Union, there are others like Nichols who have won that glittering prize yet who never quite recover from it for the rest of their lives. Into the middle years and even into old age an air of faded brilliance hangs about them, and the talent that once impressed undergraduates consorts uneasily with grey hair. So precocious was Beverley Nichols that he issued his autobiography soon after leaving Oxford and called it *Twenty-Five*, the age he had then reached. He wrote novels, plays, and reviews for which he composed the music. Famous people accepted him as one of their own, and his beguiling descriptions of them were collected in *Are They The Same At Home?* which ran into half a dozen reprintings. Society took him up and no-one blamed him for enjoying and cultivating a success so easily gained. He took to advising the readers of women's magazines on how to plan their lives, he produced best-selling books which created a pleasant illusion of ideal gardens, he meditated on the charm of cats and explained how to talk to them.

Behind the fluency, however, there was passion, and, as the years went on, a feeling of anger that his gifts had perhaps been frittered away. In old age he wrote about the sadistic father whom he once contemplated murdering, and the subject of another book was a vicious attack on his old friend Somerset Maugham. One of the themes on which he felt most strongly and sincerely was pacifism. He hated war and, on a note of hysteria, argued against it. In 1931, soon after Agate joined *The Daily Express*, Nichols wrote a play called *Avalanche* which, like his book *Cry Havoc*, was inspired by a deeply felt pacifism. *Avalanche* was given a first and very successful performance in Edinburgh. Agate heard about this and asked Nichols if he could see it. Flattered by the attention of *The Sunday Times*, excited at the thought of a possible London run, Nichols made all the arrangements the critic demanded: a quiet room in a discreet Edinburgh hotel where no-one was likely to ask questions about *louche* young guests in the middle of the night. After all, thought Beverley, the play's the thing.

The distinguished visitor from London arrived and departed. Next week a review of *Avalanche* appeared in *The Sunday Times* which attacked the play so violently that hopes of a London production had to be abandoned and all financial support was withdrawn. Soon afterwards, in *Country Life*, Nichols chanced on a quite different article by George Warrington, who went so far as to disagree openly with Agate's opinion and said that *Avalanche* had given him a lot to think about. If only, thought Nichols, Mr Warrington had been the critic of *The Sunday Times*. He telephoned *Country Life* to thank their contributor for his welcome notice. The editor seemed ill at ease. At last he revealed that Warrington was Agate.

The author of *Avalanche* put down the receiver 'trembling

with anger' and made his fury known in official quarters. Anxious meetings took place behind the scenes and intermediaries strove to placate him. What had doubtless happened was that Agate, whose patriotism was of the Kiplingesque type, had taken offence at the pacifism expressed in *Avalanche*. Afterwards, as George Warrington, he reflected that perhaps he had been too hard on a play which, however badly put together, was at least sincere, and wrote accordingly. But, as he had first observed, the piece 'lacked moral unity' and was 'about three things, all of which are dropped and none of which is related'. Professional critics are not alone in having second thoughts, and Agate, here, unfortunately made them public. When the uproar died down Nichols addressed a bitter note to him. Should there be any more trouble of this nature, he threatened, he would give the police full details of Agate's private life. Later he sent him a review copy of *Cry Havoc* with the menacing suggestion that a good notice would be desirable. Thereafter Agate treated him with respect, even if, on occasion, he unsheathed his claws for a moment, as in his observation of the revue *Floodlight*, with music by Beverley, that it was 'brilliantly scored by Mr Benjamin Frankel'. The irony in this episode of genteel blackmail is, of course, that while condemning Agate for his 'quite exceptionally scabrous' private life, Nichols himself indulged the same partiality, though more discreet, for those of his sex. Do we not, when reviling our enemies, paint them all the blacker if they happen to share some of our own failings?

Chapter Five

MAN ABOUT LONDON

'Looked in at the Ivy, which was crowded. Asked Abel if anybody was there, meaning theatre-folk. Abel said, "No, sair. Only trash!"'

James Agate

i
AT THE VILLA VOLPONE

'Why don't you write a book about your debts? Since it would be long and involved you could call it *À la Recherche de l'Argent Perdu.*'

LEO PAVIA

As one evening he entered the bar at the Savage Club, where he was a prominent and boisterous member, Agate heard someone say: 'My dear fellow, he's as movable as Easter!' It was true, he thought, when towards the end of his life he calculated that during twenty-five years of London he had moved house eighteen times. Besides his town residences he had also, at one period or another, leased houses at Beaconsfield and Barnet, and bungalows at Westcliff and Thorpe Bay. He would take a house on the spur of the moment at Southend because he had played some good games of golf on the nearby course. Once he found himself a tenant at no less than four different addresses, of which he occupied only one. He would, urged by a sudden caprice, rent a house in the country as it was 'healthier', and then as quickly get bored with it because of the long midnight journeys by car after the theatre. This meant taking another London flat, where his only link with the now forgotten and neglected country house was a shoal of final demands and writs. But at least his peregrinations brought in 'copy'. At an off-licence in Southend he asked for a bottle of good burgundy. 'I'm sorry sir,' replied the assistant, 'we haven't any Australian burgundy, but we have the French wine of the same name, will that do?'

In the nineteen-thirties he entered on semi-permanent residence, give or take a house or three, in Fairfax Road, which makes common cause with the Finchley and Belsize Roads. The building was a dingy Edwardian structure, with a nice view from the rooms at the top, and stood about half-way down on the left. A manservant, large and Falstaffian of size, ran the household and attended to debt collectors. His mate, a tiny fellow, did the housework and cooked, though his exercise of these functions appeared not to be strenuous: dust enveloped the ramshackle furniture and Agate never, except for an exiguous breakfast, had meals at home. He baptised his house, in homage to Ben Jonson, the Villa Volpone.

Jock would arrive at nine, or ten, or eleven in the morning, always to find Agate abed. Sitting up in a mass of tangled bedclothes, an old jersey slung on to keep off the cold, Agate would say: 'Good morning. Take this down.' And out would pour a flood of dictation to be recorded in longhand and then typed on a machine, ancient and decrepit, which Agate, after much prodding, had been forced to acquire third-hand by his suffering amanuensis. Sometimes in the course of an article as many as twenty books would need to be consulted, and Jock would patiently take out each from the shelves nearby. There, under the eye of Sarah Bernhardt and Réjane whose photographs peered from the mantelpiece, were the tools of his trade: the collected drama criticisms of C.E. Montague, Shaw, Beerbohm, G. H. Lewes, Henry Morley and Hazlitt. All of Balzac marched beneath, with Cerfberr and Christophe's repertory of the *Comédie Humaine,* and an anthology of French verse, Shakespeare, Boswell's *Life of Johnson* and the classic *Famous Harness Horses*.

Early morning wheezes punctuated the discourse, and there would be a welcome halt for Jock's weary fingers when

Agate sniffed at his asthma inhaler and spluttered relief. It was an opportunity to look at the morning post. This contained, as always, a letter from a madman in Tunbridge Wells who had written a ten-act verse play about Gandhi and sought an opinion by return of post; the manuscript of a novel rejected by forty publishers and a demand to know why; a plea from a lady to help her niece get a job in Fleet Street, beginning, say, as personal assistant to an Editor; an announcement that the writer owned a complete edition, all but one volume, of an Illustrated Shakespeare published in eighteen-ninety and what was it worth, please? All these, and many others, received a formula carefully devised which read: 'Mr James Agate regrets that he has no time to bother about the enclosed in which he has been greatly interested.'

For several hours dictation flowed and was halted only by the frequent shrilling of the telephone. Came the moment when a truce was declared and the receiver taken off its cradle to allow for a brief interval of music. This, chosen by Jock from among his gramophone records, might be some such programme as:

1. Gigue for strings *Baldassare Galuppi*
2. Nautical Moments *Charles Dibdin*
3. Overture: Stradella *Friedrich von Flotow*
4. Two Tudor Madrigals *Period circa Henry VIII*
5. Concerto for two violins and orchestra *J. S. Bach*

If Agate had a hand in the arranging of these little diversions to which they treated themselves the programme would almost invariably include his favourite *Symphonie Fantastique*. The only criticism he made of Berlioz was that 'this all but colossal genius' had not ended the piece with the terrific March to the Scaffold. Surely, he used to argue, the *Symphonie Fantastique* ends with the March as definitively as the railway line ends at the buffers in Euston?

Once the last notes of music died away the telephone was put back and minds refreshed addressed themselves once more to the latest piece of nonsense at the St Martin's Theatre or the new masterwork by Dornford Yates. In a typical week there were half a dozen articles to be prepared, each between 1,500 and 2,000 words long, and every fortnight the script of a broadcast. The *Sunday Times* theatre review was sacrosanct. This, drafted perhaps on a Tuesday, would be scrapped on Wednesday and a new one written. On Thursday night Agate would have second thoughts and revise it yet again until, by two o'clock on Friday morning, he was more or less satisfied. Only when the piece had appeared on Sunday and was beyond all possibility of alteration did he give up, by which time he was already worrying about next week's article. Things like his *Tatler* work he looked on as different. They, unlike the contributions to *The Sunday Times*, were a bit of fun, and an occasion for writing in a much looser and undisciplined way. Looking through some back numbers one day, he was struck by one item in particular. It was rather good, he said, pointing it out to Jock. 'Of course it is,' replied Jock. 'I wrote it!'

By two o'clock he remembered that he had a lunch appointment at the Ivy for half-past one. The oak-panelled Ivy, just off Cambridge Circus, was for many years London's most famous theatrical haunt. It had been opened in 1916 and named, according to legend, after a remark by Alice Delysia that actors 'always cling together like ivy'. The twenties and thirties were its great days, and though the glamour has faded a little now, the ghosts of Noël Coward, Ivor Novello and Marie Tempest confer a nostalgic presence. Agate made his entrance as effectively as any actor, bowler hat askew, stick clumping, monocle dangling. 'It's now or never!' he'd bellow, descending on his hapless luncheon guest who had been awaiting him for over an hour. 'That man,' said Leo Pavia, 'if invited to the Last Supper, would turn up just in time for the Resurrection.'

At four o'clock he would take a taxi back to the Villa Volpone. Taxis exerted a strange spell over him. There is but one recorded instance of his having set foot in a bus; otherwise he rode everywhere in cabs to the extent of hailing one if he simply wanted to cross the road or to travel fifty yards down the street. While absorbed in a game of bridge, which he enjoyed almost as much as golf, he would keep his taxi waiting at the door and seemed to derive a perverse enjoyment from the thought of the hours and the shillings ticking away inexorably on the meter. Although he never learned to drive himself, he owned, in the years up to 1939, a series of motor-cars driven by a procession of chauffeurs who ranged from ex-jockeys to eager youths who did not know the difference between a back-axle and a gear-box. For a month or two he had the latest Riley but quickly tired of it and exchanged the car for a flashier two-seater, congratulating himself, after intricate negotiations, that he had made a bargain, though naturally it was the dealer who had most cause for jubilation. Then, as he passed a show-room, his eye was caught by another model, grander still, and his fickle taste rejected the machine which for a week or two had enthralled him with its comfort and its speed. The Riley became a Talbot, the Talbot a Humber, and on his trips to friends in the country he was as likely to turn up in a sedate limousine as in a sporty roadster. Out driving once, and late as usual, he urged his chauffeur to go faster and to ignore the speed restrictions of a built-up area. A police motorcyclist gave chase and stopped them. The policeman dismounted, took off his gauntlets, and bent down grimly at the open window. On seeing the driver his face relaxed. 'Hello!' he said, and planted a smacking kiss on the driver's lips. 'On your way you and don't get caught again!' The car drove off.

'Do you know him?' demanded Agate in astonishment.

'I can't remember his name, sir,' answered the chauffeur, 'but we were in the Guards together.'

Between half-past four and seven o'clock he 'read' four books and wrote a twelve-hundred word article for *The Daily Express*. It was now time for the theatre. This meant either the West End, or, if the piece was 'experimental', a slog out to Richmond or Kew which a friend described as 'being the drama critic for Asia Minor'. For such remote expeditions he always insisted on the management sending a hired car, a favour they were glad to do in the hope of a *Sunday Times* mention. Whether in Shaftesbury Avenue or out at Ealing, he did not always remain until curtain-fall. An experienced taster, he contended, doesn't have to swallow whole barrels of bilge to know what he is drinking.

Round about eleven o'clock he took his usual table at the old Café Royal where, surrounded by mirrors and gilt caryatids, he relaxed at the end of the day. He needed a rest. To write at one sitting a thousand words of good prose, fictive or critical, leaves you, unless you are a Balzac or a Dickens, as exhausted as if you had been navvying all day. Admittedly Agate often relied on dictation, but the mental effort is the same. His constitution was incredibly robust and resilient, despite his nonchalance in overdriving it. The body took its revenge, and the permanent stress of deadlines to be met, the pressure of being controversial, stimulating and entertaining to order, emphasised the neuroses which harassed him from youth onwards. At the age of eighteen he had already been seized by irrational fits of panic, as when, taking his three-year-old sister for walks on the pier, he was terrified lest he should snatch her up and throw her into the sea. Having changed once for a tennis match, he went back to tidy up his clothes on the bed. 'If you do that, you will do it all your life,' he remembered telling himself. He went back, and he did it all his life. The thought of sleep-walking oppressed him, and he never slept high up in a building or without a piece of furniture against an open window. Neither did he care to have razors or matches in the bedroom. He forced himself to keep awake in railway carriages, and was scared of travelling in an empty one. Railings and lamp-posts had to be regularly touched, and cracks in pavements to be sedulously avoided. The gas was turned off four, eight, sixteen or thirty-two times, always in multiples of four. In company, when fully dressed, he observed a ritual that compelled him to touch, in repeated sequence, his left breast, his right, his middle, his sides, as if looking for something that wasn't there or as if to find continual reassurance that all was well.

'Wind' and 'nerves' were the terms he used to describe the vague illnesses that beset him. He sometimes wished that he could start the day free of worry about his health instead of waking up each morning asking himself if he was due to drop dead a few hours later. At a medical examination for insurance purposes – he had just bolted a meal of potted shrimps, boiled salmon, asparagus, Bollinger and brandy followed by a foot of cigar – the doctor tapped his chest and observed: 'It's a magnificent ruin. The quality's good, even if the fabric's impaired.' Another medical man chuckled: 'You haven't half got an aortic lesion. I could hear it a mile off!' Agate was not concerned about his heart. It was the fear of dropping down in his tracks that concerned him. He was told not to worry: there would, he was airily assured, be plenty of warning in the shape of swelled ankles and weariness. And what about his stomach? Oh, it was just jiggered up generally – couldn't be helped with the heart as it was. As he went back home in the car he evolved a brand-new phobia which involved adding up the number plates of the vehicles in front. When they came to thirteen he sweated with fright.

Even so, there were times when he had fits of insane happiness such as he knew as a boy. These moods had nothing to do with health, as he could be feeling quite ill. They lasted a good five minutes, and while they endured it seemed that he was whole again. Free of asthma, untroubled by migraine and liberated from his neuroses, he experienced life 'as it hath been of yore'. That was why, at the end of the day, he settled his bulk gratefully into a chair at the Café Royal. There he refused to talk about work after business hours. He was too tired for that, and all he wanted to do was to eat, drink, smoke and rest. Steak was served, and with it a pewter mug replenished from a half-bottle of champagne, the mug being a quaint little pretence, which deceived no-one, that he was not a champagne swiller. Around him assembled a côterie which, to one observer, often suggested Oscar Wilde and his stable boys. Leo Pavia clucked and snuffled beside him, and across the table sat his guests of the evening, barrow-boys awed by the crimson velvet and glittering pillars of the Café Royal, young men picked up from nowhere, and guardsmen. Ah, the guardsmen! Those were the days when, at the old barracks in Albany Street off the Marylebone Road, an obliging sergeant would, if handed a modest fee of ten shillings, call up a group of likely lads and parade them before an intending patron. The choice was made and a pound note changed hands. It was easy money, the guardsmen found, especially with blokes like Agate: all you had to do was urinate in his tankard of beer for him. Afterwards you just shut your eyes and thought of your girl friend.

Having left the Café Royal he would look in at the Savage Club for, perhaps, a game of bridge with his special cronies the pianists Mark Hambourg and Benno Moisewitsch, or that amusing Bohemian Hermann Finck, composer of the deathless 'In the Shadows' and provider of music for dozens of revues and operettas. As like as not Finck would annoy him by arguing that Glazounov was a better composer than Berlioz, and then win his forgiveness by saying that Basil Cameron, when conducting Sibelius, looked 'more like a tobacco pouch than ever'. As the Savage closed its doors he would make his way home reluctantly to the Villa Volpone. He hated the thought of going to bed and woke up any of his staff who might be asleep with the demand that they sit and talk with him – or rather, listen to him talking. When even they could no longer keep their eyelids open he went out into the street, desperate for company, and chatted with the first person he met: a policeman on the beat, an early-morning reveller, a milkman doing his round. At last he realized the horrible moment had come. He walked into his bedroom and undressed except for the clean shirt he had put on that morning and in which it was his custom to sleep. The asthma spray, the sleeping pill and the indigestion tablet were administered in a careful rite. And then Mr James Agate sank to his knees beside his bed, following the custom he observed each night, and said his prayers as he had when a boy raised in the Unitarian faith. He commended himself to God and asked forgiveness of his sins. That done, he used his chamber pot for the last time, though even here neurosis intervened. Where should he place the utensil when finished with? Should it go a little to the right? Or should it be positioned six inches to the left of the middle bed-spring? Perhaps it would fit nicely in the centre of the floral pattern on the carpet? Or would it be better with the handle pointing to the south-west? After some ten minutes of anxious manoeuvre he succeeded in placing it to his qualified satisfaction. He climbed into bed and slept soundly, unless, at four o'clock, a sudden remembrance of an awkward epithet in his

Sunday Times article dragged him out again to correct the manuscript on his bedside table.

ii
ABROAD

> 'At Arles met Anthony West, the son of Rebecca. He is a pleasant and extremely intelligent boy, and I liked him ten times more when I heard that after three days in Arles he was "fed to the teeth".'
>
> JAMES AGATE

In the matter of 'abroad' Agate did not go quite as far as Nancy Mitford's Uncle Matthew who believed that all foreigners are 'bloody': he felt instead a sheer lack of enthusiasm for travel. He disliked Germans, and, despite Jock's pleading, remained indifferent to Italy. The only country he readily visited was France, whose language and culture had influenced him so deeply. France, to him, meant Balzac, the Comédie Française, and a view of life which he applauded. It meant the old maiden lady behind the cash desk at his hotel, ancient and bemuffled, bemittened and hung about with small gold chains, and looking as if she had just stepped out of Balzac's *Le Cabinet des Antiques*. She had sat there, for all one knew, since the turn of the century, always complaining cheerfully of the weather, the Government, the taxes and her rheumatism, but still the embodiment of French content. The approach by train to London had an Anglo-Saxon melancholy. That to Paris breathed gaiety. On the way to the station of Saint-Lazare Agate looked out for a vast cemetery which skirted the line. Now even the French cannot prevent such a place from being full of gloom. But at the far end was a huge wall emblazoned with the sign 'Jambon Cadillac' or something like that. And on the return wall could be read another giant announcement, 'Saucisson Cadillac'. It inspired him to adapt Charles Lamb in his conversation with the tombstone: 'I am alive, I move about, I drink and eat the sausages and hams of Monsieur Cadillac. Know thy betters!'

He could never resist the lure of France. When, in May 1934, George Bishop invited him for a cruise to Marseille with a few days on the Riviera he accepted immediately. There were one or two small chores that needed clearing up before he left – his current Bentley was exchanged for a Vauxhall, five articles were knocked off in two days, a sympathetic bailiff gave advice in the matter of a dozen or so writs – and once these trifles were out of the way he boarded the P & O liner *Mooltan* with George. Excusing himself to a friend for his preoccupations, he said: 'Now you'll understand why sometimes my articles are a bit thin.' 'Thin?' was the answer. 'I wonder some of 'em don't pass away altogether.'

It was a happy cruise except for the occasional phobia. His man-overboard complex kept him away from the side of the ship, and, on a tour of the bridge, he was assailed by his fear of heights. He hastened away to review a book in the safety of his cabin, where his eye lighted fearfully on the sentence: 'Of course, he may have jumped overboard. Many people do.' In Gibraltar, where they had four hours ashore, he went through a fit of melancholy as they inspected the tombstones of sailors killed at Trafalgar. The mood vanished on a drive around the Rock. He asked the chauffeur if he knew England. 'Yessir. Verr grand country!' 'What part of England did you find very grand?' 'Barrow-in-Furness.'

On the *Mooltan* they sat at the Captain's table, where the company, which included a Governor's lady and high-ranking officers, was starchy at the outset. Before the first dinner was over Agate had them all chattering about Hackney ponies, Sarah Bernhardt and the latest play – or rather, he did most of the chattering, though no-one realized it. When the ship docked at Marseille Agate refused to go on to Cannes or Monte Carlo as Bishop had planned. Instead, since Agate wouldn't let his travelling companion go on alone, the unhappy George was condemned to spend four or five days in a town which depressed him no end. During the day they hired a car and drove about Provence. At Salon, where Captain Agate had married his Edmée sixteen years ago, they saw in the distance the grey and bent shadow of his mother-in-law. The owner of a café told them that his father-in-law had recently shot himself because of money troubles. In the street Agate caught a glimpse of Monsieur Fabre, the mayor who married them, still patting his beard in the automatic way he remembered. He felt no emotion except for a vague curiosity. It was all so dead, so long ago.

In the evening, after dinner, George was left to his own devices while Jimmie went off on his own in search of adventure. It was strange, thought the distinguished critic as he prowled sordid streets and knocked at ill-lit doors, how little fear he knew in those *quartiers chauds*. Although assassins might lurk behind the curtains of the window, although the man he spoke to through the tiny grill might be a pimp of murderous intent, he felt more at ease walking these squalid thoroughfares than he did the dark London streets. He had a wonderful time. Of course, the stevedores of Marseille and their matelot friends were expensive. The packet of banknotes and traveller's cheques that fattened his pocket soon melted away. Within twenty-four hours he had borrowed all that George could spare. Urgent telegrams flew off to his agent, to the cashier of *The Sunday Times*, to a friend in London. By the end of his stay he had spent, apart from his hotel bill and car hire, something like today's equivalent of fifteen hundred pounds and more. He usually returned to the hotel at four in the morning, a time when the saintly George had long since gone to bed, having, no doubt, read quantities of Browning, a poet to whom he was immoderately devoted. 'Hello, Jimmie,' a friend greeted Agate on his return to London. 'How did you enjoy being away with Bishop? I suppose you've now got *Sordello* by heart!'

One of his purer Gallic interests was an obsession with the Dreyfus case. This event is, in its way, as absorbing as anything else in French history, along with the Revolution and the German Occupation of 1940, which are also liable to develop into a life's study. It may have been Zola who first caught his attention with it. He had, as we know, read all of Zola, and anyone who does this cannot avoid Dreyfus, for the novelist played a very brave part in the lamentable affair.

In 1894 Captain Alfred Dreyfus was accused of having passed French military secrets to a German agent. He was court-martialled, cashiered and exiled to Devil's Island. Soon afterwards new facts emerged throwing doubt on the genuineness of the documents which helped to convict him and showing that the French War Office had suppressed certain details. A major by the name of Esterhazy was revealed as a possible culprit. After a court-martial, however, he was acquitted. Zola now published his famous newspaper article 'J'accuse' – a framed copy of which hung on Agate's wall – and incriminated the War Office. He was prosecuted for libel and convicted but escaped to England, where his worst suffering was caused by the food. Gradually the impression spread that Zola had truth on his side, and in 1906 Dreyfus was at last rehabilitated. During the long years since his first trial the whole country split into those who were for Dreyfus and those who were against him. Dreyfus was a Jew and therefore the target of anti-semitic feeling. He was loathed by the army and by the established order. He could be, according to opinion, an object of hatred or a symbol of justice. Families were divided on the question and friends turned into bitter enemies. The crisis, which left its indelible mark on French history, has political and spiritual implications which are alive still.

Dreyfus became the reason for Agate's second venture into the theatre as author. The impresario Gilbert Miller asked him to translate a German play on the subject and he resolved to find out all he could about an episode which fascinated him. He asked a well-known bookseller to send him the literature available. Where, replied the bookseller, should he deliver the many van-loads which would be necessary? Another drawback was that he did not really know enough German for the task. This was an easier problem to solve. He dragooned the erudite Brother Edward and Jock and sent them off to work on the play secluded in one of the houses he owned at the time – and not only on the play but also on the ten thousand documents involved. The evenings of a hot October were spent in making a map of the case with various scenes from the play strewn over the floor and the researchers crawling on hands and knees between them, rather, he imagined, as railway managers do when laying out a timetable. Some sort of play was distilled from the German original and the mounds of documents, whereupon a film about Dreyfus was announced and queered everyone's pitch. Gilbert Miller realized that you can, justifiably, make a film after a play, but not the other way round. The project died.

A few years afterward *I Accuse!*, as the piece was titled, came to life again. The German author had revised his first version and somebody, somewhere, asked Agate to incorporate the alterations. Once more he plunged, with assistance, into the labyrinth and breathed again the names that were magic to him: Zola, Esterhazy, Picquart, Clemenceau, Scheurer-Kestner, Labori. Performances of *I Accuse* were arranged at the 'Q' Theatre, and Agate revelled in the excitement of theatrical production with none of the financial responsibilities. The dress rehearsal lasted six hours. Should he have kept in so many details? he asked himself. Should he have taken out this, or preserved that? *The Manchester Guardian* was approached about a possible review. '*The Manchester Guardian* is very much interested in the Dreyfus case. It is also interested in James Agate,' came the answer. 'Whether it is interested in the two in conjunction is another matter.'

The play was well received. Those who knew everything about the Dreyfus case thought he had brought clarity and coherence to the murky tangle of lies, forgery and deceit. Those who, like Ivor Brown in *The Observer*, did not have the thing at their finger-tips, pronounced it 'baffling and chaotic . . . If you start with a complete knowledge of Parisian backstairs gossip in 1897 it may be lucid.' Agate had made the easy mistake of cramming in too much fact, whereas what he should have done was to throw out all the history and then begin from scratch with an imaginative reconstruction. Still, at least he had proved, to other people's satisfaction if not his own, that he was no more of a playwright than he was a novelist.

iii
THE INSANE DESIRE

'If you do not want to explore an egoism you should not read autobiography.'

H. G. WELLS

In July, 1934, a literary agent floated the idea that he write his autobiography. 'Privately printed, of course,' said Leo Pavia when the news came through. This, like the offer to become drama critic on *The Sunday Times*, was among the most important events in his life. He already kept a diary of sorts, and the balance, about seventy-thousand words, needed to be written in six weeks. A holiday in Whitby had been arranged for August, and since there were only seventeen articles to prepare in advance he reckoned that with all hands to the pumps the task could be done. Jock was firm: an extra secretary must be engaged. His employer muttered something about his habit of deserting him in a crisis. Jock coldly retorted: 'Mr Micawber never asked Mrs Micawber to type a hundred and fifty thousand words, probably four times over, in addition to looking after the twins!' Help was engaged.

What should he call his new book? Malicious friends obliged with suggestions. *Loud Bassoon* was an appropriate one, taken from Coleridge. He himself favoured *Insubstantial Pageant*. This, in five years' time, could be followed by *Pageant Fading* and, at the last, by a gentle, melancholy sequel called *Pageant Faded*. Or what about *Irresponsibility* on the lines of his early novel? Jock had the last word. It must be *Ego*, he declared without contradiction.

The volume was prepared, half in narrative form covering his early and middle years, and half in the shape of a daily journal between June, 1932 and July, 1934. Two publishers instantly turned it down. A third, Hamish Hamilton, accepted it. This, his twenty-fifth book had, he calculated, been taken on by his fourteenth publisher or so.

'Why,' he asked himself, 'am I keeping this diary? Answer. Because it is part of the insane desire to perpetuate oneself. Because there seem to be lots of things I want to say that other writers put into novels and accepted essayists into essays. Because it will be a relief to set down just what I do actually think, and in the first words to hand, instead of pondering what I *ought* to think and worrying about the words in which to express the hammered-out thought. But I cannot and never could invent a story, or be bothered to tell it, and have already published *five* books of essays, not having to do with the theatre, that have been complete and utter failures. So I am driven to this last ditch of expression.'

'Accepted essayists' – the phrase had a wistful ring. His essays had not been 'accepted' as were those of the popular E. V. Lucas and A. A. Milne, and neither had his novels or plays. In diarising, however, he found the medium that was perfectly suited to him. When you keep a journal you do not have to think up plots and create believable characters. There is no need for what E. M. Forster called the 'atavistic form' of the story. Plot is provided by chronology itself, and the characters you choose to feature depend for their success on the journalistic quality of sharp observation. Moreover, as Whistler discovered with the telegram, the brief daily entry in a journal can be an ideal chance for epigrammatic wit.

Yet though he looked on *Ego* as a more relaxed way of writing than formal reviews, when the proofs came in they gave him as much anguish as his weekly *Sunday Times* article. Some five thousand alterations were made, together with lengthy deletions, insertions and total revisions. Solicitors then examined the palimpsest and demanded further changes. At last the book was ready for printing and Hamish Hamilton asked the author to write the blurb. 'I'll be damned first!' said he with untypical modesty. His friend Meg, George Bishop's wife, did it on his behalf and described him as 'a many-sided personality . . . a connoisseur of many things, great acting, literature, champagne, harness ponies; a wonderfully fertile and ready wit; a man of moods, buoyancy outriding depression . . .' She added something about 'a Micawber-like incapacity for keeping within his income' which had immediate relevance. For *Ego* he had received £200 advance on royalties, or £180 less agent's commission. From this also had to be deducted the cost of an extra

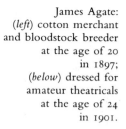

James Agate:
(*left*) cotton merchant
and bloodstock breeder
at the age of 20
in 1897;
(*below*) dressed for
amateur theatricals
at the age of 24
in 1901.

With his Commanding Officer Major A. W. Devas Jones: (*above*) in France, 1916 and (*below*) in London, 1946.

At the BBC
(*above*),
and *dans ses meubles*
(*below*).

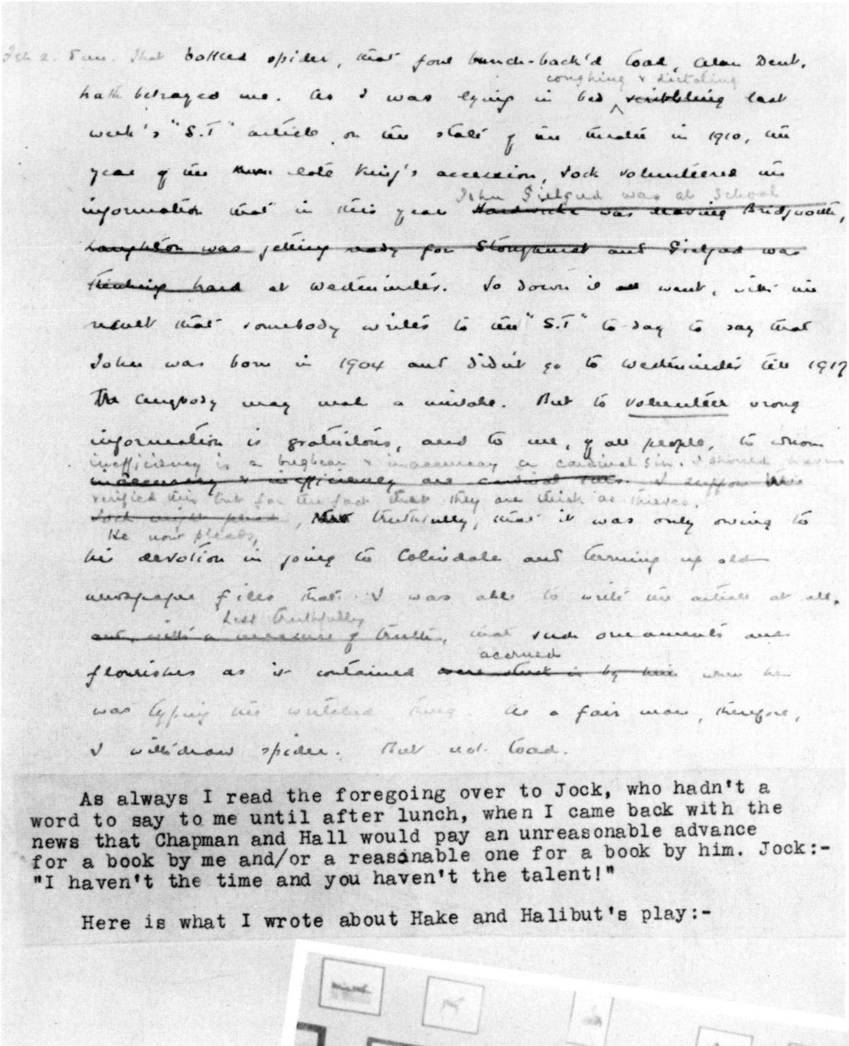

Feb 2. Sun. That bottled spider, that foul bunch-back'd toad, Alan Dent, hath betrayed me. As I was lying in bed coughing & dictating last week's "S.T." article on the state of the theatre in 1910, the year of the late King's accession, Jock volunteered the information that in this year John Gielgud was at School at Westminster. So down it all went, with the result that somebody writes to the "S.T." to-day to say that John was born in 1904 and didn't go to Westminster till 1917. The company may [illegible] a miracle. But to volunteer wrong information is gratuitous, and to me, of all people, to whom inefficiency is a bugbear & inaccuracy a cardinal sin. I should have verified this but for the fact that they are thick as thieves. He now pleads, truthfully, that it was only owing to his devotion in going to Colindale and turning up old newspaper files that I was able to write the article at all, [illegible] truthfully, that such ornaments and flourishes as it contained accrued when he was typing the wretched thing. As a fair man, therefore, I withdraw spider. But not toad.

As always I read the foregoing over to Jock, who hadn't a word to say to me until after lunch, when I came back with the news that Chapman and Hall would pay an unreasonable advance for a book by me and/or a reasonable one for a book by him. Jock:- "I haven't the time and you haven't the talent!"

Here is what I wrote about Hake and Halibut's play:-

A page from the manuscript of *Ego 2*, 2 February 1936, and (*inset*) Agate's study. The draft was, as usual, heavily revised for publication, and in the end only a rewritten version of the typed paste-over remained.

An 'official' portrait by Angus McBean (*above*). (*Below*) In the hall of Queen Alexandra Mansions beside his Sarah Bernhardt.

(*Right*) George Felton Matthew, aged 39 in 1936, and (*below*) Bertie Van Thal, watched over by Agate on the wall above him.

holiday
h Leo Pavia
ht), and
the roof
h 'Peter'
1943
ow).

Consulting the menu
in his spiritual home,
the old Café Royal.

secretary at £70, another £15 for illustrations, £8 for typing and £7 for indexing. This left some £80. Was there a profit? No, because, in addition to his author's six free copies, he sent out presentation copies to various friends which all had to be paid for, besides giving lunches and dinners to celebrate the event. It seemed, as with his collections of essays and drama criticisms, that he would still be dependent on his income from journalism.

At two o'clock in the morning of 24 January, 1935, he looked out through his bedroom window at the deserted street and quoted Gray's line to himself: 'And all the air a solemn stillness holds.' He bedded down and awoke to morning tea with the line still in his mind. As his man Arthur administered pot and cups he said: 'Good morning, Arthur, I don't know what sort of day it is, but *all the air a solemn stillness holds*.'

'Not half, Sir,' replied Arthur with a touch of Cherubino. 'Even the coal-men are crying their wares in hushed voices!'

The Times Literary Supplement did him well and remarked: 'A philistine with the conscience and equipment of an intellectual is enough to upset anybody.' Indeed, the reviews generally were the best he'd ever had, and the finest of them came from Rebecca West, who concluded: 'It is not enough to read and possess it. One would like to organise some graceful national demonstration in its honour. For symbolic homage there might be put an end to the pretence that the agate is only a semi-precious stone. Really, there is not anything much better than our Mr Agate, save Mr Pickwick and such bright diamonds of literature.' *The Church of England Newspaper* was less enthusiastic. 'Why,' it enquired austerely, 'should we be interested in Mr Agate's milkman?'

The first edition sold out by the end of the month and two reprints followed close on each other, half a dozen errors having been corrected thanks to the vigilant eye of Edward Marsh who was now doing for Agate the same service he rendered to Somerset Maugham and the proofs of his novels. Perhaps, if Eddie had worked on the first edition, he would have noticed the reference to 'Johnson's *Boswell*' which escaped everyone else until the last minute and necessitated urgent re-paging. *Ego* had gone off with a resounding bang – 'a stupendous book' wrote Allan Monkhouse, his old Manchester colleague – and Victor Gollancz offered to publish *Ego 2* next year. And still the splendid notices went on appearing. Jock, reading the *Punch* review, snorted: 'A fearless and enormously recondite critic be blowed! I'm your recondity!'

Ego may have done wonders for his reputation but it contributed nothing to his bank account. A bill of £65 for extra proof corrections disposed of any profit he hoped to make. How do people live who depend on writing books? he wondered. Without journalism he would starve. Amid all the excitement an Essex newspaper reported that James Agate, 'described as a dramatic critic,' had been committed to prison for debt. Fortunately his little mare 'Black Tulip' and the pony 'Smokeless Diamond' performed well at a horse show and won nearly enough to settle the amount of the writ. Alas, the news item alerted many other creditors and the storm raged full blast. To get away from it all, and to fête the birth of *Ego*, he went off for the weekend in his new Bentley with Leo Pavia. Leo was in good form. 'Business as usual during the deteriorations,' he remarked as they passed workmen tampering with a lovely old Georgian building. On the breezy front at Worthing he struggled simultaneously to keep his hat on and to quote Homer. 'I can't see why you don't preface your new Diary with another account of your life,' he said across the breakfast table. 'It could be quite different and you could call the book *Alter Ego*.' They drove through Hastings and Leo stared at the buildings: 'They could,' he remarked, 'be divided into two styles, Early Wedding Cake and Late Water Closet.'

These jaunts outside London – to Southend for golf, to Newmarket and Norfolk for horse shows, to Brighton for air – were agreeable interludes in the working round. Other trips were dictated by speaking engagements. His post-bag each morning bulged with requests for him to address the Amateur Dramatic Society in Thurso, the Rotarians of Plymouth, the Music Appreciation Group of Selly Oak, usually in return for payment of one guinea and a cup of tea. Most he turned down, though he always accepted an offer to speak in Oxford or Cambridge. On his rare visits there he felt an odd twinge of nostalgia. Was nostalgia the right term to describe an indefinite homesickness for something he had never known, for a place he had never been to or at? Added to this was the realisation that those young people had the whole of life before them while he could give them forty years on. He was proud of their invitations to talk, his vanity was touched, but he would lie awake at night and feel acutely miserable. The obituary which he wrote for himself at the suggestion of *The Daily Express* contains the remark: 'He felt keenly the lack of a university education, and was jealous of the Foreign Office accent. His shop-window was superb, and perfectly concealed the meagreness of the academic stock within.'

Still, his shop-window served to impress undergraduates, even when he simply read extracts from *Ego* ('Originality is the thief of time'), and at Oxford he paid them tribute with a carefully thought out appreciation of the O.U.D.S. *Hamlet.* The youth of Cambridge, with their easy talk about a life he never knew, at once elated and saddened him. It was as well they had not overheard his conversation with Fred, his man of the moment, before he visited them:

> *Fred.* I've put in two shirts, two collars, two white ties, both dirty, and two waistcoats, one of which looks all right. And you'll find the notes for your speech in your breast-pocket along o' your 'ankercher.
>
> *J. S.* But I haven't written any!
>
> *Fred.* I found some old ones in a drawer and they'll do.

Back in London reviews of *Ego* continued to arrive. Some of them asked why Mr Agate did not comment on politics or world affairs. None of these things, he answered, was his individual concern, since he was keeping a personal diary. The depressed areas of South Wales, the anomalies of the Divorce Laws, the problem of Fascism, were not his responsibility. His aim was to give an account of a particular life lived at a particular time, and that was enough for one man's energies. The concept of *Ego* filled his mind to the exclusion of nearly all else: he thought *Ego*, talked *Ego*, dreamed *Ego*. The manuscript of *Ego 2* which he eventually delivered to

Gollancz went through at least half a dozen versions. After he worked on the galleys it would have been hard to find fifty unchanged sentences. When the page proofs came in he made several thousand more alterations, the reason being, as every writer knows, that the typescript of a book reads differently in print. He also found, to his embarrassment, that his afterthoughts were always better than the passages which he had thought over most deeply, and that his best writing, like Balzac's, was to be found in the margin of the proofs. Leo Pavia reassured him: 'Afterthoughts my foot! Don't you know that Dickens wrote the whole of Mr Dick's King Charles's head stuff on the page proofs of *Copperfield?* That those two marvellous octaves at the beginning of the slow movement of the Hammerklavier Sonata were an afterthought, sent by Beethoven to the printers? So cheer up.'

He avoided cant about the Spanish Civil War by declaring that it must be fought over without him. There were difficult days when Jock was upset by the possible destruction of the Goya frescoes and the Velasquez's in the Prado and could hardly work. Agate ploughed on and simulated concern for the numbers of people killed, although it was all so far away and really much less important than next Sunday's review. As for the state of affairs in Germany Leo asked him what Hitler could do to stop world-famous pianists from being Jews? 'Teach Christians to play the piano,' suggested Agate. 'Half the Jewish world-pianists are Christians in disguise,' snapped Leo. Ten minutes later he withdrew the remark. 'Only a Jew would think of it!' he added.

Strangely enough, for a man totally uninterested in current affairs unless they were of the amorous variety, Agate spoke out forcefully on one controversial topic. The Deutsche Akademie invited him to a festival on behalf of 'the Art and Culture of the Contemporary German Theatre,' and included among its inducements to visit Munich a first performance of Richard Strauss's latest opera *Der Friedenstag*. He wrote back:

> 'Dear Deutsche Akademie,
>
> I am obliged to you for your invitation, which I must decline in the most emphatic manner possible.

My mother was educated in Germany, and I have been accustomed to hearing German from the cradle. All my life I have found my best friends among Germans. I have spent half my leisure time listening to German music. I immensely admire all that Germany has achieved since the war.

But I will not set foot in your country so long as you persecute Jews. We will not argue whether this is an offence before God; it is an abomination in the sight of man. I regret to have to write like this. But I feel deeply on the subject, as do hundreds of thousands of Englishmen who, like myself, have no drop of Jewish blood in their veins.

Yours faithfully,
James Agate'

In this letter the man who was so often accused of living a narrow boulevardier's life restricted to the theatre and Hackney ponies displayed a perception and an outspokenness denied to many more 'serious' commentators at the time.

iv
ENCOUNTERS

'I see now that, unloved as you may be, you are the least loathsome of your tribe or species.'

CLIFFORD BAX TO JAMES AGATE

At a West End Turkish Bath frequented by men eager for adventure Agate met one afternoon an acquaintance with whom he was to sustain over the years an odd relationship alternating between affection and contempt. Nowhere else are youth and beauty more prized than in the homosexual world. There are, however, members of it who like their trade to be older than themselves and fat into the bargain. Physical plainness is no bar to people who cherish this refinement of deviance, and pot-bellied Mr Agate was delighted to find that his partner was one of them. As the two men relaxed afterwards he learned that his younger admirer was the novelist Hugh Walpole. He promptly touched him for a loan of twenty pounds.

Walpole could afford it, since at this time he was accustomed to receive the modern equivalent of twenty thousand pounds and more in advance on a novel. His London flat at No. 90, Piccadilly, looked over the park and was filled with beautiful furniture and pictures. At his country home in Keswick he assembled a magnificent library which specialised, among other things, in the manuscripts and books of Walter Scott. These were the rewards of an industrious career which produced over thirty novels written at speed before he died in his late fifties. The 'Jeremy' books inspired by his boyhood made the name so popular between the two wars that innumerable male infants found themselves saddled with it for life. From realism he moved to fantasy, romance, even mysticism, and he beat all his own best-selling records with the vast family saga called *The Herries Chronicle*. His gift was for exciting narrative, and he could tell a story with sparkling verve. Readers thrilled by quick-moving incident and surprise developments tended to overlook the shoddy character-drawing and the mediocre prose.

His lively imagination so boiled over with stories clamouring to be told that on occasion he was busy on four novels at the same time. *The Cathedral* stands up to re-reading, and of his prolific output the stories with a macabre tinge are perhaps likeliest to survive – *The Old Ladies, The Killer and The Slain, The Man with Red Hair*. This is an unexpected side to a man who in private life was the sunniest of characters. He could not understand why intellectuals disdained his novels, and he believed that adverse criticism was the result of personal dislike. Any reviewer who spoke ill of his work was sure to receive an invitation to an expensive lunch and a friendly chat that put things right and left him with the feeling that Hugh was the nicest of men – which he was, a thoroughly good sort and inexhaustibly kind. He went on lecture tours of America, speaking not only about his own books but also those of others, and he helped considerably with the Book Society. These social activities may have given Somerset Maugham the idea for a malicious portrait of him as the self-seeking novelist in *Cakes and Ale*. Although

Maugham pretended that he had not intended to satirise him, Walpole knew that he was the target and felt deeply hurt. He put on a brave face. 'I shan't forgive Willie easily,' he told Agate. 'The beggar had drunk my claret!'

All his life Walpole sought what he described as the ideal friend. For a time he found it in the mountainous opera singer Lauritz Melchior, whom he adored as man and artist. Eventually he formed a permanent attachment with a brawny policeman who left the service and gave up his pension rights on the promise of a bequest in Hugh's will. Here was his defence against the envy of the literary world and the unkind people who denigrated his success. Happiness was his, he bore a grudge against no man, and his loud ringing laugh confirmed the serenity of a well-filled existence crowned with a knighthood. He lacked vanity and had few illusions about his own work. His reverence for Virginia Woolf, an author who could not have been more different from him, was typical of his humility. It was this humility which, every night, made him kneel down at his bedside and say his prayers like a child.

Night-time prayers and sex were the few things he had in common with Agate. Soon after their meeting in the Turkish bath he was, 'rather reluctantly', lending the critic £200, a very large sum in the early thirties. Hugh divided those he knew into 'friends' and 'enemies', and Agate was classed from time to time as one or the other according to circumstance. He was an enemy if he wrote cruelly about a new novel. In the pamphlet entitled *A Letter to a Modern Novelist* Hugh assaulted him roundly. Agate replied by savaging the piece in *The Daily Express*. Hugh protested and he replied: 'I wonder you can do that, attack me in a *book* – a tiny one but a permanent thing – and expect Puss not to scratch back.' But Agate could be, unexpectedly, a friend, as when he praised *The Apple Trees*, an autobiographical work, and Hugh began to wonder what he would do without this 'enemy' to fulminate about. Thus, when Agate next came to lunch at 90, Piccadilly, and flicked his cigar ash into a wooden bowl painted by Gauguin, and admired the scarab ring that belonged to Oscar Wilde, and appraised the new Matisse pictures, Hugh was in his pinkest and most cherubic mood and ready to lend Agate another hundred or so.

What most upet this gentlest of men was the accusation of insincerity. He once thought Agate had charged him with this and fell into a state of hurt indignation. Agate replied: 'Is the Keswick air too strong for you? I did *not* say that your mysticism is *not* sincere. Of course it's sincere – and that's what's so funny about it. Now do please try to come out of your summer mist and get the exact value of my next sentence. *You are a bad mystic in the sense in which Martin Tupper was a bad poet.* And heaven knows that nobody ever accused Tupper of insincerity.' They met for lunch and sweetness was restored. Doubtless Agate was tactful enough not to speak of an incident which occurred at the first rehearsal for a stage adaptation of *The Old Ladies*. Hugh went up to Edith Evans who played a leading role and said: 'I hope you liked the novel'. 'Oh!' she blurted out, looking him full in the face, 'Is it from a book?' Lilian Braithwaite, chuckled Agate to himself, would have said that if she had known the novel by heart.

Another Walpole–Agate clash arose from arguments about the historical novel as a genre. 'You know my passion for everything that concerns Johnson and Boswell,' wrote the critic. 'Heaven forfend that I should ever read a novel about them! Biography is a form of history; fiction never can be, and I, personally, don't want it to try. I want history to be nothing but history and fiction to be wholly fictitious. 'Let us have no meandering," said the old lady who won David Copperfield's caul. I am equally firm for no tampering.'

This was a skirmish, a mere aside, compared with the battle when Hugh, exasperated by Agate's criticism of his writing, forbade Macmillans to send his new novel to *The Daily Express*. Agate offered him space in one of his *Ego* books to explain why, and ended his letter: 'Come, you old badger, let me draw you.' Hugh was drawn, and replied that he did not want him to review his books '. . . because you don't read them. What you do is open my new book, find a piece of English that isn't *your* English, pick it out, pillory it under your fat caricature in your paper, make a mock or two, and so leave it.

'Now you are a first-class journalist and I always read you with joy, but I can never reconcile your serious, devoted attitude to the theatre and your flippant, casual patronage of current literature.

'I *doubt* if you've ever read a *whole* book by anyone right through in your life! Have you? If so, what?

'Now, you may be right in your attitude to current literature, but, as *you* know, a book *is* a book to the author of it. One has been a year or more living with it, caring for it, cursing it. Why should one deliver it over to someone who will certainly mock it without reading it? All the same it *would* be so delivered over were it not for the second reason.

'. . . I have a great regard for our friendship. It has had some ups and downs, but by now I value it for its entertainment value and because I like you. Now, I know that a contemptuous review by you who have *not* read my book will only make me, for a time at least, think you a patronising, job-shirking bastard. Of course, you are *not* that, but I, in company with others whom you have mockingly patronised, would for the moment think so. As you are not that I don't want to think you are.' It was typical of him that he should sign this letter as 'Your affectionate friend'.

The thrusts and parries and reconciliations continued until Walpole's death. Though Agate could not tell a story, and admitted it, he prized words and the meaning of words. Inexactness jarred on him. 'A flock of angels cut the brilliant air like a wave breaking through mist.' How could a writer allow himself a simile of that nature? But Hugh was incorrigible, and however much Agate twitted him his smile remained steady and his blue eyes shone with the enjoyment of life. Amid the lovely surroundings of his Keswick home he wrote in his diary: 'Even Agate I don't *really* dislike. If he came tomorrow up the garden holding out his hand, I'd take it and be delighted.'

Another of Agate's rich friends was Montague Shearman, barrister, art collector and something in the Foreign Office. He inherited a large fortune which enabled him to take life not very seriously and to build up a valuable collection of modern pictures. It was Monty who, when Agate moved into one of his many new houses, gave him a Chirico to hang on the wall. He was amiability itself and raised no objection on hearing that his grateful friend decided he did not like it and had exchanged it for a Guevara which he had long coveted. There were many others where it came from, including canvases by Matisse and Utrillo, of whom he was a pioneer in England. They hung in 'the Room', that section of his apartment in the Adelphi where he held what could only be termed a *salon* and where some of London's best talk occurred around midnight. Next to them were canvases by Renoir, Monet, Sisley, Rouault, Vuillard and Bonnard. His English discoveries numbered Sickert and Duncan Grant. In 1936 Agate dedicated to him a book entitled *Kingdoms for Horses*, a harvest of essays about his various sporting passions with exquisite illustrations by Rex Whistler. The dedication read: 'To Montague Shearman, who at the Oxford Agricultural Show turned his back on the ring and read Horace.'

There was an eighteenth-century flavour to this genial *bon vivant* who knew more than any man about Cruickshank and Rowlandson. He always reminded Agate of Johnson's verdict on Burke: 'His stream of mind is perpetual.' Yet although he stood over six feet tall and weighed sixteen stone, he never really felt well and was a hypochondriac who had to struggle with genuine illnesses in addition to the melancholia that beset Johnson and Chesterfield. Perhaps, with better health, he would have gained the rewards that he saw, without bitterness, his inferiors achieving. Why, Agate asked him, did he give up the Bar? 'I was a poor advocate,' he replied. 'I defended twelve murderers, and they were all hanged.' His friend suggested that they were guilty. 'Yes. But I prosecuted on twelve occasions. And they all got off!'

Agate dragged him once to Ireland for the Dublin Horse Show and could not help feeling boredom at Monty's ecstasies over the Georgian architecture and the aesthetic appeal of a fifth-century graveyard. He got his revenge by lunching, to annoy his old friend, on lobster and sparkling Burgundy, and feeling triumphantly well afterwards. Monty just smiled, for he was a tolerant man – and a generous one too, both in his patronage of young deserving artists and of middle-aged not so deserving drama critics. He kept, unknown to all, a diary himself, and it contained such entries as '. . . I know J. A. hates to be told that his work is not indispensable to the *Sunday Times* and is not creative! Must stop this. After all, who am I to criticise anybody?' J. A., says this frank document, barks boorishly, cannot control his manners, is a bilker, and can be very tiresome abroad. On other occasions he is 'very good'. Then: 'James's new *Ego* is out. Very vulgar. What a contrast to Chesterton's delightful Autobiography!'

Most of Agate's friends were less austere towards the *Ego* books and even provided him with material for them. Bertie van Thal, for example, pretended that he was keeping his own diary modelled on *Ego*. It began: 'The season has opened brilliantly with the death of old Lady Tweedle . . .' Bertie first met Agate, who thought him 'a pleasant young man', in 1932. He had been impressed by the critic's review of Wycherley's *The Country Wife*, a piece of writing that gave the lie to Agate's mischievous description of himself as so mixing up 'the plays of Congreve, Wycherley, Vanbrugh and Farquhar that he carried in his waistcoat-pocket a note of what each had written in case somebody should stop him in the street to ask'. Agate was flattered by Bertie's remarks and often took him to first nights. The Restoration dramatists were only one of Bertie's loves. He had immense knowledge of Victorian literature which extended to a minute acquaintance with the novels of Mrs de la Pasture and of Eliza Lynn Linton. Although he was one of the earliest publishers to recognize the talent of Hermann Hesse, his greatest pleasure lay in discovering neglected writers like George Gissing and Theodore Hook. In music he was a keen opera lover and would often be seen scouring remote neighbourhoods like Hammersmith in pursuit of a rare revival of Cilea's *L'Arlesiana* or Massenet's *Cendrillon*. He loved books above all, and he often championed lost causes unselfishly and at no little expense to himself. Agate described him as 'looking more than ever like a sleek, well-groomed dormouse' out of Tenniel.

Such Bertie was, with his dapper suit, natty bow tie, glittering monocle and black shiny shoes.

They made a typical excursion together in 1938 to the Malvern Festival where Shaw's *Geneva* was being given for the first time. Agate, as always, arrived to pick him up an hour late. 'Time, you know, means absolutely nothing to me, nothing!' Then the harassed critic remembered that he had forgotten his spare walking stick, a stout silver-topped malacca affair, and they had to drive back to the Villa Volpone where the cook handed it to a manservant who passed it on to a chauffeur who was obviously in a state of nerves at the prospect of driving his cantankerous employer. On the way Agate stopped the car frequently to jot down ideas for his *Daily Express* column. Eventually he fell asleep. Next day, to recover from the rigours of *Geneva*, which is not one of Shaw's best plays, they sneaked off to Birmingham where Sir Seymour Hicks was playing a matinée. Their companion was Peter Page, a journalist who wrote the 'Mr Gossip' column in the *Daily Graphic* and who is credited with the shortest drama criticism ever printed: his notice of a play called *Oh, Yes!* consisted of the two words 'Oh, No!' He was tall, Oxford-educated and a skilled musician, and he had, unlike most music critics, conducted performances of opera. Perhaps it was this experience which made him agree with Arnold Bennett's remark that opera is only tolerable if given in a foreign language. 'I remember going to the theatre in Athens and seeing a play called *The Sister of the Mother of Karolos*,' he told Agate. 'It was an hour before I found out that the play was a Greek version of *Charley's Aunt*.'

Peter – he had been christened Philip but disliked the name – lived at Colville Hall in Essex, a mansion built around 1593 which was the sort of place where you are warned: 'Be careful with that door-handle. Henry VIII wrenched it off the last time he dined here.' Surrounded by hamlets with names like Margaret Roding, Abbess Roding and Rambouillet Roding, it was an appropriate setting for this great-grandson of Charles X. He, wearing his ancestor's coat of flowered satin, entertained his guests with anecdotes which challenged them to distinguish lies from truth. At a mention of Timbuctoo he would dismiss it, in actor's jargon, as 'any Number Three town' – but he had, in fact, stayed there and knew the place. You realized, though, he was fantasticating when he spoke of going on to the Solomon Islands and dining with head-hunters whom he found indistinguishable from any party at the Savoy Grill. He also had an unbelievable story that when he was initiated into Freemasonry his sponsors were Willie Clarkson, the famous theatrical wigmaker, and Lord Kitchener of Khartoum. This happened to be the absolute truth.

So they went off to Birmingham, Jimmie and Bertie and Peter, and there they dined with Seymour Hicks, the actor and playwright who could challenge Peter on his own ground as a raconteur. Peter told of a luxury cruise when his boat stopped at a tiny islet in the Marquesas which was visited every five years or so. Having gone ashore he met a youth wearing nothing but a pair of dirty shorts. Peter addressed him in his best French and strove to bring him up to date on all the news he had missed living on this deserted spot. 'I suppose,' he added, 'in view of your isolation, you must find it a great treat to talk to anybody?' The young man, who had been staring at him perplexed, answered in broad Cockney: 'I don't know wot you're talking abaht, sir. I'm a steward on B deck.'

Seymour Hicks kept them up with his stories until after midnight as the waiters, forgetful of unwashed dishes, crowded round to listen. He spoke of the time when he and Peter, in solemn mood, had undertaken a pilgrimage to the Richmond tomb of Edmund Kean. It was the great romantic actor's centenary, and they wished to honour the occasion by laying a wreath. They had trouble, however, in finding the vault which contained his remains. The oldest inhabitant came along and told them it was in another part of the church. This happened five times with five different oldest inhabitants, the wreath wilting and fading as they tramped hopefully around the building. At last they identified the correct vault and paid their homage. Seymour wiped his brow and said: 'With all his vaults we love him still.'

The Seymours, the Peters, the Berties, were just the type

of friends you would expect to associate with a gregarious journalist. A more surprising companion was the gentle Clifford Bax. He was the brother of Arnold, composer and in time Master of the King's Musick, and, member of a rich family, played the generous host at his manor house in Wiltshire and at his London flat in D2, Albany. Posterity has treated him worse than Arnold, whose music is still sometimes to be heard. His poetry and plays are seldom mentioned today, and his name does not figure in the standard reference books. His many plays mostly took historical themes: *The Rose Without A Thorn* celebrated Lady Catherine Howard and had two last acts which, in Agate's opinion, built up 'extraordinary tension'. *Socrates* cleverly utilised the Platonic dialogues for theatrical purposes and gave Agate 'a lovely afternoon in which the mind, having had its bath of pure sublimity, was permitted those commoner emotions for which actors and the theatre exist'. As Bax grew older his neatly bearded features took on an even more ascetic cast – a combination of 'Shakespeare, Charles I and Beecham,' said Agate – and he delved into Buddhism and other mystical pursuits. Once, after giving Agate dinner in Albany, he offered to put on a gramophone record of somebody dead speaking at a Spiritualist séance. As it was two o'clock in the morning, the agitated critic flatly refused to hear it.

'If you had more sensibility and less bounce, what an attractive man you would be . . .' Bax told him. 'The world (the reviewing world) hates me because I am a temperamental aristocrat: lots of people detest you because you have not my aloofness and my "despise" of The Little Man and Journalistic Cheapjacks.' Agate retorted: 'But consider where I should have been without "bounce!" You are a born Londoner, your appearance is elegant, you have always known everybody, and you have always had money. With your talent and these advantages it would have been disgraceful if you had not made for yourself a place in English letters. Now consider my case. I am a provincial of commonplace exterior who began his assault on London at the age of forty-one without a ha'penny and with no influence. Was I to make modesty trumps? No. I decided to put on the whole armour of Balzac, and not to make the mistake Goldsmith made when he tackled London "without friends, recommendation, money, *or impudence.*"' That 'commonplace exterior' reminded Bax of some Roman slave who might have been in attendance at Trimalchio's Banquet.

'Agate's least admirable characteristic was to play the bully, as Dr Johnson did, threatening both foes and friends with the terrible effects of his displeasure,' thought Bax, 'and the best in him was shown by his entirely disinterested championship of culture – that is to say, of the well-cultivated mind.' In a magazine article Bax accused him of being ready to sacrifice a play or a player 'for the sake of the second-cousin of a poor pun'. Agate burst into fury and threatened him with a libel writ and a trouncing in his next *Ego*. Nothing came of this 'flustering of an infuriated fish-wife,' and the two men were soon back on good terms. 'I have improved upon Goldsmith's Mr Hardcastle,' Agate wrote to him. 'I like old manners, old books, old wine and old women. And, old friend, I like you.'

One of the reasons for this unlikely friendship was a mutual love of cricket. Agate would forgive Bax anything for having introduced him to the cricketing giant C. B. Fry, who was not only a first-class athlete but also a first-class scholar. 'I always wanted to be a minor poet,' Fry confided in Agate. 'I remember when I did my record long jump saying to myself when I was in the air half-way, "This may be pretty good jumping. It's dashed poor minor poetry."' Man's universal desire to shine at something else did not, however, persuade him to accept the Crown of Albania when that nation, impressed like the rest of the world by his brains and his personality, offered him the throne. Agate pressed him to name the world's greatest batsman. He declined to compare Grace and Ranji, but he inferred that the order of precedence was Ranji, Grace, Trumper, Bradman and Hobbs, and he revealed that the secret of Jessop's quickness lay in the fact that he was double-jointed all over. As for the mentality of cricketers in general, he allowed himself one small touch of malice: 'If they were mice you wouldn't be able to teach them the way to their holes!'

The closest of Agate's many acquaintances and friends was George Felton Mathew. They had met in 1932 at *Country Life* where George then laboured and where Agate, under his 'Warrington' pseudonym, wrote the drama reviews. He was the great-grandson of Keats's friend, a man whom the poet described as possessing 'An Elegant, Pure and Aerial Mind' and whose signature may be seen in the visitors' book at Keats House. George was thirty-five or so but looked a disillusioned twenty-four and had the air of a bemused St Bernard dog. It was difficult for him to tell right from left, and when asked which was his right hand he needed to think for a moment to decide it was the one he wrote with. During his service in the Navy he was instructed to haul a rope with his right hand: this he absent-mindedly did with his left instead and released a string of mines in the direction of the Grand Fleet. Later he was ordered to row a pair of officers to their ship. The more he rowed the more the ship receded, and in the end the astonished crew on board saw two officers rowing George.

Behind this dream-like manner there was a sharp mind. As an editor George cut to the heart of things and never let a misprint get past him. He scrutinised *Ego* proofs with a steady gaze and helped to avert many a small disaster. Agate had a genius for persuading his friends to help him out of difficult situations, and George's talent was soon pressed into service for tasks more creative than reading proofs. He grew used to the urgent telephone call at six o'clock in the evening which explained that Agate was unable to go to a film première and would dear George attend in his place? All he need do was write a quick review and drop it in the letter-box of the Villa Volpone on his way home so that the Agatian trade-mark could be applied to it. The good-natured George never let him down, and Agate, despite himself, often wondered at his 'whimsical tolerance of me in all my moods from the monstrous to the petty'.

Often they supped at the Café Royal and wandered the streets talking until three in the morning. George wanted to produce one witty book before he died. He had written novels for their witty passages and plays for the sake of chances given by the dialogue. Agate told him to save enough money to keep himself for two years while he lived in a garret and wrote. But he could not make up his mind. He was a mixture of the audacious and the timid, an artist whose best things disappeared in the evanescence of talk, a modest man who, when offered promotion, recommended someone else. His conversation astonished Agate, who had never heard anyone else use the word 'esurient' in everyday talk before. He had heard his own father say 'eleemosynary' and another friend drop the epithet 'ineluctable'. Now it only remained for him to hear someone say 'jocund'. And George was so full of charming theories. Had he not pointed out that Bach has only two tunes, one grave and the other gay? Had he not further insisted that the gay tune was only the grave one played faster?

For fifteen years George was a foul-weather friend, ever reliable, endlessly helpful. And it was to George that Agate spoke the last words he uttered on earth.

Chapter Six
EGO

'I did so enjoy your book [Ego]. Everything that everybody writes in it is so good.'

Mrs Patrick Campbell

i
DIARIST

'I don't think my importance warrants immortality. But I want my work to last, *and so that it may perpetuate itself, not necessarily me.* I must perish; so be it! But that is no reason why the things I have loved should perish.'

JAMES AGATE

Ego 2 appeared in 1936 and established what became a regular event in the publishing season whereby every year or so Agate brought out the latest instalment of an autobiography which maddened some as intensely as it pleased others. Among the former were Humbert Wolfe, who summed up the author as 'blissfully certain of his own importance and the unimportance of general standards of taste', and spoke disdainfully of 'a noisome self-satisfaction unequalled since Pepys'. Admirers included Noël Coward, Hugh Walpole and the faithful Rebecca West, who wrote: 'I shall keep these journals as I keep the Goncourt journals, as records of their time more truly historical than history.'

Pepys and Goncourt! Who could ask for more? True, these were journalistic, on-the-spot reactions. There were no Pepysian revelations in *Ego 2* and no frankness in the manner of Rousseau. Instead of Flaubert, Gautier, Turgenev and George Sand who were the Goncourts' subjects, Agate had to make do with Noël Coward, Hugh Walpole, Clifford Bax, J. B. Priestley and Marie Tempest. What he does give is an entertaining picture of a certain group of people living a certain life at a certain time in London, together with a self-portrait that is always absorbing. A diarist does not necessarily rely on famous or attractive people for his material. Paul Léautaud's journal is among the finest of its kind, though its hundreds of characters are mostly unknowns. A more serious accusation is that Agate fails to reveal all about himself as Rousseau did. It is, though, easy to read between the lines, and it would have been impossible for him at the time to tell the whole story. Pepys, we must remember, wrote in code. Agate wrote for immediate publication. He tried to analyse his reasons: 'Why do I write it? For immortality? But how much immortality? Ten years? A hundred? Ten thousand? '*La gloire est le soleil des morts*.' Yes. But does it warm them? I enjoy keeping this diary, yet would not write a word except with the notion that some day somebody may read it. Would a painter put anything on canvas if the canvas were never to be seen by living eye? Is not a writer without readers like an actor without a public? Compare the poet in *Le Lys Rouge* who cared so little for any earthly future that he wrote his poems on cigarette paper. 'Thus my verses retain only a kind of metaphysical existence.' But what a purely metaphysical young man this pure young man must have been. There is an essay here, and I am wasting money.'

The full flavour of the *Ego* books cannot be appreciated without reading them through consecutively. So much depends, as in a musical composition, on the individual themes which are stated, taken up, varied, developed, and then succeeded by other motifs that recur at given points. A daily entry can be as short as half a dozen words or as long as a complete essay. Sometimes Agate gives way to an obsession and drops in some sprawling piece, under the guise of an 'intaglio' on, for example, the Dreyfus affair. If one's interest in Dreyfus is faint one skips it, although, on later readings, one finds oneself looking through it, anxious to squeeze the last drop from these idiosyncratic books just as one gladly ploughs through the genealogical ramblings of

Saint-Simon. There are passages on golf, cricket and Hackney ponies which cannot be avoided and which may be appreciated by laymen for the sake of the energy and obvious enjoyment which pervade them. In any case, they represent an essential side of the man's character, and without them the portrait would be incomplete. Besides, they often inspire him with a perfect *mot* in other contexts. When asked whom he considered the better actor, Olivier or Gielgud, he would quote the judgment of an ancient caddie at St Andrews on who was the better golfer, young Tom Morris or Bobby Jones: 'Baith o'them played pairfect gowf!'

Less excusable is his habit of reprinting, in extenso, a *Sunday Times* review which happened to have pleased him, or an article of which he felt especially proud, the point being that *Ego* is here being wasted on stuff available elsewhere. The letters he features are a different matter. His correspondents were numerous, and anyone who wrote him a quaint or amusing or witty epistle could rely on seeing it in the next issue of *Ego*. One of them was George Richards, né Reichardt, cat-lover and frustrated drama critic who poured out his views in copious missives. He lived at Poole, and one weekend Agate and George Mathew stayed at a hotel in Bournemouth where he joined them for dinner. Afterwards they retired to Agate's bedroom for more whisky and conversation. They had Agate's tooth-glass and George's, which he collected from his own bedroom, but lacked a third glass for Richards. The latter said, 'No problem!', left them for a moment, and, presumably having robbed a vacant bedroom of its tooth-glass, returned with one in his hand. In the early hours of the morning, when their conversation had ended, George Mathew escorted Richards to the lift and saw him off. On the way back to his room George saw a pair of lady's shoes left out for cleaning: they contained two sets of false teeth. Next day at breakfast George saw a lady guest observing him intently with a suspicious eye. 'No, Madam,' he thought to himself, 'it was not I who violated your dentures.'

A star correspondent was George Lyttelton, 'a nice, large affable creature in the sixties,' as Agate described him when they met for lunch at the Ivy after many letters exchanged.

He taught English to generations of small Etonians and divided his spare time between marking examination papers and writing to people. In retirement he kept up a fortnightly ping-pong with the publisher Rupert Hart-Davis, an ex-pupil, and carried on this interminable correspondence to the extent of six volumes in which he occasionally spoke of his previous target, a little ungraciously, as 'old Agate'. His periods were, however, smoother than those of the anonymous letter-writer who could never forgive Agate his adverse criticism of W. C. Fields as Micawber in the film of *David Copperfield*:

W. C. FIELDS AS MICAWBER
De mortuis nil nisi bonum
You
Self-advertising
Flamboyant
Swollen-headedd
Utterly bloody
Bastard.
God wither your right hand!
To James Agate
Queen Alexandra Mansions
Sour Grape Street
WC2

(Agate was then living in Grape Street.)

A dull trip to Bexhill in 1934 is transmuted thus: 'Aug. 21, Tuesday. Autobiography accepted by Hamish Hamilton, and get £200 on account of royalties.

'Went South and set off for short jaunt with Leo Pavia. The old thing is more unprintably witty than ever. Spent our first night at Bexhill-on-Sea. (The turn of this sentence reminds me of a Shakespearean postcard Bruce Winston once wrote to Sybil Thorndike: 'Lay last night with your husband at Tewkesbury.') Filthy hole, dull and, I gather, purse-proud. After dinner sat on the front in a green alcove rather like an outdoor setting for *Much Ado*, and watched a worn moon preside over a green sea and a silver taffrail. Nobody passed. Complained of this to girl at hotel cash-desk who said icily:

"How many people do you require?" Collected luggage and left Bexhill.'

Excursions like this one are varied by an entry for November 5:

'My day:

10.30. Sat for James Gunn [the portrait painter].

1.00. Film lunch at Claridges.

2.30. Appointment at Hamish Hamilton's.

3.16. René Clair's new film at Academy Cinema.

6.00. Ernest Fenton's.* Reviewed six books for *D. E.* article, 1600 words. E. told me this pathetic story. One evening shortly before the war he and Arthur Roberts [the comedian] were walking down Panton Street where, outside a public house, an old man was mournfully playing on a penny whistle the old waltz "Love's Golden Dream is Past". It was five minutes to closing time, and as they passed the old man, Arthur said, "Hurry up, or you'll be too late to have one!" The old man replied, 'Sorry, Mr Roberts, but I can't hurry up. You see it's marked Adagio.'

10.00. Lay down for a snooze.

11.30. Got up, dressed and went to Peter Page's masked supper given in conjunction with some Russian Princess. Wouldn't have gone only don't want to appear to slight Peter.

3.30. Bed.'

The outside world of 1935 sometimes looms:

'*Oct. 2. Wednesday.* Jock entirely refuses to take the war danger seriously. His comment on the alarmist newspaper placard 'Italians in Abyssinia' is: "Sounds like an opera by Rossini." *Oct. 3. Thursday.* War starts, all the same.'

* Ernest Fenton, who stood over six feet tall and looked like a vicious Renaissance cardinal out of a play by John Ford, began his stage career as a chorus boy in musical comedies. He never progressed much further, and this may have accounted for the feline bitterness of his wit. He was, for a short time in his chorus days, beloved of Oscar Wilde. This interesting link with the past, as Max Beerbohm might have called him, obligingly acted as a go-between when friends wished to use his Holborn rooms for lovers' meetings in secret.

It comes even nearer:

> '*Nov. 25. Monday.* It is known, indeed I boast of it, that as a hay-purchasing officer in the Bouches-du-Rhône I was, throughout the entire war, further from gunfire than any British officer. This explains Reggie Pound's interruption when I was holding forth at the Club today about going to war to stop Germany's ill-treatment of Jews and my willingness to enlist:
> *R.P.* "Nonsense, James. Tanks don't eat hay!"'

And it will not stay away:

> '*Dec. 10. Tuesday.* At half-past one this morning turned on the wireless and heard a delightful performance of *Tyl Eulenspiegel* from some German station. Had to be very soft because of the people above, in fact pianissimo all the way through, but it was delightful and at that hour secret communion with a great race, despite the Nazis, blast 'em. Fred Leigh was entranced too. We often have a quiet hour like this with a couple of pipes and not a word spoken.'

Fred Leigh was one of his most loyal retainers, a man 'who, with his height, tummy and yellow hair looks like a German tenor's Siegfried, has been many things – currier, railway-painter, actor, singer, boxer, and the youngest publican that ever held a licence in the Midlands . . . During the war when in France with the R.G.A. he used to carry 6 hundred-pound shells, 3 in each arm, down the duck-boards to the gun. In November 1917, when strafing Fritz at Metz, in one morning he lifted two thousand hundred-pound shells on to ten men's backs, to put beside a 4-gun battery.'

Note the journalist's attention to precise detail: the 6 hundred-pound shells, the 3 carried in each arm, the two thousand hundred-pound shells, the ten men's backs, the 4-gun battery. This care for accurate reporting is shown in a story told about Dennis van Thal, Bertie's brother, 'a personable youth of twenty-four'. Dennis wanted to work in the theatre and obtained an interview with André Charlot, the famous impresario whose productions inspired even C. B. Cochran. 'Mr Charlot,' said Dennis, 'I want to conduct a revue.' 'Can you?' said Charlot. 'I can.' 'Prove it.' So Dennis then assembled, in Agate's words, 'an amateur band of 10 instruments – 2 violins, 1 cello, 1 double bass, 1 pianist, 2 saxophones (doubling clarinets), 1 trumpet, 1 trombone, 1 drummer.' He rehearsed the band, engaged a hall, and invited Charlot, who arrived on the dot. They played a bit from the overture to *The Barber of Seville*, two fox-trots, 'and a thing called *Nola*'. At four o'clock that afternoon Charlot gave Dennis a contract to conduct *Hi-Diddle-Diddle* on its provincial tour and then in London. This was the first time, said Agate, 'I have ever known an aspirant do anything except aspire, and the only time I have ever known a theatre manager act promptly.'*

Agate was a hypochondriac who often had genuine cause to worry about his health. Even when feeling at his worst, however, he could always summon up the striking epithet, as in the first word of the following entry:

> '*July 22. Monday.* Sumptuous day of wind, nerves, asthma, etc., ending with the doctor coming at two in the morning to give an adrenalin injection.'

This vague malady of 'nerves', which he shared with charwomen and elderly bachelors, can inspire amusing writing:

> '*Nov. 21. Thursday.* Driving back from lunch today had an attack of nerves. At Oxford Circus was on my deathbed, going up Great Portland Street was dead and buried, along Albany Street calculated estate available after insurances raked in, horses sold and debts paid, passing Stanhope Terrace made my will, ascended Primrose Hill and descended to the Everlasting Bonfire simultaneously, and as we turned into England's Lane was critically considering Jock's first article as my successor on the *S. T.*
>
> All this turned out, of course, to be merely what Doctor

* Some two or three shows later Dennis saw Agate getting into a taxi in the Strand. They exchanged greetings and shared the taxi. Dennis seized the opportunity to tell him he had written the score for the opening of the show that night. Result: Agate gave two of his numbers very bad notices. This did not prevent Dennis from going on to become a very important figure in the cinema, TV and theatre as a founder of the influential London Management Agency.

Rutty, the Irish Quaker, called "an hypochondriack obnubilation from wind and indigestion".'

No illness, real or imaginary, was allowed to obscure his sharp eye for the sights and sounds of the London around him:

'Coming down Primrose Hill saw a perfect Manet, three French nuns in total black walking against a background of trees.'

Other people's witticisms, even directed at his own vanity, are included if they are good:

'*May 21. Tuesday.* Ivor Novello, on being asked his opinion of my Diary, said he was entranced but that he thought the Grossmiths' Diary of a Nobody was better. I suspect Bobbie Andrews [the actor, Ivor's close friend] of putting him up to this. At the wedding of Dorothy Hyson and Robert Douglas, the clergyman summoning bride and bridegroom to the altar and addressing them inaudibly and interminably, Bobbie was heard to whisper: "I think he's trying to sell them a play."'

The diarist's tangled finances, or lack of them, often intrude:

'*Feb. 21. Thursday.* Driving Leo to lunch today I said I was surprised to see that a well-known Bond Street money-lender who died recently left no more than £12,000. Leo puckered up his old face and said: "I expect that's what you owe him!"'

Everything, though, is subordinated to work:

'*April 1. Monday.* National celebrations like public holidays are a curse to the journalist, who has to deliver his copy a week earlier, and sometimes finds two weeks crowded into one. Here is my little lot for the next six days.

Monday.	Book article	1,600	words
Tuesday.	Causerie	1,500	„
Wednesday.	Film article	1,200	„
Thursday.	Pseudonymous article	1,500	„
	ditto Jubilee article	2,000	„
Friday.	Theatre article	2,000	„
		9,800	„

'Fortunately there is only one play this week. But I have still to tackle the films and the books, and these include Cronin's recent dollop of 701 pages! Blast these talkative writers who don't know how to stop!'

On public holidays he was miserable, with no telephone ringing and no crisis to stimulate him:

> '*Christmas Day, 1935* . . . In the evening sat, Scrooge-like, at the Café Royal, friendless and deserted. Finally encountered another lone soul whom I hadn't seen for years and gave him dinner.
> '*Boxing Day*. Pub-crawled.
> '*Dec. 27. Friday*. Thank Heaven work has started again.'

Work, for him, signified the maximum output. Like a gardener cherishing the progress of a giant marrow, he kept rigorous tally of all the words he had written and, at the end of the year, summed up the grand total. On the 31 December, 1935, he arrived at this figure:

Sunday Times	100,000	words
The Tatler	60,000	„
Pseudonym, No. 1.	60,000	„
Pseudonym, No. 2.	85,000	„
Daily Express	80,000	„
BBC	50,000	„
Ego	100,000	„
Odd articles	20,000	„
	555,000	„

In addition he had visited between 100 and 150 plays, 50 films, glanced at 500 books and more or less read 200. The famous word count did not include books he himself had published during the year. This would have been cheating since they mostly comprised old stuff worked up. He once boasted to Jock about the lengthy list of his publications. 'I am astonished, Jock, at this reverence of yours for Max Beerbohm when he has published so few books.' Jock reported: 'But surely, Jimmy, you are confusing sheer quality with sheer quantity.' A black look was darted and the subject was quickly changed.

The quotations in this chapter are typical of the *Ego* books. You may complain, as many have, that in such an apparently voluble and egoistic writer who is eager to talk about himself at length, it is strange to find no mention of his intimate life. To which the answer is that he drops many clues and that the fun lies in deciphering them. On a visit to the highly respectable town of Bognor, for example, he writes: 'The names of Bognor's streets are in black letters on a white ground. At the corner of my road I saw dovetailed into the lettering the pencilled scribble: "B. M. loved T. B. H. here twice."' It is a good story considered on its face value alone. The informed reader, even in those reticent times, would have been able to extract another layer of meaning from it, since "T.B.H." in gay slang between the wars, and still among more mature adherents of the cult, stands for 'to be had'.

ii
PROTÉGÉS – AND A TRIP TO NEW YORK

> 'Well, Jock can say of himself what he likes, I know, and put on record here, that the first day I set eyes on him I recognized the strange beauty of his mind and spirit, and that I have not been deceived, or ever thought I could be. He has been my friend and counsellor, pupil and sometimes mentor; and never does, nor can, his wit run dry.'
>
> JAMES AGATE

On the 1 September, 1936, he celebrated the tenth anniversary of Jock's arrival on his doorstep – or, rather, Jock celebrated it by taking him to lunch at Rules in Maiden Lane, then the haunt of publishers and editors, now the preserve of advertising men and television executives. With them was A. D. Peters, Agate's literary agent and firm friend of many years, and Gerald Barry, who, as editor of the *Saturday Review* in 1926, had at Agate's prompting accepted Jock's first article. Rules was where Agate had first asked

Jock to lunch, and the champagne they drank in 1936 belonged to the year of their original feast.

Jock was only one of the many protégés Agate adopted over the years. Young men who wished to be writers, poets, actors, musicians, were for ever drifting in and out of the Villa Volpone to be counselled, lectured, taken up, and as often dropped by their disappointed patron when his efforts at launching them foundered on the indifference of an uncaring world. Agate was a kind man in many ways. He admired, quite unselfishly, youth and talent and did his best to encourage those who possessed them. Thus he satisfied a frustrated paternal instinct. It also helped him to feel that once in a way 'I am doing, or helping somebody else to do, something creative instead of this perpetual criticising'.

Two early recipients of his patronage were Kenneth Allott and Stephen Tait. The young men, both in their early twenties, lived in Newcastle-on-Tyne, and had written a play which they described to him as the best comedy of manners since Congreve. It had also, they added, been rejected by the best actresses and managers in London. He sent them a telegram: 'Letter received five minutes ago. Sit up all night typing play and I will do ditto reading it.' Two years later, after much harassing of theatre managements, badgering of literary agents and bullying of the would-be playwrights to improve their plots, he saw at the Q Theatre a production of *The Prickly Pear* which they had written. He gave it a critical but sympathetic notice in *The Sunday Times*. Were it not that the two young authors were masters of dialogue, he concluded, the piece would be insufferably tedious. As Tait and Allott faded into the past, to be succeeded by other protégés. he murmured to himself: 'Shall always like these children.'

Their place was taken by Alexis Kligerman, a Russian Pole who showed signs of virtuosity as a pianist. Agate once more felt the urge to help, perhaps because Kligerman 'will be a change from the hordes of mediocrities who pester me with their lack of talent'. The accompanist Gerald Moore and the music critic Ralph Hill were commanded to hear him. They praised his technique but were ominously reticent about his musicianship. In the silence that followed Leo

Pavia took over at the piano and improvised a paraphrase on Strauss waltz themes. 'This is the first real piano playing we've heard this afternoon,' whispered Gerald Moore.

Agate and Pavia set to work. They stormed at the sulky Slav, they tore his playing to pieces, they fought to inculcate in him the lightness and the delicacy he needed for Chopin and Schumann as a counterweight to the Lisztian bravura he already possessed. Would he always be a virtuoso and hardly ever a musician? groaned Pavia, absent-mindedly filling his pipe from Agate's pouch. Would he always play Beethoven as if he had a grudge against him? At the same time Agate told everyone about his new discovery and vaunted his talent on all occasions. Even that gentle musician Basil Cameron was unable to prevent a glazed look coming into his eye. Jock showed unwonted jealousy. Agate reminded him tartly of the incident some years ago when, 'on the strength of a few lines scribbled in a notebook, I gave a talented boy of twenty-one his first chance. On the strength of a few bars overheard in the foyer of a suburban theatre I am moving heaven and earth, Myra Hess, and Thomas Russell [manager of the London Philharmonic Orchestra], to give his chance to a talented boy of twenty-two . . .'. Jock relented and confessed a recent dialogue between himself and a friend. Jock: 'I'm devoted to James, but just at the moment he's a terrible bore about some young pianist.' Friend: 'My dear, he was a terrible bore about *you* fifteen years ago!'

Heaven was moved, and earth too. Walter Legge, the emperor of HMV, was enlisted to organise a recording session. A concert agent was drawn in and recitals were arranged in places like Burnley and Aldershot. Although he was infuriated by Kligerman's Slavonic moods, Agate could not help feeling proudly that all the trouble was worthwhile when he heard him give the last movement of the Tchaikovsky piano concerto more breadth and dignity than he ever knew it contained.

A little later Agate was thrilled to discover a new talent in the young violinist Yfrah Neaman. Here, he decided, was playing of the Heifetz order, and he wrote a sensational piece about it in *The Daily Express*. This time Gerald Moore protested at his flamboyant praise and was, as a result, told to use his 'loaf'. Did he not realize, Agate said, that in popular journalism there was no grade between nonentity and world celebrity, and that it was essential to use the sort of clichés *Express* readers would understand? Moore remained unconvinced. 'Mush, my dear Jimmie,' he replied.

The case of the young poet Kenneth Hopkins was rather different. He had published *The Grasshopper Broadsheets* which included poems by himself, Charles Williams, Sylvia Townsend Warner and Stevie Smith. A copy was sent to Agate who reviewed it kindly in *The Daily Express*. He did not like this modern stuff which grated on an ear more attuned to the mellow verse of Tennyson – but he was ready to give it a cautious recognition. Hopkins entered into a sprightly correspondence with him. It ended with a P.S. from Agate inviting the 'delicate' Hopkins to come and see him. The poet did so, and Agate listened with delight as the lad explained why he was the greatest living poet. He went further and severely warned Agate to give up his *Ego* books at the first sign of being written out. This was the sort of impertinent talk Agate enjoyed. In the taxi afterwards he rested an exploratory hand on the young man's knee. It went no further.

Later Hopkins enchanted Agate with a review of *Ego 5* for *Time and Tide* which, in four hundred words, embraced quotations from Chaucer, William Morris, himself, Belloc, Drayton, Shakespeare, Praed, Humbert Wolfe, Johnson, Samuel Butler the elder, Theodore Hook and Cowper, so challenging Agate on his own ground of quotation and showing that it wasn't necessary to rely on French. Agate declared it the best review he'd ever had. Both men emerged well from this curious encounter: Hopkins as the champion of the new order and Agate as the defender of the old, and despite their obvious differences they ended up respecting each other. The critic avowed, rather sadly, to him: 'In my life I have tried to dissuade three people from pursuing what they felt to be their vocation – Alan Parsons, the journalist and critic, and Robert Speaight and Reginald Tate, the actors. They all made brilliant careers. I have tried, contrariwise, to encourage young men, all of whom have failed, with the notable exception of Alan Dent.'

Which brings us back to Jock sitting with his guests amid the Edwardian splendour of Rules. Jock was no more the humble secretary. A year previously Ivor Brown had invited him to write drama criticism for *The Manchester Guardian*, an invitation which, to Agate's private alarm, he accepted. 'Splendid, Jock – but you'll never be able to do it. Get me a taxi right away!' he blustered, and drove to the paper's London office where he berated them for robbing him of his valuable secretary. Having found out that the new drama critic's salary was to be £250 a year, he asked Jock to take something less than the £7 a week to which he had lately promoted him because, having to attend the theatre professionally four nights a week, there would be less time for secretarial duties. They argued, they snapped at each other. In the end Scotland beat Lancashire and Jock kept his salary intact.

Resigned to the inescapable fact that the apprentice was turning into a master, Agate took Jock to a Bridie first night and suggested he write a practice drama criticism by way of dress-rehearsal for *The Manchester Guardian*. Between the end of the play and twelve o'clock Jock scribbled his piece and sent it to the Villa Volpone in an envelope bearing a midnight post-mark which showed he had kept his word. It was good, thought Agate, and, apart from signs of stage-fright, tellingly expressed. Jock afterwards confessed that the moment he had consigned his criticism to the post-box all sorts of witty things bubbled up in his mind. Henceforth, suggested Agate, he should sign his articles 'E. de l'E.', for *esprit de l'escalier*.

A week later Jock was installed at *The Manchester Guardian*. His articles continued to inspire Agate with pride and disquiet. A reference to Frank Vosper acting 'as it were, uncrushably' reminds you instantly of this player's silky accent and sleek smile. Here was cause for pride. Disquiet began when Agate realised that the younger generation was knocking at the door, not once, but continually, and with increasing persistence. His contract with *The Sunday Times* was due for renewal in two years. Suppose, by then, Jock's excellence were to give him the succession? Suppose, equally appalling, his drudge, amanuensis and ghost were to leave him without the stimulus of his golden mind – and, more practically, wasting hours searching for a line in Cowley when Jock could have told him where to find it in Crashaw?

At the Rules luncheon these horrid possibilities were not mentioned. When Gerald Barry, then editor of *The News Chronicle*, offered Jock between courses the post of drama critic, he turned it down, preferring to stay with *The Manchester Guardian*. In this, thought Agate, he rose superior to Mrs Micawber, who, after all, was never put to the test.* Jock reminded him that at their lunch ten years ago he had borrowed the money from Peters to settle the bill. Agate, secretly, rather hoped that, to complete the pattern, Jock would do the same.

Within a few months Jock did, in fact, take over from Agate at *The Sunday Times*, though only as a locum tenens. The occasion of it was Agate's excursion to New York where the paper sent him to report on the state of the American theatre. His companion was a Jewish doctor friend, and, since the liner they travelled on was the *Bremen*, he prudently asked the shipping company whether there would be 'any Nazi nonsense' on board. The clerk replied that the company did not allow politics to interfere with business. An admirable Jewish maxim, thought Agate.

On the 28 April, 1937, Jock saw him off. Agate recommended him to shine, but not, he added thoughtfully, to outshine. The Southampton Sewage Works bloomed with flowers and greenery as the boat cast off, and Agate, all his complexes in full swing, anxiously asked his doctor friend whether, in a crisis, he could do a tracheotomy. 'Yes, if you've a penknife,' was the cheerful reply. He rose abruptly from the breakfast table, and, bowler hat firmly jammed on to defeat the wind off the sea, he padded the deck with unease.

* 'Emma, my angel!' cried Mr Micawber, running into the room, 'what is the matter?'

'I never will desert you, Micawber,' she exclaimed.

'My life!' said Mr Micawber, taking her into his arms. 'I am perfectly aware of it.'

'He is the parent of my children! He is the father of my twins. He is the husband of my affections,' cried Mrs Micawber, struggling; 'and I ne-ver-will-desert Mr Micawber!' (*David Copperfield*)

The aeroplane has made these long luxurious voyages a part of history. For six days Agate consumed food and wine excellent beyond belief. Whenever he raised a cigar to his lips a silent presence slipped a matchbox into his hand. A bandbox smartness pervaded the ship. He did not really know what to do in this gilded idleness, and he felt like a dog which, on the leash for years, had suddenly been liberated but had forgotten how to frisk. He soon remembered, though, when he appraised the lift-boys who, in their sweet white uniforms, looked like tap-dancers in a revue.

On the 3 May, in a slight haze, the Brooklyn gasometer peered out from starboard. On the left the Statue of Liberty took on the aspect of a big girl about to have a baby. Then the New York skyline ever so slowly emerged with its resemblance to those scenes in stencilled cardboard that used to be a feature of the London theatre. The famous but not luxury hotel where he stayed amazed him with its prices, though fortunately *The Sunday Times* was paying. He walked down Broadway and saw it as a film version of the Place Clichy with a hint of Shepherd's Bush. Central Park was a smaller and shabbier Hampstead Heath, like a crater with walls made of surrounding skyscrapers. At a matinée of Housman's play *Victoria Regina* he admired 'An excellent Prince Consort' played by Vincent Price. The impresario Lee Shubert heaped attentions upon him and even offered to lend him money. New York, as Agate quickly found, could be even more expensive than Marseille.

At lunch with John Mason Brown, drama critic of *The New York Post*, he spoke of Mrs Patrick Campbell, the actress who was spending the last days of a faded career in a lonely New York hotel. 'She is committing the wittiest form of hara-kiri,' said Brown. Agate went over to West 49th Street and took her out to lunch. The star of the nineteen-hundreds had been a famous Paula in *The Second Mrs Tanqueray*, a ravishing Juliet, an unforgettable Mélisande, an exquisite *comédienne* who was the first to play Eliza in *Pygmalion*. Now she lived like a hermit with only a snappy little white Pekinese called 'Moonbeam' for company. For twenty years she had the world at her feet, and, with suicidal contempt, she kicked it away. Indeed, she preferred to exercise her often very cruel wit. At a party she went up to a clever little *ingénue* who happened to be standing at the side of a distinguished actress in her sixties. 'My dear, how young you look, next to everybody,' she said.

Sarah Bernhardt had told May Agate that 'La Patrick Campbell' was the only woman player of genius in England. Bernard Shaw called her 'a perilously bewitching woman'. Even for Max Beerbohm, who was not to be gammoned, she had 'a quiet and haunting realism of which the secret is hers,' together with glamour and a subtle and potent art. But she was also capricious and wilful. True, the gibes which made her so many enemies were delivered impartially against the famous as well as the unknown. When young she took the lead in a stage version of a then very popular novel by Hall Caine, the prolific and best-selling novelist whose books were read by millions. At rehearsal he ventured to suggest a few stage moves. 'You don't mind, do you?' he asked politely. 'Oh dear, no, Mr Caine,' Mrs Campbell sweetly answered, 'my greatest desire is to achieve success for *your* sake. By the way, have you ever written anything before?'

The devil within her inspired sallies which burned her mouth as money burns the pocket of a spendthrift. To them she sacrificed her art and finally herself. Of a famous prima donna with an enormous jowl she remarked: 'My God, she looks like I do in a spoon!' An elderly scientist drooling on about ants being wonderful little creature with their own police force and their own army was stopped in his tracks when she said: 'No Navy, I suppose?' A famous theatre director was told: 'You are a wonderful producer. No-one else could have made me look like a little, old, bow-windowed chest of drawers!' And she once threw away untold dollars on a telephone call from New York to Hollywood just to say: 'I've had a cable from England. They want me to play Oscar Wilde.'

Agate took her out to lunch at Voisin's but never noticed what they ate and drank, so compelling was the talk of the irrepressible seventy-two year-old. Neither could he even remember paying, which was just as well. He thought he had never before been exposed to a mind so frivolous and yet so big. She analyzed Schnabel playing Beethoven as being 'like the winds of the air and the waves of the sea, without shape'. She referred to an American actress as having such a beautiful voice 'that you won't understand a word she says'. The same actress, she added, was 'such a nice woman. If you knew her you'd even admire her acting.' And she admitted: 'Many people say I have an ugly mind. That isn't true. I say ugly things, which is different.'

They touched on Somerset Maugham's novel *Theatre* which had just come out. It is one of Maugham's cleverest performances and, as always, irresistibly readable. The heroine, a celebrated actress, is observed with venom and represents all the leading ladies Maugham had known in his long career as a dramatist. Agate was outraged by the portrait. Yes, he argued, Rachel had also been a slut, but she was an august slut who thought nobly of her art. Maugham's heroine was nothing more than a bitch who had no reverence for genius and who could not possibly have been a great artist. She plays with the idea of acting *Phèdre* but decides against it because the leading lady does not appear until the third act. Rachel, thought Agate, would never have approached Racine's masterpiece in this shabby spirit.* Mrs Pat dismissed Maugham. 'He has never met a great actress. No actress could be great in his presence. He has a worm in his brain. He lives in hell and likes it.'

Their conversation in the taxi as they went for a sightseeing drive after lunch was varied by stories about her beloved Pekinese Moonbeam and argument with the driver. They talked of Sarah Bernhardt. 'I toured with her for five months,' said Mrs Pat, 'sat on her bed till five o'clock in the morning, and never heard her say a word to which a child could not have listened.' Four hours later he returned to his hotel. Suddenly he became aware that he was holding a velvet geranium which, in one of the altercations with the

* Neither Agate nor any other critic noticed that Maugham made a mistake here. Phèdre actually comes on as early as the second scene of the first act. But the argument, so far as Maugham's heroine is concerned, remains valid.

taxi-driver, had fallen from her hat. Mrs Pat seemed to dog him throughout his New York trip. Next evening he called on the English actor Maurice Evans who had established himself there more or less permanently. He told Agate that she had said, after his first night, 'I liked it all except the honey-coloured hair.' Then, turning to an immaculate blonde, 'I always think fair hair destroys personality, don't you?'

Dutifully he toured the sights, inspected New Jersey and Coney Island, went to a boxing match at Madison Square Garden, and even, with the urge to see and hear all, submitted himself to the frenzied noise of Duke Ellington at the Cotton Club. A visit to Grant's tomb gave him a notice which he bagged as a collector's piece: GENTLEMEN ARE REQUESTED TO REMOVE THEIR HATS WHEN ENTERING THE TOMB. On top of the Empire State Building he shivered with fear and dared not approach the parapet: something swayed, but he could not tell whether it was himself or the structure. The skyscraper views he saw as he emerged from the Plaza Hotel on Fifth Avenue made London, he thought, look like a collection of native huts. At his English bank's office in Wall Street he was pleased to learn that the cashier who attended him had never heard the phrase 'ten grand' – something which every cinema-going child in England knows to be the most American of idioms.

A weekend in Atlantic City suggested to him Blackpool without the crowds. The nine miles of hotels, casinos and fun-palaces were deserted. A Horse Show was in full swing there, and he admired the five-gaited horses (the required gaits being walk, trot, canter, slow and the rack), which flaunted long tails that were 'miracles of science and adjustment, like huge interrogation marks'. From the sun-baked sands of Atlantic City he drove to the cooler green of New England and the famous Hackney pony stud at New Marlboro. He looked at the registers and picked out the names of brood mares he had known and thrilled to for years: Bricket Fuchsia, Colne Marvel and Eastertide. A small pony of impeccable descent enraptured him. Its name was Cassilis Sonnet, its age four and its appearance perfect.

Cassilis Sonnet, he reckoned, was likely to be a great performer. There and then he bought the attractive creature to be shipped back to England with him.

What he saw of the New York theatre impressed him. Although he was in general wary of musicals, a eupeptic *Babes in Arms* at the Shubert Theatre enlivened him with its Hart and Rodgers score written in an idiom which was theirs and no-one else's. He enjoyed every minute of Clare Boothe's acid comedy *The Women*, whose theme was summed up in a remark by one of the characters: 'The man who can think out an answer to that one about the husband who adores his wife while making love to another woman is going to win that prize they're always giving out in Sweden.' How would he cast the thirty-five women in the play for an English production? He would need, he reckoned, at least Marie Ney, Jean Cadell, Martita Hunt, Olga Lindo, Margaret Rawlings, Isabel Jeans, Greer Garson and twenty more of equal calibre, 'including somebody who can suggest a discomfited giraffe'.*

Tobacco Road, a dream entirely American, left him bewildered in a maze of frustration and incest. Another quintessentially American piece to defeat him was *High Tor*, a fantasy with comic interludes which he found desperately unfunny. Transatlantic comedy was easier to appreciate. *Room Service* reminded him of Aldwych farce in its plot about a theatrical company stranded at a hotel and unable to pay the bill unless their play is a success. From this developed a zany narrative put over at a furious pace and ending with the play being acted in a theatre belonging to the hotel. 'Perhaps this will be the first hotel to win the Pulitzer!' declared the

* He had already crossed swords with Greer Garson, then a new arrival on the West End stage and later to become a Hollywood star. His Victorian attitudes offended by her excessive *maquillage* in a recent performance, he wrote that she should not her 'multitudinous nails incarnadine'. The future Mrs Miniver retorted in a witty pastiche:

'The fault, Sir Critic, is not in ourselves,
'But in our text which strictly sets it forth
'That Fanny's finger-tips and toe-tips too
'Must scarlet be – a fashion I detest,
'And much it grieves me that this point offends.
'What? Multitudinous nails incarnadine
'Making the green see red . . .!'

triumphant manager. The smash hit of the season was Hart and Kaufman's *You Can't Take It With You.* Again the visiting English critic discovered that it is impossible to predict what will amuse a foreign race. He relished an exchange between a boy and a girl – 'I won't deceive you for all the rice in China'; 'Is there much rice in China?' – which he thought was good Noël Coward. To his surprise nobody laughed. They roared, though, at the speech: 'The reason Mother writes plays is that eight years ago a typewriter was delivered here by mistake.'

The drama critics of New York did honour to Agate. Brooks Atkinson of the *Times*, John Mason Brown of the *Post*, Burns Mantle of the *News*, Joseph Wood Krutch of the *Nation*, John Anderson of the *Journal*, and George Jean Nathan who wrote for all the other papers, came together and gave him lunch. Who, they asked him, were the Irving and Ellen Terry of the contemporary English theatre? John Gielgud and Edith Evans, he told them, with a reservation in favour of Laurence Olivier as the most promising young actor. A few days later he dined with the Beckfordian columnist Lucius Beebe at the Twenty-one. Beebe, who was immensely rich, wrote his daily article for fun and cultivated an aura of eccentricity by changing his clothes seven times a day. He confessed pride in being called the American Bayard. 'Sans peur mais avec beaucoup de reproche,' noted Agate in malicious dog-French.

On the last day of his visit George Jean Nathan took him to tea with Lillian Gish. The star of those Griffith epics *Intolerance*, *Birth of A Nation* and *Broken Blossoms* entered the room looking just as she did in *Way Down East:* the little face was pinched and sad, the eyes woebegone. She had left films to play Shakespeare and Chekhov. 'I came from the theatre, and I am glad to go back to it,' she declared. Agate chattered about her old films as she sat in silence 'nodding like some grave flower'.

At the end of a hectic month he embarked on the liner *Deutschland* for the journey home. The May morning was stifling hot with the odd quality of steam-heat he ever after associated with New York. The mist was pierced by the Empire State Building and later by the distant glimmer of

Radio City. The skyline of New York vanished and left as a souvenir the refrain of 'Where or When' from *Babes in Arms*, which his travelling companion insisted on whistling. Musical comedy though it was, he had enjoyed it most of all his theatre visits.

London seemed drab and small. The Café Royal had shrunk into provincial banality, and England become a land of warm soda-water and tepid lager where everyone went to bed at eleven o'clock. He felt melancholy and unsettled, and could not even face taking up drama criticism again. In the attempt to pull himself together he plotted with his stud manager to launch Cassilis Sonnet, the pony he brought back with him from America. At the Royal Show in Wolverhampton Cassilis Sonnet put up a dazzling display, half on his hind legs and the other half on his front ones, and was, rightly thought his disappointed owner, placed last by the judges. What else was there? He went to Lord's and saw Kimpton hit 45 runs in 24 minutes – a great bat in the making, though again the worm attacked the bud: Kimpton was Australian! Then Lord Kemsley, owner of *The Sunday Times*, invited his drama critic for a yachting weekend, and Agate turned up at Southampton arrayed in a new yachting-cap, expensive gaberdine trousers, blue double-breasted blazer from Moss Bros and darned white socks, this last, he thought, being a very neat touch. Waiters in snow-white jackets kept a glass of whisky and soda miraculously replenished as he dozed in the sunshine over his review copies. They were at Deauville by eleven on Saturday morning, and on Sunday the yacht was gliding up the river Seine. That afternoon Agate and Beverley Baxter played bridge on deck with Kemsley and his partner.

His spirits were beginning to rise again and his *joie de vivre* was returning. While he was away in America Jock had written damnably clever stuff as his deputy on *The Sunday Times*. Jock was feeling very tired, and at the approach of his last weekend stint he asked whether he, Agate, would write his article for him. And for how much? This gave Agate his first real laugh since his return. He began to feel better.

iii
DEATH MASKS

> 'Dame Madge Kendal dying this morning, with the result that the whole day has been given up to the nerve-wracking business of telephoning editors and rushing special articles. The journalist is like the undertaker: a death is just a job.'
>
> JAMES AGATE

Three months after the trip to New York he found his sixtieth birthday looming upon him. This was a milestone that called for celebration, and on the 9 September, 1937, he gave a luncheon party at the Ivy. Jock, of course, was there, and so were his sister May, Hamish Hamilton the publisher of *Ego*, and Hugh Walpole, who at that moment was passing through one of those phases when he considered Agate to be a 'friend'. The stage attended in the persons of Marie Tempest and of Gladys Calthrop, the artist and intimate of Noël Coward for whose productions she designed sets and costumes. As a birthday present she brought with her a drawing which had been part of the décor for a recent Coward show: a confection half ancient Greece, half peppermint rock, which showed two pink and white stallions gracefully curvetting. There was a hint of Chirico about it, and the picture might indeed have been a copy.

In the evening he went to a Sibelius concert at the old Queen's Hall and listened to his favourite second symphony. Later there was a boisterous supper party at the Villa Volpone which erupted into the morning hours of 10 September. His sixtieth year had been lavishly fêted. Every birthday is, though, a *memento mori*, and by the time you reach your sixtieth, or even earlier, you have become used to the death of friends. Having heard that Walpole, his birthday guest, had suffered a bad heart attack, Agate sat up late one evening writing him a long letter in which he attempted to reconcile affection for him as a friend with disapproval of his literary style. He was too late. Walpole did not live to receive the letter and died at the age of fifty-eight. In his diary Agate noted: 'Balzac writes somewhere of 'l'honnête artiste, cet infâme médiocrité, ce coeur d'or, cette loyale vie, ce stupide dessinateur, ce brave garçon.' Heart of gold, soul of loyalty, tried and trusty friend – Hugh was all these, but the rest of Balzac's judgment would not be too severe. His tragedy was that his fine qualities have nothing to do with being a great novelist.' On that note their relationship ended. Hugh had earlier, in a generous review, observed, 'There's no doubt about the readability of *Ego*, its glitter, its sense, its thumping good humour.' Agate wrote an obituary for the *Express* and quoted from *Hamlet*: 'Now cracks a noble heart.'

Marie Tempest, another of his Ivy guests, died the year after Walpole. She was then Dame Marie, queen of the English theatre and as much a famous personality as an actress. Though trained for a singing career and specialising early in light opera – experience which doubtless helped to perfect her immaculate timing and exquisite diction – she became a monarch of light comedy. Perhaps her greatest triumph was as Judith Bliss, the dominating actress in *Hay Fever*, which Noël Coward wrote especially for her. Marie Tempest was a glittering ornament of the West End stage who loathed touring. But even she had to play the provinces, and she would lament to Agate '*quelle vie de DOG!*' Her husband was Graham Browne, a competent actor who wryly dismissed his own career with such remarks as, 'My Rosencrantz was not up to much, but my Guildenstern was immense!' His main purpose in life was to regulate the high-powered machinery of Dame Marie's talent, and Agate believed that 'Willie's best claim upon the theatre of his time is that he nursed a miraculous little engine and kept it running.' Agate often lunched at the Ivy with the Brownes and was content for Marie to shine unimpeded. On one of these occasions she had had a rare flop. Agate consoled her. 'My dear Mary, if you were three times better than Irene Vanbrugh you wouldn't be half so good!' She smiled bravely and said that, after all, anyone at the beginning of their career must expect reverses. She was then sixty-five.

In 1935 there had been the affair of her Golden Jubilee to celebrate the fifty years which began with her first appearance in Suppé's operetta *Boccaccio*. A grand *Matinée* was organised at Drury Lane with King George Vand Queen Mary in the audience. The preparations for this were long and arduous, necessitating many committee meetings over lunch at the Savoy. The dramatist Barrie gave a mawkish address at one of them and reduced Marie to tears. (Or Mary, as her friends called her, for her true name was Mary Susan Etherington.) Somebody wondered if the tears were real. 'Of course they're real,' said Agate, 'everybody knows she can cry off stage.' And he told the story of how her husband came down for breakfast one Sunday morning to see Mary in floods of tears and screaming: 'James Agate says I can't cry, and damn it, he's right!'

The point about Marie Tempest, said Agate in a broadcast talk on the *Matinée*, was that 'she is not one of those intellectual players who have to deliver themselves of some world-redemptive gospel in order to make it worth anybody's while to listen to them. She can very nearly do without a play, and Heaven knows that sometimes she has to! She is mistress of all the forgotten arts of the stage – the art of walking, talking, and wearing clothes. She is mistress of the forgotten art of being a lady – an art almost entirely lost in these days. Marie Tempest is an actress of wit; and if that quality had not been in the world, she would have invented it.' A friend of his once observed her walking down Piccadilly one sunny morning. On the way she stopped to inspect Fortnum and Mason's window. It was, he said, a perfect performance.

This *monstre sacré*, thought Agate, was an actress of the first rank, despite never having played in Goldsmith, Sheridan, Pinero, Wilde, Galsworthy or Shaw. Wisely, she ignored new movements and cultivated, within its limitations, a flawless gift overlain with a patina that resulted from years of study. Although she did not have pathos, she had everything else: unsurpassable elegance, poise and an exact sense of proportion. Off stage he found her a perpetual delight. There had been a fire at her pretty little St John's Wood house, and he arrived in the morning to commiserate. She, wearing pyjamas, was rampaging through the mess brandishing a coal hammer and about to demolish a grand piano. It would look better for insurance purposes. He protested that it wouldn't seem at all like fire damage. She reversed the hammer and bounced the spike along shelves of rather shabby calf-bound books. Again he protested. 'The hose-pipe, dear,' she reproved him in her patrician voice, 'the hose-pipe!'

Madge Kendal had already gone, in her eighty-seventh year, a Dame like Marie Tempest and an even greater *monstre sacré*. Agate remembered her with awe and with affection. She was the twenty-second child of an actor-manager and sister to the playwright Tom Robertson, author of *Caste* and *Society*. Not unsurprisingly she went on the stage in her earliest childhood and soon became an outstanding actress. She played Shakespeare because it was the thing to do, but her real forte was light comedy. Agate never forgot her in some farce where she was required to sit upon an oak chest containing her husband's mistress. As she drummed her heels on the chest she sent her delinquent partner away on an imaginary errand. 'R-run like the swift hare!' she trilled at him, enjoying his discomfiture before turning to deal with the luckless woman in the box.

Her sense of fun, and the pathos she could evoke, made her, Agate firmly declared, 'the greatest English actress of my time'. Bernard Shaw agreed with him. She was also a Tartar, both on stage and off, and died alone except for her doctor, having been estranged for many years from her four children. Agate recalled one of his meetings with her shortly before her death. She had been at Drury Lane, she told him, to rehearse. 'Rehearse?' he echoed incredulously. 'Yes,' replied the octogenarian Dame. 'I have to make a speech there tomorrow, and as I have never acted on the stage of that theatre I wanted to know exactly how to pitch my voice. So I went down to Drury Lane, walked to the place where I shall stand tomorrow, and said to the charwomen cleaning the gallery: "Ladies, can you hear me?" They said, "Yes, Mum." I said, "Can you hear me perfectly?" and they said, "Yes, Mum." So now I know I shall be all right.'

This staggering illustration of the thoroughness of the old school would have appealed to Sir John Martin-Harvey, another whose death-mask Agate was soon to fashion. Both he and his wife were extremely kind people. Agate once confessed to a sore throat while talking with them back-stage during an interval. Next morning, at eight o'clock, the Martin-Harveys' chauffeur drove up from their country home to deliver not only an infallible remedy but also the inhaler with which to administer it. They took Agate on a convalescent drive to Frinton, he in the back of the car with Lady Martin-Harvey while Sir John sat next to the driver. A desolate Essex village came into view and the gentle knight said: 'My dear Agate, do you mind sitting in the front? We are about to pass through the village where I proposed to my wive, and I should like to hold her hand.'

He was, Agate thought, 'a great little actor in the more wistful kinds of melodrama . . . Nature had not given him the physical attributes essential to the great actor; the mould in which she made him was too small. Realising this, Martin-Harvey determined to be the best purveyor of romantic entertainment *with something in reserve*.' Often Agate went down to Sheen where the actor and his wife lived in retirement. They sat around the little garden and then went indoors to a candle-lit supper. Here Lady Martin-Harvey presented him with what became two of his most treasured possessions: the photographs of Irving and Ellen Terry which for twenty-five years had hung on either side of Irving's dressing-table at the Lyceum. Sir John showed another aspect of his character: a sense of humour. He pointed at a pair of very ornate street lamps at the foot of the staircase which, claimed the dealer who sold them to him, had come direct from the Vendramini Palace on the Grand Canal. 'I did not tell him,' said he, 'that I recognized them as part of my production of *Othello*!'

Agate was one of the few mourners at his funeral. He was shocked to find not an actor, not a critic there: only the Martin-Harveys' chauffeur who had driven him in the past and who remembered him.

The obsequies of Lady Tree drew a larger house. She died in the very year of Agate's sixtieth birthday, a long time after the final exit of her husband Sir Herbert. Agate enjoyed her reply to a compliment on the way she had arranged her hair: 'How sweet of you to call it my hair!' He wrote: 'So Lady

Tree has gone. A kindly soul and a delicious wit. It is always said that the line in Barrie's play à propos of boiler-scraping – "What fun men have!" – was one of her dress rehearsal impromptus. I remember how, about to recite at a charity matinée, she advanced to a gold chair, and, swathed in heliotrope tulle, said smilingly, "I want you all to imagine I'm a plumber's mate!" In her early years her extreme plainness was a handicap. In later life her face became her fortune; it was that of a benevolent horse. In her old age she was an admirable actress who made the most of a good part, and got a lot that wasn't there out of a bad one.'

How he loved these vintage actors and actresses! Seymour Hicks, for example, was the incarnation of theatre, a man who would never have been taken for anything else but an actor. Seymour not only acted, he also wrote or adapted dozen upon dozen of plays, produced a hundred others and managed his own theatre. In Edwardian days he had made his name – and that of his beautiful wife Ellaline Terriss, herself a daughter of the famous Fred – with entertainments such as *The Earl and The Girl, The Cherry Girl, A Runaway Girl, The Circus Girl, The Shop Girl*, and, as if to make quite sure, *My Girl*. The tenor of these 'naughty' pieces is obvious. Straight plays, musical comedy, variety, all were one to him and he excelled in whatever genre he chose. He even built and ran two London theatres – one of them was the Aldwych and the other the Globe, known to audiences in its early years as the Hicks Theatre. His acting was above all notable for the impression of spontaneity. Agate wrote of him as giving 'his oldest sketch with inconceivable *brio* and as if the thirty-year-old jokes were occurring to him for the first time. I can understand an actor being brilliant on a first night because of the critics. But I can never understand how he can continue night after night and long after he has exhausted invention. It must be as tedious as driving a bus. That, in my view, is the real paradox of the actor.'

Hicks was, too, a scintillating talker. Disappointingly, though, no-one has captured the spirit of his conversation, which was said to be fleeting, mercurial, and often libellously funny. The epigram which, in Hicks's velvet tones, convulsed his hearers, dies a mute death on the printed page, and his impromptu mimicry at the Garrick Club is left unrecorded. He once suggested Agate as a member there. 'O vision entrancing!' was the response. 'How all other passions fleet to air.' W. A. Darlington, theatre critic of *The Daily Telegraph*, was to act as proposer. Alas, there were members who objected. An actor whom Agate had offended? A dramatist whom he had crossed? He decided it would be prudent to withdraw and avoid possible humiliation. The incident hurt, although he made a joke out of it. Returning from his New York trip he mused that he had become eligible for blackballing at the Traveller's Club as well as the Garrick. After his voyage on Lord Kemsley's yacht he thought of writing to Seymour to tell him that he now qualified for black-balling by the Royal Yacht Squadron in addition to the Traveller's and the Garrick.

One death-mask he prepared but never delivered took the form of a tribute to Arnold Bennett's *Journals*. His article was, as we have seen, kept out of *The Daily Express* by a more topical need to print lists of winners in the Irish Sweep. The *Journals* had been the inspiration of his own diary, although he admired Bennett for many other reasons: his industry, his craftsmanship, his critical flair, his wide appreciation of French literature. Always ready to do a friend a good turn, Bennett had written a long thoughtful preface to Agate's collection of drama notices entitled *The Contemporary Theatre 1926*. He gave him useful advice, too, of the sort which he dispensed in his 'self-help' books. Agate arrived late for the theatre one evening and pleaded over-work, saying it would kill him. 'People do not die of too much work, but of badly organised work,' Arnold reproved him.

After Bennett's death his manuscripts came up at Sotheby's. Agate went expecting all the world to be there but finding only some fifty dealers looking like auctioneers out of Balzac. The material was sold in bundles at six or seven pounds each and comprising blocks of foolscap pages covered in Bennett's neat small handwriting. There were other treasures to be saved from the cold-eyed dealers, among them letters written by Agate's old colleagues in the Manchester days, Allan Monkhouse, C. E. Montague and George Mair. 'The thought of all this lovely stuff perishing makes me sick at heart,' noted Agate. His relationship with Bennett had always been a little uneasy. The novelist's outward appearance of North country toughness masked an artist of quivering sensibility, and Agate's vivacious manner tended to jar on him. Agate knew this and was pleased when, some years after Bennett's death, the latter's wife wrote to say that 'A.B. thought quite a lot' of him really but that their temperaments were violently opposed. 'If you had had mumps in the jaw, he'd have had them in the foot.'

A Bennett of a different hue was the music-hall comedian Billy, always listed on the programme as 'Almost A Gentleman'. Introduced by the stirring refrain of 'A Fine Old English Gentleman', he would roll on stage wearing shabby soup-stained evening dress and would recite 'The Green Tie on the Little Yellow Dog', a parody of that once-popular monologue 'The Green Eye of the Little Yellow God', or 'The Charge of The Tight Brigade', or an outrageous version of 'Mandalay': 'By an old white-washed Pagoda/Looking eastward to the west/There's a Burma girl, from Bermondsey,/Sits in a sparrow's nest.' His humour was surrealistic and featured Irish Eskimos, whiskered grapes, spanners for milking cows, railway engines that went in two directions at once, and ducks with tonsils. 'Where has the kidney bean?' he would demand in bibulous tones. 'What made the woodbine wild?' An old *Manchester Guardian* tradition venerated the music-hall, and Agate continued it. 'Bennett's grossness had that gusto about it which is like a high wind blowing over a noisome place,' he wrote. 'He never meant more or worse than he raucously proclaimed. Sometimes you said to yourself in half-delighted, half-fearful apprehension: "Surely he isn't going to suggest . . ." Which was foolish of you, because Bennett never suggested anything. He said what he had to say, and emptied his mind of the matter very much as our eighteenth-century caricaturists would show viragoes at upper windows emptying their wrath and other things on the heads of those below.

'Nobody who saw him is ever likely to forget that rubicund,

unaesthetic countenance, that black, plastered quiff, that sergeant-major's moustache, that dreadful dinner-jacket, that well-used dickey and seedy collar, the too-short trousers, the hob-nailed boots, the red silk handkerchief tucked into the waistcoat, the continual perspiration which was the outward and visible sign of a mind struggling for expression – these things will not be forgotten. His best witticism was that in which he deplored his permanent non-success at Huddersfield – "They take me for a baritone." He raised every night in the week to the level of Saturday night, gave his audience infinite amusement, and never uttered a word at which sensible people could take offence.' Off-stage, Agate added, his manner was quiet almost to shyness, in keeping with his gentle and wholly nice mind.

At a luncheon given by the Variety Artists' Federation Agate happened to sit next to a taciturn little man whom he did not know. Anxious to fit his conversation to the mood of the gathering, he told his neighbour how he had recently seen a very funny sketch called *Fishing* given by Harry Tate. He spoke of how Tate had inadvertently thrown ground-bait at a red-nosed man in a bowler hat two sizes too small for him, how the man was furious, how Tate said that he'd mistaken him for a swan, how the man enquired, 'Do I look like a swan,' and how Tate roared, 'Not now you've turned around!' Agate bellowed with laughter at the recollection. Not a muscle in his neighbour's face moved. 'Must have been very funny,' said Harry Tate, who, on stage, wore an immense property moustache and who in private life was unrecognizable.

His most famous sketch was *Motoring*, a lunatic diversion on the quirks of the motor car. During the 1914–18 war he was driving with his company to an engagement in Plymouth. On the way they saw a group of wounded soldiers sitting at the roadside. Harry stopped and gave an impromptu performance of *Motoring*. This went on for ten minutes without raising a smile. At last one of the soldiers removed a cigarette from his mouth and observed, 'Bloody fool – thinks 'e's 'Arry Tate!' Agate particularly enjoyed his sketch about Big Business. Harry, striding into the office, moustache twitching, would roar, 'Any letters?' No, he was told. 'Then we must write some!' Taking up a parcel he demanded, 'What's this?' 'Don't know, Sir,' replied the office-boy. Harry banged it on the table. 'Send it to Milan!' Agate was sure of Harry's place in the annals of music-hall. 'This marriage of imbecility and observation was the core of Harry's fun, which swept like a gale through the British music-hall for forty years.' But, as Agate found when he sat beside his unknown neighbour at the V.A.F. luncheon, the private Harry 'was difficult to talk to because he did not listen, being too busy with intellectual gestation of his own, the labour pains ending nine times out of ten in something quite unintelligible.'

iv
THE NIGHT HAS BEEN UNRULY

> 'In the dug-out read Noël Coward's new book of extremely witty short stories. When I came to "There was a signed photograph of Sarah Bernhardt looking like a sheep in white lace" I found I had forgotten about the air-raid.'
>
> JAMES AGATE

At the end of 1938 he made up his usual score for the past year. It amounted to 448,000 words, a quarter of that being *Sunday Times* work and the rest articles for the *Daily Express*, *Tatler*, *Ego* and pseudonymous articles. Was there not an ever so slight falling-off here when compared with last year's total of more than half a million? He reassured himself with the thought that he earned more money in 1938 than in any previous twelve months, a sum of up to six thousand pounds, which then had sixteen times the purchasing power it has today.

It had been a good year in other ways. His massive panoply of golf clubs was now complemented by an array of walking-sticks which it delighted him to take out, spring-clean and gloat over. The prize item was Henry Irving's walking stick, a present from Audrey Lucas, daughter of E.V. Fred Leigh gave him the silver-topped malacca cane that belonged to the Victorian actor-manager John Hare who had, at the first performance of Pinero's *The Profligate*, received it from the playwright himself, as the inscription attested: 'John Hare, from A.W.P., 24th April, 1889.' Agate remembered having seen him carrying it in Manchester some time in the eighteen-nineties. Barry Lupino presented him with Harry Lauder's walking-stick and also the one flourished by Vesta Tilley in her music-hall act. Another, owned by Gladstone, came from a retainer in the politician's family, and a sixth, with a complicated provenance, had once been the property of the Emperor Franz Joseph. A fine example in malacca had been owned by the novelist Harrison Ainsworth, and the collection was soon to be graced with a stick that had come down through the years from Hogarth himself. To those were finally added a malevolent knobkerrie passed on to Agate by George Robey, he having had it from a Zulu who moulded it out of a club used by his grandfather in the battles with Cetewayo.

Ego 3 had sold out its first edition of two thousand and was to be reprinted. Would he, his publisher George Harrap asked, make a list of any corrections? This he did, finishing at two in the morning and then starting his *Sunday Times* article which he completed at four. Jock typed it until six, dozed for an hour, and by seven was off to the country. As an interim report Brother Edward offered his thoughts on the latest instalment: 'I find, in your *Ego 3*, the same eminent quality of readibility, the same remarkable zest for life, and the same vulgarity which characterized the two earlier volumes . . . And your friends! And your bedlamite behaviour! Those peregrinations into inaccessible spots by motor-car at dead of night; this invention of parlour-games; this flirting with phobias. You and your friends remind me of a disused pack of cards – all knaves and jokers; and their proceedings take me back to *Bouvard et Pécuchet*, with a touch of *Gentlemen Prefer Blondes* thrown in.'

But 1938 had brought war and rumours of war that penetrated even so far as the Villa Volpone. Mr Chamberlain flew to Germany for his interview with Herr Hitler, as he always spoke of him, and Agate resolved to make a dug-out in the back garden. Fred Leigh, two of his ex-music-hall friends and the chauffeur began casting up the clods of earth. There were no bags of sand to be had, so Fred, through his acquaintanceship with a girl at the grocers, obtained sugar packets which were cut up and made into the right size. A middle-aged gentlewoman reminiscent of a character in a Dodie Smith play called to measure Agate for a gas-mask. She avowed herself ready to be killed on the job. 'How can man die better than facing fearful odds?' she chirruped. 'Lord Macaulay, you know. I learned the verse when I was a girl. Still quite apt, don't you think?'

Fred Leigh scoured the neighbourhood for sheets of corrugated iron needed to complete the dug-out and scrounged the last half dozen available. Yards of substitute for cellophane paper were bought up and used to make a gas-proof room at the Villa Volpone. The back garden started to look like Flanders field. Agate couldn't make up his mind whether to volunteer for something. If so, what? Out of respect for the worsening international situation he postponed trying on a new suit he had ordered.

Mr Chamberlain flew off again and met Herr Hitler in the company of Signor Mussolini and Monsieur Daladier. They reached an agreement, and the crisis, for the time being, was ended. Mr Chamberlain and his famous umbrella reminded Agate of Dickens's General Choke in *Martin Chuzzlewit*: '"We are a new country, Sir," observed the General. "Man, Sir, here is man in all his dignity. Here am I, Sir," said the General setting up his umbrella to represent himself – and a villainous-looking umbrella it was, a very bad counter to stand for the sterling coin of his benevolence – "here am I with grey hairs, Sir, and a moral sense!"'

So the threat of war faded and 1939 opened, as the New Year usually did, with a note from the Inland Revenue demanding immediate payment of current tax and arrears to the amount of £1,841, not forgetting a bill of £292 for horse-keep. He did a quick sum and found that, if called on within twenty-four hours to pay all he owed, including money-lenders and bank loan, he would be £4,000 in the red.

Another difficulty was that there had been no new plays since Christmas and so nothing for him to dilate on in the *Sunday Times*. An E.V. Lucas could write about anything. A drama critic must have a play on which to string his gems.

He relished crises, and the challenge of putting together an article about non-existent plays was summarily dealt with in the early hours of Friday morning. The Inland Revenue posed a more difficult problem, however. Happily, a few weeks into the New Year, he met a tall, elegant man called Alfred Chenhalls, baldish, with an egg-shaped head and a sympathetic wife. They entertained him in their Marylebone flat where, a bottle of champagne at his elbow, he played early Beethoven sonatas very sketchily on their magnificent Bechstein. Chenhalls offered to sort out his financial affairs. Agate denied such a thing was possible and said his resources were mortgaged up to the hilt. 'My dear fellow,' laughed Chenhalls, 'you don't know where the hilt is!'

Chenhalls was ruthless. The horses must go, he announced, and so must the valet and the chauffeur. Even Fred Leigh and Jock trembled in the balance. 'The invariable result of inviting somebody to straighten out your affairs is that he flattens *you* out,' commiserated Peter Page. Within six months all of Agate's income tax up to the end of 1938 had been paid and only the current demand remained – this, of course, in addition to stud bills, money-lenders and bank loans. What was to be done about them? Chenhalls described the situation as 'frankly desperate'. Agate's solicitor, Stanley Rubinstein, spoke of it as 'almost rosy'. Agate decided to let Rubinstein take over and salved his conscience by dedicating *The Amazing Theatre*, his latest volume of drama criticisms, to the amazing Chenhalls. After all, the latter's wife Gwen had not only wit: she had humour as well, and was among the few women who could keep him laughing over dinner from eight to midnight.

A complex equation evolved by Rubinstein allowed for frenzied monthly payments to the Inland Revenue and other creditors. Domestic staff at the Villa Volpone were sacked, the car was turned in, and Agate's income was taken over – or at least as much of it as he admitted to Rubinstein – in exchange for a cheque-book marked 'Private Account' to be credited with a pittance each Monday morning. Agate felt, he said, like a remittance man who had *not* been packed off to Australia.

Suddenly a demand arrived for surtax dating back to 1933. How could he make the Inland Revenue understand his method of working? At dinner in the Café Royal someone would tell him a story, an anecdote, which made the article in which it appeared. Why did they not see that his dining out was essential for the raw material of his job? Would they prefer him to sit in Bognor producing dull articles and drinking cups of cocoa? Both he and Rubinstein decided against bankruptcy. By taking over all Agate's earnings and paying him a small allowance, at the end of 1941 Rubinstein had paid off 52 creditors, two money-lenders, the bank, and all tax arrears. A total debt of £5,000 had been reduced to £1,500, although the horses to which Agate clung despite everything were still eating their, and his, head off. 'Would you,' Rubinstein enquired, 'like to take over the management of *my* affairs and try and be as clever!'

Undeterred by financial troubles rumbling permanently in the background, he did not lose his zest for making more discoveries and new acquaintances. One of the most exciting was a book called *The Quest for Corvo*. This classic biography of Frederick Rolfe – pederast, sponger, paranoiac, author of mad and vivid fictions – inaugurated something of a cult for 'Baron Corvo' as he dubbed himself. *The Quest for Corvo* appeared in 1934, though Agate only read it in 1939. Rolfe, he thought, seemed like a composite portrait of people he knew: the venom was pure Leo Pavia and there were ummistakeable traces of Brother Edward and even of Jock. The name of the biographer was A. J. A. Symons, and he had begun his 'quest' after hearing of Rolfe from the London book dealer Christopher Millard. Now Pavia had known Millard. 'He was a schoolmaster with ideas about the relationship of pedagogue and pupil centuries behind his times!' remarked Leo. 'His enemies said he got into all sorts of trouble; it would be truer to say he got into only one sort. He had enormous intellectual pride backed by colossal brains, was always half-drunk, and never went to bed for the normal reason. He was the most splendid anachronism I have known.'

Agate was thrilled by the *Quest for Corvo*, fascinated, bewitched, infatuated. In one week he wrote five times to Symons, and the flattered author addressed him in his replies as 'Egomet Bonmot'.* In Corvo Agate saw, besides Leo, Jock and Brother Edward, himself as well: the lover of exotic words and extravagant prose, the sybarite, the chronic debtor, the connoisseur of boys. He never said as much, but the inference is clear. Symons was invited to lunch at the Ivy and revealed himself as a dandy and a gourmet, a collector of music boxes and fine wines. His ambition, he said, was to write the definitive life of Oscar Wilde, though he would not begin it until all the interested parties still living had agreed that he should have a free hand. A year or so later he fell ill and died of encephalitis. 'He was the best kind of highbrow,' mourned Agate.

Symons would probably have been the ideal biographer of Wilde, but he never started, let alone completed, a book that might have rivalled *The Quest for Corvo*. Agate, for his part, had a strangely mixed view of Wilde. The blunt, hearty side of him could not stand Wilde the aesthete, the self-described 'lord of language', the drawing-room wit. 'The basis of Wilde's wit is the dressing-room of the chorus in any theatre,' he snorted. 'Produce far enough, in Euclid's sense, the wit of any gigolo, and you get Wilde. Produce that kind of wit to infinity and you do not begin to get Congreve, Fielding, Swift, Sheridan, Thackeray, Sydney Smith.' Yet he quoted Wilde more often than any of the other names he mentions, and, although he spoke contemptuously of Wilde's 'scented output', he admitted that the Irishman had written 'the wittiest light comedy in the language'.

He learned a great deal more about Wilde from Lord Alfred Douglas, that repellent left-over from the Nineties who lived in threadbare retirement at Hove. No longer the Prince

* This was the pseudonym of Thomas Griffiths Wainewright, critic, friend of Charles Lamb and murderer. Wilde observed of him: 'The fact that a man is a poisoner is nothing against his prose.'

Charming known to Oscar, Douglas in manhood and old age was a litigious bully who displayed some of his unspeakable father's worst characteristics and who, indeed, served a prison sentence for a criminal libel on Winston Churchill. That part of his time which was not taken up by lawsuits he devoted to writing poems with titles such as 'My Soul is like a Silent Nightingale'. Some of them, for example 'Impression de nuit', which evokes the lights of London by night, are pleasing enough trifles. He set too much store by them, however, and believed himself to be 'a first-rate poet', that is, one who belonged in the company of Shakespeare, Milton and Wordsworth. It is a judgment posterity has not been able to accept.

Douglas had written to Agate about the author of a play called *Charles the First*, in which Irving gave an unbearably moving performance. The combination of Irving, Douglas and Wilde was not to be resisted, and Agate went down to Hove for a meeting with the self-styled 'major poet'. They had a gracious and pleasant meal, with Douglas obviously on his best behaviour. He disclosed that *The Importance of Being Earnest* had originally been conceived as an eighteenth-century piece with costumes of the *School for Scandal* period. According to Douglas, it was at his suggestion that Wilde changed the setting into a contemporary one. Oscar always named his characters after places – Worthing, Goring, Basildon – and Lady Bracknell was 'Lady Brancaster' in the first draft, Brancaster being a town in Norfolk where Douglas at the time was studying with a tutor. He later switched the name to Bracknell, which was the railway station for the country house owned by Douglas's mother. Another mystery: what were the origins of a four-act version in German of *The Importance of Being Earnest?* Douglas believed that the original manuscript could have been stolen when the contents of Wilde's home were being sold up. All sorts of letters and documents vanished on that occasion, and the thief may well have sold it later to a dealer from whom the German translator bought it.

Prickly though Douglas was, Agate decided that he should like a little of him very much. The feeling was mutual. Douglas wrote to him: 'Devouring time that blunts the lion's paws has slightly modified my feelings of dislike towards you.' He was, he told Agate, heaping coals of fire upon his head by giving him all that inside information about *The Importance of Being Earnest*, bearing in mind the less than enthusiastic reception the critic gave his poetry. They continued to argue about Douglas's true rank. Agate classed him as a 'third-and-a-half rate poet', not so good as Housman but better than Wilde. Douglas riposted charmingly: 'Mon pauvre monsieur, are you not aware that seventeen of my last sonnets were written in Wormwood Scrubs?'

While Douglas worried about his literary reputation in Hove, political crises abroad flared or faded according to which newspaper you read. *The Observer* thought that things were worse than ever. *The Sunday Times* remarked that little was going on. *The Sunday Express* believed that a great deal was happening. In the very hot August of 1939 Agate prepared to go on holiday for three weeks. He took Leo Pavia with him to Southend and installed himself in his favourite hotel where the big writing desk faced a statue of Queen Victoria. At Burnham-on-Crouch he defied doctor's orders and played golf – twenty-four shots with a No. 2 iron and mashie borrowed from a friend as he'd left his own in London. There were no ill effects except a touch of asthma which he suspected was coming on anyway.

After a fortnight in Southend he cut short the holiday and returned to London. War definitely threatened, and he wondered what he should do. *Ego*, of course, came first, and he prudently laid in manuscript paper for a year. Jock asked him to guess what was the one thing any actor would defend with his life, even if all his other most treasured belongings went up in smoke? The answer was that uniquely valuable possession, his book of old press notices. A less amusing conundrum was what to do with Brother Edward? He had suddenly grown into an old man, very worn, very ill. He spoke dismally of failures being the best kind of bomb-fodder. Agate persuaded him, after a disagreeable scene, to go to York, where their brother Harry would look after him and perhaps find him a job. As the train moved out Edward handed James a slip of paper. On it was written: 'Evacuating a genius at the cost of a £2 railway ticket is what I call reasonable!'

On the 3 September Mr Chamberlain announced the declaration of war against Germany. Minutes later an air-raid warning sounded. Agate and Fred Leigh retreated into their garden dug-out. Nothing happened, and in half an hour the all-clear was heard. Jock called to collect his gas mask. He reported that the air-raid sirens had caught him at breakfast in Lyons' Strand Corner House and driven him into the basement. His first irritable reaction had been: 'What a *very* unattractive crowd of people to have to die with!'

Barrage balloons floated in the air and the setting sun turned them into golden asteroids. Fred Leigh and Agate took it in turns to sleep as, not waking easily, they didn't know whether they would hear the sirens. Soon they gave up the watch business and snored in unison. But Fred's snore developed into an ominous warble too like the siren itself, and Agate moved from the Villa Volpone to a bedroom at the Savage Club. He walked through a blacked-out London where the ladies of the street flashed pocket-torches into the prospective client's face and murmured 'Coming home, dearie?' Surely it would be better, he thought, to flash it on their own? Later, he recorded in his diary, coming out of the Café Royal 'into the pitch darkness of Piccadilly Circus, I heard a man playing 'How sweet the name of Jesus sounds'. This had a half-eerie, half-emotional effect on the crowd, which was standing still to listen.'

Chapter Seven

DRITIC

'Most dramatic critics (why shouldn't we call them Dritics, for short?) have seemed to me fantastically conceited; and the reason is, of course, that the giving of opinions goes to their heads.'

Clifford Bax

i
BRIEF CHRONICLES

'. . . the abstract and brief chronicles of the time.'

HAMLET, ACT II, SC. 2

From his bedroom window at the Savage he could view a panorama that swept from the Horse Guards by way of Parliament and the Abbey to end at Westminster Cathedral. It shimmered hazily in the hot sun which blazed throughout the last weeks of September. A break in the trees showed a stretch of the lake in St James's Park that he always associated with Chekhov's *The Seagull*. White birds skimmed over a surface fringed with silvery shrubs, and here, he thought, Konstantin might have reflected on his play and Trigorin pondered his metaphors. As he scribbled away on the rickety table beside the window he remembered a satirical picture by Gustave Doré. It showed a monk writing in his cell while all around a terrible battle raged. The monastery was about to collapse, a hand-to-hand fight was going on in the doorway, but the monk, oblivious, kept his nose glued to his manuscript. So, Agate resolved, should he keep his nose glued to

Ego. When *Ego 4* appeared a few months later a friend remarked: 'It means that you regard your Diary as more important than the war.' Agate replied: 'Well, isn't it? The war is vital, not important.'

In March, 1940, he decided to evacuate himself from London. Partly, he decided, he needed a rest-cure, and partly he was suffering from 'specialised funk': how could he smoke his asthma cigarettes through a gas mask? Dullness being essential for a rest-cure, he chose Bognor Regis. Within ten minutes of emerging from the railway station he had seen and rented a furnished flat for a year. He took with him a new house-boy – 'My name's Charlie, but I answer to anything!' – and Leo Pavia. It was Leo's birthday. 'I'm sixty-five today,' he said. 'For the first five years they despaired of my life; for the last fifty it's my death they've despaired of!'

Bognor was good for his vanity. No one recognized him and his name in the shops caused little interest. For the first time since he was a boy he led a normal life: breakfast, shave, newspapers, snooze over books, lunch, tea, supper and bed. Only Leo and George Felton Mathew on his occasional visits disturbed the absolute dullness of the place. Such tranquillity couldn't last. He chafed under it, longed for the gaiety of the Villa Volpone, and was soon back in London for the biggest air-raid to date. He watched it from the roof of the Café Royal and thought of those old posters for *A Royal Divorce* showing Napoleon's cavalry against a background of red flaming ruin.

Most evenings now he seemed to spend eating sandwiches and playing rummy in the dug-out with Fred Leigh and Charlie. He decided, feeling like a coward, to run away. After all, he could do nine-tenths of his work as well outside London as in it. Stanley Rubinstein lent him a cottage in the Chilterns for ten days or so. Then he moved for a longer stay to Oxford, where Bertie van Thal's friend, the actor John Byron, found rooms for him and generally succoured him. Taking the Oxford air one morning he saw two women vainly exhorting a dog to get into a car. He prodded it with his stick and quoted from *Cyrano de Bergerac*: 'Monte donc, animal!'

The elder woman looked at him severely. 'I think,' she said, 'that was most uncalled for.'

Soon after he arrived in Oxford the post brought a gift from an unknown donor. The parcel contained four small volumes of drama criticisms taken from London newspapers for the years 1885 to 1893. A later package of cuttings continued the story from 1897 to 1906. Here were rare contemporary accounts of Henry Irving and Ellen Terry, Bernhardt and Réjane, Mrs Kendal and Beerbohm Tree, exciting stuff and invaluable for historians. He winnowed through the collection and produced an anthology called *Those Were The Nights*. A little later he was to do the same thing with the scrap-book of Clement Scott which the latter's daughter passed on to him. He entitled it *These Were Actors* and affixed the dedication: 'To John Gielgud, our first player.'

Already, in 1932, he had compiled an anthology called *The English Dramatic Critics, 1660–1932* which he culled from volumes in his own library and which features critics whom he looked up to as masters of his trade. The book opened with Flecknoe on Richard Burbage, the first actor to play Hamlet, Lear and Othello, and with Steele reviewing Mrs Bracegirdle in *Love for Love*. Garrick was seen through the eyes of Francis Gentleman, and Mrs Siddons was evoked by Leigh Hunt and Hazlitt. G. H. Lewes examined the greatness of Macready and analysed the art of Rachel, 'the panther of the stage; with a panther's terrible beauty and undulating grace she moved and stood, glared and sprang.' Irving was glimpsed by Clement Scott on a night of 'nervousness and paralysing excitement', and by Max Beerbohm, whose mocking wit spiced an ingenious tribute. All the leading authorities of the past are included in what deserves to be a text-book on the subject, and it ends in the twentieth century with, inevitably, Agate himself and Charles Morgan, the novelist and successor to A. B. Walkley on *The Times*.*

Besides rescuing so much material from the past Agate wanted as well to preserve his own best articles. His motives,

* Morgan's reviews, though well written, were noted for their high philosophical tone. Leo Pavia called them 'Morgan Voluntaries'.

as all human motives are, were mixed: the impermanence of journalism, the urge to perpetuate his name, and the need for cash mingled with a disinterested wish that later generations should know about the acting he had seen in his time. In all he brought out fourteen volumes of collected criticisms. The most useful of them are the three which appeared during the war under the imprint of Jonathan Cape. Each of them bears that familiar wartime notice: 'Book Production War Economy Standard. This book is produced in complete uniformity with the authorized economy standards'; yet each is a model of elegant printing and design that could challenge many books issued today. Although they contain drama criticisms reprinted in some of his other volumes, their particular advantage is that they handily group together the main categories of play Agate saw between 1920 and 1943: Shakespearean, contemporary, and light entertainment.

The performer dazzles and is gone. 'The moment at which I speak,' says Pascal, 'is already far away from me.' Nothing can recapture that fleeting magic born of the relationship between actor and audience, and it fades as soon as he leaves the stage. Words are powerless to re-create images left in the memory of those who were present, even if a great writer is using them. When Charles Lamb writes about Munden in his well-known essay, he convinces us that the actor was a great comedian, not by attempting to detail his performance but by describing the effect it made on him and his own delighted response to it. This was Agate's method. He spoke with such authority about fine acting that you realized something important had occurred. Plays themselves, new or old, did not interest him so much as the performance itself. It was the art of acting which drew him to the theatre. As well as reviewing a play he would also develop an argument or elaborate a theory. He could be headstrong and capricious but always stimulating, and when people disagreed with him he was gratified, for he loved a debate more than anything. Like Dr Johnson, he argued for victory and enjoyed opposition from those who took a different view.

Yet if acting was his prime concern, there were plays which he knew by heart and which from his earliest days he had loved for their beauty of language and their portrayal of the human heart. Such were the plays of Shakespeare. *Brief Chronicles*, which appeared in 1943 with the sub-title 'A Survey of the Plays of Shakespeare and the Elizabethans in Actual Performance', ranges over the whole canon and even includes the 'doubtful' plays *The Two Noble Kinsmen* and *Arden of Feversham*. Although he reviews eight different productions of *Hamlet*, a like number of *Othello* and seven of *Macbeth*, he has something trenchant to say on each occasion and is never at a loss for ideas.

As Baudelaire observed, criticism is only justified when it is partial, passionate and wholly personal in a way that opens up the widest horizons. Agate is frank about his Shakespearean likes and dislikes. He avows that he finds *Love's Labour's Lost* 'a tedious masterpiece' with lovely bits in it, and that *The Comedy of Errors* strikes him as 'the most excruciatingly boring farce ever devised by a man of genius'. Indeed, he would almost prefer to see *Volpone* rather than any of Shakespeare's comedies, although perhaps the unfamiliarity of the one and the over-familiarity of the others may have something to do with it. There is little for him to admire in *Timon of Athens* because here the poverty of invention results in expressing the same thing over and over again. *Macbeth* is his favourite among the tragedies, with *Antony and Cleopatra* a near rival. A serious competitor, though, is Marlowe's *Dr Faustus*, where the speech 'Sweet Helen, make me immortal with a kiss' seems to Agate not exceeded by *Antony and Cleopatra* for glory of pure passion. Neither is 'Oh, thou art fairer than the evening air' excelled, in his view, even by Perdita's flower speech.

Agate lived at a time before directors gained the dominance they have in today's theatre. As far back as the nineteen-twenties, however, he was complaining 'there's nowt so queer as folk' in his remarks on a production of *King Henry IV, Part 2* which mangled Falstaff's part and tampered with some of his best speeches. He also deplored the habit of staging Shakespeare in modern dress. Directors argued that they could make Shakespeare's import clearer thus by relating it to contemporary experience, and that, after all, had not the plays originally been staged in the dress of Elizabeth's day? Agate replied that the Elizabethan playgoer at an Elizabethan play heard language his ears were attuned to and saw costumes to which his eyes were used. No ambiguity intervened. Two minutes after the performance had begun, he suggested, the Elizabethan forgot all about costume and was wholly absorbed in what the actors were saying. When you play Shakespeare in twentieth-century costume a vast discrepancy between speech and dress instantly arises. The spectator never stops thinking about costume and has less attention to spare for what is being said. It was the same with stage design. The first function of scenery, declared Agate, was to be forgotten in any play that spoke to the mind. The choicest designs of Craig, Komisarjevsky, Bakst and Picasso would have been thrown under foot and trampled on by Shakespeare. The dramatist himself would have preferred the strictly representational. Any old battlement would do for *Hamlet*, and any old pair of red curtains for Gertrude's bedroom. Agate did not believe that 'a mind completely filled with one thing can have room for any other thing,' and Shakespeare would have belonged to the school of Beerbohm Tree, with its real forest, its real water and its real rabbits. Agate did, though, allow that there were plays like *Much Ado About Nothing* which, not taking up all one's attention, might lawfully be treated as masques.

He was old enough, and lucky enough, to have seen great acting. The giants of his youth were Irving, Forbes-Robertson, Charles Hawtrey, Ellen Terry, Mrs Kendal and Janet Achurch. Among the French had been Coquelin, Lucien Guitry, Baron, Brasseur, Sarah Bernhardt, Bartet and Réjane. Like most critics from Hazlitt onwards he insisted that the physical side in acting came first. An actor must have presence above all, an attractive physique, and a resounding voice that can thunder like Wotan. Agate would not agree that subtlety of interpretation makes up for physical deficiency. A chubby Hamlet, a plain Romeo, an insignificant Othello, a little Lear, all were unacceptable to him. When people challenged him with Irving's raven croak, the ungainly limp, the slurred consonants, he replied that, as in the case of

Garrick and Kean, genius blinded the spectator to their failings. The faults of the great actor were more impressive than the virtues of the player who only had talent.

If the legendary players of his early days had vanished, there were quite a few actors still about who excelled in character parts. Hay Petrie was the finest Shakespearean 'low comedian' in his experience. As Costard in *Love's Labour's Lost* Petrie breathed the very spirit of an Elizabethan numskull yet contrived to be amusing in a very modern way. His Shylock even restored comedy to the part, although his Thersites in *Troilus and Cressida* was a misshapen dwarf, malignant, lurking in the shadow, hardly perceived yet dominating the entire stage. His colleague Baliol Holloway made an excellent Falstaff, who had fatness in his very bones, 'a great man in full sail, trimming with infinite condescension his course to the mean necessities of his purse'. Wilfrid Lawson, a sadly doomed actor whose talent rarely found the opportunity it deserved, made a disastrous Antony but an exquisite First Gravedigger.

Among the women, Agate prized Edith Evans in the unexpected part of Rosalind; she acted it with just the right note of mischief and love-lorn *nuance*. She was a Queen Margaret in *King Richard III* who walked like a queen and ranted like one also, though her attempt on Cleopatra had not enough passion or vulgarity. Her Nurse in *Romeo and Juliet* upset the balance of the whole play: she ruled the roost with a grandeur and pathos in such a way that it was as if the Porter were the centre of *Macbeth*. Another actress, Sybil Thorndike, as the Wife in *The Knight of The Burning Pestle*, imported a Lancashire accent and a wealth of warm-heartedness. The Queen Katharine she portrayed in *King Henry VIII* showed that there was only one answer to the question as to whether she was a great actress: 'Yes, in a great play.'

If we except John Barrymore's Hamlet and Paul Robeson's Othello, which were isolated phenomena, the most promising Shakespeareans in Agate's time were John Gielgud, Laurence Olivier, Ralph Richardson and Donald Wolfit. Agate was on friendly personal terms with Gielgud and had known him since 1930. 'He was very kind and sympathetic to me,'

Gielgud remarked once. They lunched together at the Ivy on alternate Mondays, paying for the meal, at Agate's suggestion, on equal terms. One day Gielgud bought him a bottle of champagne. The following week Agate returned the compliment with a miserly glass of lemonade. He was full of advice, often delivered in a curiously brutal and insensitive way. After admiring the first act of a *Macbeth* which Gielgud produced early in his career, he went backstage in the interval and said: 'I only want to tell you that the murder scene was the best I have ever seen. I know you can't keep it up to the end of the play so I've come round now to tell you.'

It was the nervous side of Gielgud's acting that appealed to Agate. Although he complained that Gielgud's 1930 performance of Richard II, one of Shakespeare's most subtle characters, neglected the artist in the king, the element that makes a beautiful pattern out of misery, he praised the elegiac effect and the beautiful speaking of the soliloquy 'What must the king do now?' Gielgud's Lear fell foul of the critic's belief in the need for physical attributes. Lacking the means to build up something patriarchal, the actor, who was only twenty-seven at the time, had decided to show a man prematurely old. A later assault on the rôle in 1940 found Agate still dissatisfied: Lear's rages did not go beyond petulance, and although the speech 'Do not laugh at me' hung on the air, a miracle of pathos, it remained a youthful air indistinguishable from the actor's Romeo when he spoke 'Eyes, look your last!'

Gielgud's Romeo, thought Agate, carved the verse exquisitely. As a performance it was a lovely exercise, better as absolute rather than programme music. Macbeth was, of all Shakespearean rôles, the most difficult to interpret, and the difficulty increased if you took into account Goethe's opinion, which Agate often quoted, that the play should have been called *Lady Macbeth*. Gielgud's Old Vic appearance in 1930 was probably the one where Agate delivered the shattering judgment mentioned above on his visit backstage. If so, he was proved completely wrong, and admitted as much in his notice. For the first time in all his playgoing, he said, this Macbeth held him to the end. After the banquet scene the part is nearly over, and during the apparition interlude Macbeth is virtually a spectator. Following the murder of Lady Macduff, the business about Malcolm, the revelation to Macduff and the sleep-walking scene, 'Macbeth's next appearance is with Seyton, and whether the play is to stand or fall depends upon the power of the actor to suggest the ravages of mind, soul, and even body endured since we saw him last. Mr Gielgud did not begin again as so many Macbeths do, but came on the stage as though he had lived the interval . . . in the old phrase, the actor carried us away.'

Agate's view of Hamlet was clouded by the memory of Irving's pathos and daemonism. Neither of these qualities, he judged, did Gielgud possess in 1930. Yet, given his physique, Agate did not see that he could have played better. He was as good as any reasonable person might ask because the part made demands that were unreasonable. These demands included every grace of body, mind and heart, together with the power of expressing intellectual and spiritual ugliness. Hamlet should make us cry one minute and shudder the next. Gielgud's Hamlet was at least an exploration of the part rather than an exploitation of the actor. The play scene and all that followed were taken at cracking speed and with the right kind of nervous energy until, at the 'All occasions' soliloquy, the rate deliberately slackened for one of the finest pieces of sheer exposition Agate had ever heard. Altogether he saw Gielgud in four productions of *Hamlet*, and it was the last that he found most moving. The actor had, in 1944, reached the right age and the height of his powers. 'He is now unchallengeably this generation's rightful tenant of this "monstrous Gothic castle of a poem",' he wrote. 'He has acquired an almost Irvingesque quality of pathos, and, in the passages after the play scene, an incisiveness, a raillery, a mordancy worthy of the Old Man. Tonight he imposed on me all this play's questing feverishness; the middle act gave me ninety minutes of high excitement and assured virtuosity; I don't remember that Forbes-Robertson was more bedazzling in the "O, what a rogue and peasant slave" soliloquy. Indeed, I think there is no doubt that this is, and is likely to remain, the best Hamlet of our time, and that is why I shall urge John to stick to the mantle of tragedy and leave lesser garments to others. For, like John Philip Kemble, he is not really a comedian.'*

Agate's relationship with Laurence Olivier was decidedly chillier than the one he had with Gielgud. Indeed, Olivier, who regarded drama critics as 'those bastards', told Donald Wolfit that he had once hit Agate 'in the stalls of a darkened theatre'. Yet Agate was by no means unappreciative of the actor's work. While he thought that Olivier's Romeo missed the poetry, he praised the 'infinitely touching' gestures used in the balcony scene and the imaginative play of arm. The line 'Is it e'en so? Then I defy you, stars!' came over tonelessly and thus with the highest effect. All in all, this was the most moving Romeo Agate could remember. Two years later, in 1937, he was not so impressed by Olivier's Hamlet, a Dane without melancholy or madness, despite the cogency and fire that marked the soliloquies.

Olivier as Macbeth drew him twice in 1937. At his second visit he reflected that, except for Garrick, there had been no great Macbeth in the calendar. Why, then, be hard on an actor whose voice was too high for the 'Tomorrow and tomorrow' and the 'Sere and yellow leaf' speeches which should vibrate like a cello? Macbeth required the momentum of age, and Olivier would doubtless play the part twice as well when he had twice his present years. In the meantime there was his Coriolanus, magnificent of voice and extraordinary in range of tone, a performance physically admirable which contained one startling leap and a superb fall at the end. 'I banish you!' was given with Phelps' 'cold sublimity of disdain', and the climax, with all stops out, brought the house to its feet cheering. This was in 1938. By 1944 Olivier's playing of Richard III left Agate in wonderment. 'As I sat attentive at this admirable performance I seemed to see an extraordinary succession of images – Charles II plotting mischief, any old actor's Robert Macaire and Alfred Jingle, any good actor's Iago and even Iachimo, and, above all, a great deal of Irving's Mephistopheles . . . Yes, there was a

* *Ego 7*, Oct. 18, 1944, pp. 219–220.

great deal of Irving in Wednesday's performance, in the bite and devilry of it, the sardonic impudence, the superb emphases, the sheer malignity and horror of it.'*

Whereas John Gielgud revived *The Importance of Being Earnest* and Maugham's *The Circle* only to demonstrate in spite of himself that his gifts lay with tragedy, not with comedy, Ralph Richardson's problem was just the reverse. His 1931 performance of *Henry V*, a part which demands every physical grace an actor can summon up, went awry in its attempt to portray Harry as a human being. His Othello proved that Nature had showered upon him the kindly gifts of the comedian but refused him any tragic facilities whatsoever. The broad, moony countenance gave Othello's rolling eyes the faintly comic look of Harry Tate. With Falstaff, however, he created a great piece of acting: here, in person, was the 'stuffed cloak-bag of guts' as well as 'reverend vice' and 'grey iniquity'. There were parts that Richardson could not play, bringing to them no more than 'the competence of a fine actor labouring at the uncongenial.' As Falstaff he had everything required and more: exuberance, mischief and gusto.

And last we come to Donald Wolfit. He made 'a splendid mouthful' of Volpone and spoke the verse as one in Johnson's day must have spoken it. In the role of Antony he was handicapped by his chubby looks, although he played magnificently as Richard III 'in the back-of-the-pit, Saturday-night vein demanded by this roaring melodrama.' The eerie and the macabre eluded him, there was little subtlety in his speaking of the verse, yet he terrified the playgoer. His Lear in 1943 convinced Agate that he must be 'relegated to the category of the immensely talented; *he does nothing which we cannot explain*.' Moreover, Agate insisted, his blubbered mien was not the face of a tragedian. He could never be anything more than a first-rate compromise in rôles of a melancholy or patrician nature. His face was too round.

In 1944, the year after *Brief Chronicles* appeared, Wolfit gave a classic performance of Lear and obliged the critic to

* *The Contemporary Theatre 1944 and 1945*, p. 110.

reverse his judgment. Having earlier said that Wolfit did nothing that the spectator could not explain, Agate recanted entirely. Wolfit, he said, now did nothing which one could explain. The audience surrendered to something without quite knowing what. Lear was not a young man's part, for no young actor, however brainy, could ever venture upon this Colossus of heathen antiquity. Wolfit had the minimum number of years needed to accomplish the most tremendous task confronting any player. He had already given full and overflowing measure as Othello, Richard III, Shylock, Bottom, and Falstaff, not to mention such 'trifles' as Volpone, Ford's Giovanni and Ibsen's Solness. His Lear was the summit, a performance which triumphantly combined all that was needful; majesty, moral grandeur, a 'ruined piece of nature', and enough voice to dominate the thunder, yet a spent voice. 'Mr Wolfit had and was all the things we demand, and created the impression Lear calls for. I say deliberately that his performance on Wednesday was the greatest piece of Shakespearean acting I have seen since I have been privileged to write for *The Sunday Times*.'*

Even in wartime London Agate's review caused a stir. Wolfit's manager telephoned him to say that as a result the theatre was sold out for the season. 'Every Inch King Lear' was the headline of Agate's review, and he continued to think so for the rest of his life. Not long before his death he told Robert Speaight that Wolfit was the greatest actor he had seen since Irving. The wheel had come full circle.

ii
RED LETTER NIGHTS AND IMMOMENT TOYS

'You *may* abuse a tragedy, though you cannot write one. You may scold a carpenter who has made you a bad table, though you cannot make a table. It is not your trade to make tables.'

DR JOHNSON

* *The Contemporary Theatre, 1944 and 1945*, p. 54

To the astonishment of author and publisher alike, *Brief Chronicles* sold out immediately on its appearance. The book had everything against it; a volume of reprinted drama criticisms, and Shakespearean at that, it came at the height of war in 1943 when one might have assumed readers to have more urgent preoccupations, and yet the total edition of 3,500 copies was quickly bought up. In normal times Agate would have been resigned to sales of no more than 800 or so. The reviews, too, were glowing. They spoke of his gusto, his pretty wit, his vivacity, and *The Times* pointed out that 'the quiddity of Shakespeare's drama lies not in story, not in character, nor in any sort of "message", but first and last in poetry. Mr Agate has a passion for poetry, and an ear for it worthy of his passion.' At last, he thought to himself, someone had seen that beneath his bookmaker's exterior there was a love of something which exceeded ponies, golf, music, the obsession of Sarah, whisky, cigars and even vice itself.

Jonathan Cape demanded a sequel and Agate speedily obliged with another selection of articles on the post-Elizabethan drama in performance between 1921 and 1943. A title evaded him until George Felton Mathew suggested: 'Why not Red Letter Nights?' 'That's it!' said Agate, and *Red Letter Nights* duly appeared the following year.

In 1926 he had published a little book containing a table of plays other than musical which achieved a run of more than twelve months during the period from 1900 to 1924.* Nearly all the fifty-four titles listed are forgotten now, and the two most successful were *A Little Bit of Fluff* and *Romance* with well over a thousand performances each. Barrie had four plays and Galsworthy and Maugham but two. Shaw was represented only by one, the minor *Fanny's First Play*. Would the evidence be equally depressing in the similar span covered by *Red Letter Nights?*

On this occasion Agate did not bother with runs long or short, and concentrated instead on what he believed was artistically important. During those twenty-two years he

* A Short View of The English Stage, 1900–1926, pp 29–32

reckoned to have seen up to five thousand plays. He opened the book with an account of the Restoration revivals London had witnessed and went on to give an almost complete record of Ibsen which bagged even hole-and-corner productions of *The Vikings at Helgeland* and *Little Eyolf*. Ibsen he held to be the greatest playwright since Molière and one to be placed in the Shakespeare class – the class which includes Aeschylus and Molière, Corneille and Congreve, Racine and Goethe and Victor Hugo, and 'probably' Bernard Shaw. The only difference between Ibsen and Shakespeare, he found, was that the former had no humour and was shy of beauty and charity. Chekhov he also placed very high, and if, today, his praise seems conventional, it should be remembered that when he saw *The Cherry Orchard* in 1925 both play and author were largely unfamiliar to London. His intuition did not let him down and he burnt his boats with enthusiasm. Here was the critic's true function, that of discovery and the excitement of spreading the news. 'I am always being asked which is the best play in London. This is. For the high-brow? Yes, and for butcher, baker, and candlestick-maker as well. I suggest that *The Cherry Orchard* is one of the great plays of the world.'

About other foreign imports he was equally decisive. Pirandello baffled him and he was not afraid to admit it. This dramatist had the technical facility of an Ibsen or a Labiche, and he used it, complained Agate, to hide the fact that he had nothing whatever to say. Strindberg, on the other hand, in *The Dance of Death* and *The Spook Sonata* proved that art possessed a logic of its own which might with impunity run counter to any other sort of logic, for his characters were touched with a kind of greatness and he could not handle any subject without saying anything worthwhile about it. The French, of course, did no wrong, especially Jean-Jacques Bernard, son of the humorist Tristan and author of plays very different from his father's rumbustious comedies. His *Théâtre du Silence* emphasised, as in music, the importance of silences, and the delicate adjustments of human relationships were expressed in half-formed sentences that revealed half-formed thoughts, impulses, motives, which presented life as people really lived it. Other visitors from over the Channel were the Comédie Française who ravished the ear in the Spring of 1939 with the Chopinesque atmosphere of Musset's *Le Chandelier*. Even Cocteau's bag of tricks *Les Parents Terribles* impressed with its theatrical brilliance.

The new plays reviewed in *Red Letter Nights* include some that are gilt-edged and some that are rarely even mentioned today. Among the latter are the conversation pieces of James Bridie, the doctor-playwright whose prolific wit and joy in argument held the stage of the thirties and forties. Maugham is now a period piece, and although, as Agate said, in *Our Betters* he rewrote 'one of Henry James's short stories in the manner of Congreve,' his plays can only be revived if as much care is given to the settings and costumes as to the acting. The uneasy limbo in which J. B. Priestley finds himself is not the fault of the deft artistry or the cunning structure which Agate detected in his work. *I Have Been Here Before*, like *Time and The Conways*, struck the critic as 'metaphysical bosh', although it threw up at least fifty different ideas. Perhaps Agate unknowingly hit on the reason for Priestley's future neglect when he described how, in his stall, he was suddenly reminded of Henry Arthur Jones's old melodrama *The Liars* and realised that *I Have Been Here Before* was, too, no more than the oldest play in the world rewritten by a dramatist of talent.

The success of Bernard Shaw's *St Joan* reminded Agate that Shaw's plays were the price that had to be paid for his prefaces. That to *St Joan* was full, as were all the others, 'of awful sanity, incredible erudition, and unbelievable flippancy. There is enough horse-sense in these sixty-odd pages to keep the solar system going for a twelve-month.' But in actual performance of the play Agate found that he was exhausted by the time of the Cathedral scene because he had already worn himself out grappling with Shaw's exposition of Church, Inquisition and Feudal System. He was happier at *Heartbreak House*, four hours of persistent button-holing with Ibsenite overtones which, though a failure as simple entertainment, as a great testament was exhilarating and moving. Shaw was right, Agate thought, to claim that the intellectual content of his plays was greater than that of Shakespeare's. Shaw's theatre concerned itself with enquiry into matters which might properly have been the subject of Royal Commissions. There was very little humanity and still less poetry in it, and his drama seldom, if ever, contained any drama, whereas Shakespeare contained all of human nature and the finest poetry that ever sprang from the human mind. As drama Shakespeare's plays had never been, nor ever would be, surpassed. But in intellectual content they were not the equal of Shaw's.

The humanity which Agate could not find in Shaw was supplied in full measure by his compatriot Sean O'Casey. *The Plough and The Stars* created, as did Balzac and Dickens, a whole new gallery of men and women. There was an Elizabethan richness about them: young Covey and his Pistol-like emphasis, Fluther and his Falstaffian ring, old Flynn as Shallow all over again, and Rosie as pure Doll Tearsheet. The richness, indeed, threatened to overpower everything else, since the characters talked too magnificently but not dramatically enough. In print the play read superbly and the eye could linger on beauties scattered with a prodigal hand. For the ear it was different, and the dialogue was crammed with chunks of verbiage that any actor must find impossible to deliver effectively. Still, as the Scotchman described the dish of singed sheep's head he was eating, it had 'a deal o' find confused feedin' aboot it, let me tell you.'

If O'Casey was too generous with feeling, in Agate's view, then Noël Coward was too miserly of it. At a time when Coward had four plays running simultaneously in London Agate remarked that all of them were 'as barren of emotion as a moneylender is of generosity.' The average playgoer was crying out for emotion and all he got was a Noëlism. The characters in *Design For Living* prated eternally of love, though in fact none of them loved anybody at all, for to love in any grown-up sense you must be grown up, which these people were not. 'They are naughty children occupying the same perambulator and sharing a bag of sweets which they snatch from one another. Does this make an entertaining evening, or does it not? For me, not.' Agate was even more severe on *Fallen Angels*. It contains a scene of drunken women which, at the time, created a genuine shock. Now Agate, despite his private life, was not a conscious hypocrite. He knew Coward, enjoyed his conversation at the Ivy, and admired him as a born playwright. The hectic shimmer of *The Vortex*, the impudent fooling of *Hay Fever* and the subtle modulations of *Private Lives* charmed him with their professional smoothness. But he could not swallow *Fallen Angels*. He was a Victorian born and bred, a product of chapel life and nonconformist Manchester, and it is significant that the only play of Coward's to which he responded wholeheartedly was *Cavalcade* with its spectacular scenes of Mafeking Night, the evocation of Queen Victoria's funeral and the strains of old music-hall songs.

What of the acting he saw? Once again he picked out Wilfrid Lawson in a Priestley play. 'Is this a great actor? Let me shelve the difficulty by boldly stating that he is a grand one, whose present performance is something to dream about.' Once again, too, he had to urge the merits of Edith Evans upon unheeding theatre managers. Although in later years a celebrated figure, in the nineteen-twenties and even in the thirties her light was still partly hidden under a bushel. Agate described her in *The Way of The World* as England's most accomplished of living and practising actresses. 'Her Millamant is impertinent without being pert, graceless without being ill-graced. She has only two scenes, but what scenes they are of unending subtlety and finesse! . . . There is a pout of the lips, a jutting forward of the chin to greet the conceit, and a smile of happy deliverance when it is uttered, which defy the chronicler. This face, at such moments, is like a city in illumination, and when it is withdrawn leaves a glow behind.' To *The Beaux' Stratagem* she gave a modern but wholly justifiable emotion which Farquhar never glimpsed: 'Great playing has this merit, that it makes the mind free of time and space, and sends the imagination of the spectator blowing where it listeth.' In a totally different play, Ibsen's *Rosmersholm*, she did something which audiences up to then had often found hard to accept: she persuaded them that the haughty Rebecca had at last dominated her all-conquering egotism. 'Certainly the printed page has never made one quite believe in the possibility of this, and it required the very finest art of Miss Edith Evans to achieve the complete triumph. This superb artist – and I use the word deliberately, accepting all the challenges it implies – had already in the second act given us one great moment, that of the rejection of Rosmer's love. In the third act she really did convince us of the translation of clay into spirit. Here the play took on the simplicity of the great prophetic truths, and to ask oneself whether people in real life would behave like this seemed beside the point and meaningless.'

Another Ibsenite who caught Agate's eye was Donald Wolfit. Despite the handicap of make-up suggesting by turns an amiable gorilla and a seaside phrenologist, he put forward an immensely cogent case for Solness in *The Master Builder*. 'Look, whether he has not tears in's eyes,' Agate murmured to himself as he watched this bravura performance. At a production of *Peer Gynt* he was confounded by the acting of Robert Speaight, a young man whom he had once firmly advised against entering the profession. Speaight admirably suggested the impetuosity, the vanity, the adventure and all the excitement of living in a way that bluntly contradicted Agate's pessimistic advice. But the most fragrant Ibsen memories of these years were provided by Eleanora Duse. With Duse, in *The Lady From The Sea*, speech was silver and silence golden. 'The voice seemed to me to be just as exquisite as ever; the arms, with their grave dance, eked out the old insufficiency of words; the face, in moments of emotion, lit up from within as though a lime had been thrown upon it. There was the old ineffable grace, the childish importunacy, the raising of human dignity to a power undreamt of . . . Her features have the placidity of long grief; so many storms have broken over them that nothing can disturb again this sea of calm distress. If there be in acting such a thing as pure passion divorced from the body yet expressed in terms of the body, it is here.' When he saw her in *Ghosts* he came nearer to analysing the paradox. 'Duse is a very great artist who, nevertheless, gives one the impression of scorning to be an actress. She has nothing of what the Germans call *Humor*, and only the aftermath of passion. One feels that she would play Lady Macbeth like a wounded dove. She is always herself, her fastidious, beautiful self. So, you say, was Bernhardt. But Bernhardt had a hundred different ways of being the same person. She could shake Heaven and Hell; Duse breathes only a sigh. Sarah, in the mind, still flames and glows; Duse lingers like some exquisite, faint regret.'

It was mainly in Ibsen, Chekhov and the Restoration comedies that opportunity for the best type of acting arose. There were occasional examples in modern plays – the American Pauline Lord as O'Neill's *Anna Christie* had the indefinable sense of the great player, the gift of melancholy, a face which in repose showed the ravages of past storms, and in *Richard of Bordeaux* John Gielgud had begun to show the attributes of greatness – but on the whole the classics and Shakespeare remained the only testing ground of real mastery. Meanwhile one had to make the best of plays like Molnar's *Liliom* with Ivor Novello: 'His body was a river of grace, his thighs were a cascade of loveliness, and his soul shone with a glow like that of a fountain lit up by coloured electric lights.'

Red Letter Nights was as successful as *Brief Chronicles*, and once more Jonathan Cape asked for a sequel. A second gleaning would not do, so Agate decided on a volume covering the theatre's lighter side over the past twenty years. On a Monday in 1944 he started wading through his old notices of musical comedies, revues, music-halls and pantomimes. At Thursday noon, having snatched a few hours only for sleep, he handed the complete manuscript to Cape. It bore the title *Immoment Toys*, a quotation from *Antony and Cleopatra*:

> 'Say, good Caesar,
> 'That I some lady trifles have reserved,
> 'Immoment toys . . .',

which was meant to hint that writing about rubbish is no reason for writing rubbish. Indeed, if you write about *Hamlet* or *Mourning Becomes Electra* it does not matter very much how you express yourself since the material is 'carried' by the subject. Since, however, there is nothing to be said about *Funny Face* or *The Du Barry*, the way you say it becomes of the first importance.

Throughout this appraisal of light entertainment between 1920 and 1943 he is exasperated again and again by the idiocies of musical comedy. 'There are mornings when the sky hangs over me like a pall made of porridge, all my faculties are numb and the world seems to have lost definition,' he laments. 'My breakfast-knife turns into india-rubber, and with a pointless fork I stuff my mouth with pieces of bacon made out of Berlin wool. I do not summon the doctor because he would be of no avail. What is the matter with me is that I must that evening at eight o'clock undergo a musical comedy.' A classic example of the *genre* was *Oh, Kay!*. Of this work by Guy Bolton, P. G. Wodehouse and George Gershwin, he writes: 'In so far as I can make anything of this imbroglio of a piece it concerns a cretinous earl so harassed by super-tax that he is reduced to rum-running in his last remaining possession, his yacht. With him is his sister, who is apparently called Kay. Kay, clothed in a mackintosh, makes a burglarious mid-night entry into the house of one Jimmy Winter, whom she has previously saved from drowning. Jimmy, who is arranging to marry a second wife before completely divorcing the first, now falls in love with Kay. It also happens that another rum-runner, one 'Shorty' McGee, has chosen Winter's house in which to store without permission his stock of illicit liquor. The establishment possesses forty unexplained housemaids and a baker's dozen of inexplicable footmen, who from time to time interrupt such action as there is. This is the entire story, and I can frankly say that I have known nothing in the musical-comedy line of greater melancholy.'

If Agate came back today he would be horrified to see that the London theatre was actually reviving some of the very musical comedies through which he groaned and snored his way in the nineteen-twenties. Many of them, nonetheless, were fated to vanish for ever, and he rose to the challenge with dogged versatility. His review of *Waltz Without End*, a spectacle which cynically plundered the music of Chopin, was cast in the form of a judge's summing-up against Eric Maschwitz, the author, in that on the 29th day of September, 1942, he destroyed the reputation of Frédéric Chopin. In a notice purporting to describe *Fritzi* he digressed charmingly on that eccentric forgotten dramatist Népomucène Lemercier and concluded that *Fritzi*, too, was not immortal. *The Golden Toy*, a ballet extravaganza, enabled him to quote at length from Thomas Love Peacock and to praise Ninette de Valois whose choreography so neatly utilised a small space that 'she must be our first authority on how many angels can dance on the point of a needle.'

A 'comédie musicale' is not, happily, the same thing as a musical comedy, for which reason the evenings he spent at Sacha Guitry's seasons in London were enchanted ones. Sacha's *Mozart*, with his then wife Yvonne Printemps as the child prodigy, gave him an emotion of the sort Bernhardt and Duse had awoken for him in the past. 'It is not exaggerating to say that on Monday evening people were observed to cry, and by that I mean shed tears, when Music's heavenly child appeared at the top of the stairs and came down them to kneel at Mme. d'Epinay's feet. Those who like to resolve a theatrical emotion into its component parts may find here something of a stirring of the sensibilities always occasioned by radiant happiness in conjunction with youth, something of their own unceasing wonder at that genius whose pure loveliness of achievement has never been surpassed, something of that sympathy which a certain quality of magnetism in certain players can evoke before a word has been uttered, something of recognition that the piece which M. Guitry has written to Mlle. Printemps should so obviously be an act of adoration.' In *Mozart* Sacha himself played the worldly-wise Baron Grimm, and, to music confected by the elegant Reynaldo Hahn, Yvonne Printemps embodied the wayward pathos of immature genius moving imperceptibly between speech and song. Moreover: 'Our visitors are great artists in this, that having provided a good thing they take care not to give too much of it. In both acts the curtain came down ten minutes too soon – in other words, it fell at exactly the right moment.'

There was the same artistry in *Mariette*, for which Oscar Straus provided Sacha with the music. Sub-titled 'How history gets written', this was a lightly cynical illustration of the fact that even those who have taken part in great historical events are apt to give highly misleading accounts of them. 'The theatre is in every Frenchman's blood: it is a part of his consciousness whereas it is an imposition upon ours,' wrote Agate, echoing Max Beerbohm. 'The French are a nation of actors in the best sense, by which one means that their temperament is more fluid. "I am, therefore I act", is the French dictum.'

Yvonne Printemps was to return, this time in Noël Coward's *Conversation-Piece*, and gave a faultless exhibition of wayward charm. 'There is probably more art behind this blob of heavenly nose than the casual spectator might imagine, and this highly talented actress has to thank Nature for yet another gift – that of self-caricature. She can be more like Yvonne Printemps than Printemps has right to be, and it is then that her art attains the most significance.' Although Coward's *Bitter-Sweet* did not have Printemps, it at least could offer Ivy St Helier, a reminder of Yvette Guilbert so potent 'that if this were the 'nineties, all the highbrow essayists would be dithyrambing about her.'

These occasional patches of civilised entertainment were surrounded by arid tracts of Sigmund Romberg and Buddy da Sylva. Agate took comfort from the little-known discovery that the march in *The Desert Song* echoed the chorus 'Fling Wide The Gates' from Sir John Stainer's oratorio *The Crucifixion.* He amused himself spotting the bits from Liszt, Mascagni, Rimsky-Korsakov and even 'The Londonderry Air'. Was it not prudent of Mr Romberg to have realised, early in life, that a man who is going to compose some fifty musical plays must be sparing of original inspiration? The performers themselves gave scope for lethal blandness: 'Mr Heddle Nash sings beautifully, and acts as tenors should.'

Clowns and drolls, however poor their material, usually found Agate at his best. In moments of ecstasy Leslie Henson looked at you 'out of eyes bulging like those of a moth which has eaten too much tapestry.' Those Crazy Gang anarchists Jimmie Nervo and Teddie Knox performed a version of the Russian Ballet which inspired him to write: 'At the Palladium we behold half our pair semi-swathed in leopard-skin but otherwise *décolleté.* This moiety pursues the other, whose description calls for a fresh sentence. Imagine a haphazard assemblage of arms and legs, crowned with an auburn mop, invest the trunks with wisps of clothing from the Nellie Wallace collection, endow the whole with all that "joy and gladdery" of which Beachcomber's Miss Violet Cork alone has the secret – achieve this ideal portrait and embellish it with the leaps and lollings, pirouettes and prancings of the classic dancer's repertory, and you will have some poor notion of the "winsome madcappery" of this superb droll.'

He relished the patina on the ancient quips thrown off by George Robey as Widow Twankey, the blend of pathos and grotesquerie in Will Fyffe's daft loony, and the gladiatorial stance of Kate Carney as she belted out

'Are we to part like this, Bill;
'Are we to part this way?
'Who's it to be, her or me?
'Don't be afraid to say.'

Most of all he loved Marie Lloyd. In a famous article he quoted the two bookmakers who had heard, unbelievingly, the news of her death. 'She had a heart, had Marie!' 'The size of Waterloo Station,' rejoined the other. 'Our Marie' was frank as Rabelais and outspoken as a page of Fielding. She employed a whole armoury of shrugs and leers, and each articulation of the body to reveal every craving of the mind. 'Yvette Guilbert harrowed the soul with the pathos of her street-walkers; Marie Lloyd had intense delight in her draggle-tails. She showed them in their splendour, not in their misery; the mopishness and squalor of their end were not for her. And that is why, when she came to the portrayal of elderly baggages, she refrained from showing them as pendants to her courtesans.' Her hands and feet were beautiful, and she had the most expressive Cockney face on the stage. Of course she knew every inch of the boards and was technically perfect. 'I hope,' she said in a little speech before her last appearance, 'I hope I may, *without bigotry*, allude to my past triumphs.' 'Poor soul,' remarked Agate, 'it is we who should ask to be delivered from that vice. She broadened life and showed it, not as a mean affair of refusal and restraint, but as a boon to be lustily enjoyed.' Which is more than he could say of Pirandello.

iii
AROUND CINEMAS

> 'The film shattered one of my fondest hopes. For years I have wanted to see Joan Crawford in a gas mask.'
>
> JAMES AGATE

The three volumes of criticism I have touched on so far cover two decades and more of the London theatre in all its moods from Shakespeare and Ibsen to Grock and Sophie Tucker. In 1946 Agate issued a collection of film criticisms as *Around Cinemas*, a title which echoed Max Beerbohm's *Around Theatres*. A second volume came out posthumously in 1948. For the sake of completeness, in this dritical chapter, we may as well look at them here.

The first collection was dedicated to Caroline Lejeune and Dilys Powell, film critics respectively of *The Observer* and *The Sunday Times*. He often disagreed with these two writers and loved to tease them with provocative statements to which they fired off brisk counter-charges. In such a friendly spirit were their debates conducted, the two young women regarding him as a mischievous uncle and he them as a pair of wayward nieces. The cinema had developed, as he saw it, like this: 'Think of great whales, of tumbling oceans. Of lazy, tropic beaches and feathery trees. Of mountain tops that freeze. Of earthquakes and cataclysms. Of all the things that film can do magnificently and the theatre cannot look at. And then the time came when even the film-makers got tired of looking at it, and decided that there was more 'to' the pictures than the mere presentation of the outdoor and the outsize. Hence those warning shadows, those garrets under Paris roofs, that swirl of skirts above a dropped dance-programme, those enigmatic sledges, those equivocal glooms.'

Films began turning to novels for their material, and finally the theatre was laid under contribution. How, said foolish people, Shakespeare would have welcomed films, quoting in support the Chorus:

> 'Think, when we talk of horses, that you see them
> 'Printing their proud hoofs i' the receiving earth.'

They did not stop to reflect that when you see horses prancing and curvetting there is no longer any need to put that prancing and curvetting into words. Agate recalled a phrase of Neville Cardus which described the cricketer Woolley's off-drives as being 'like butterflies going into the flame.' He was writing for a public which had not seen Woolley's innings. Agate sat next to Cardus that afternoon at Lord's, and what he said was not 'look at that butterfly going into the flame,' but 'Well played, Sir!'

Agate's experience of film-going stretched from pre-1914 Bioscopes via the coming of sound to *The Wicked Lady* and *Gone With The Wind*. His first article about a film concerned Chaplin's *The Kid*, and his last, in 1946, an English war epic called *Theirs Was The Glory*. He made a careful distinction between the cinema and the theatre. Because a cinema was built like a theatre the average playgoer imagined that anything he saw on the screen was a play, and a visit to a film became equivalent to a visit to a theatre. This was not so, for the theatre, which talks about things rather than shows them, calls for a certain amount of imagination, whereas the film, by showing everything, calls for none at all. A spectacular film like *Sanders of The River* gave Agate the same pleasure as a grand entertainment in the order of a circus or a rodeo. It had nothing to do with art. Theatre-going was one thing and film-going another. There was, however, one test of whether a film was good which it had in common with plays, books or music. In the case of a play did he want to come back after the interval and hear what A was going to do next or B to say to C? In the case of a book did he want to turn over the next page? If he were at a concert did he secretly hope there was a gramophone record of the piece? If at the cinema, did he want to go on looking at the film?

He had, as in the theatre, his blind spots. He disliked Technicolor in which pinks resembled raspberry sauce, reds turned to sealing-wax, blues shrieked of the washtub and yellows became Yorkshire pudding. In the early days a fan of Mickey Mouse, he came to loathe the raucous fowl Donald Duck and only approved reluctantly of *Bambi* and *Fantasia*. One of his sharpest disputes with Caroline Lejeune centred on the merits of Fred Astaire, which, he argued, extended no further than the ability to give twenty minutes of pleasure in the deserts of witlessness his films usually were. For years he was pursued by correspondents furious at his dismissal of W. C. Fields as Micawber in *David Copperfield* – a master comedian, he granted, in *My Little Chickadee*, but, in a rôle demanding genteel orotundity, horribly miscast. *Citizen Kane* and all the works of Orson Welles he regarded as highbrow bluff. About other films now elevated to the pantheon of cinémathèques throughout the world he was more enthusiastic. Dovzhenko's *Earth* moved him with pictorial values and compositions worthy of a Picasso or a Cézanne. 'In fact,' he added, 'the effect of the picture on me has been so great that if for the next ten days anybody mentions to me the names of David Wark Griffith, King Vidor, and Cecil B. de Mille, I shall merely laugh!' And although Eisenstein had a risible fondness in his writing for phrases like 'theoretical postulates of discontinuity' and the 'non-coincidence of the syntactic articulation with the metrical', he could be absolved because *Thunder Over Mexico* was a film of rare and astounding beauty.

As a Francophile Agate welcomed René Clair's *Sous Les Toits de Paris* and *Le Million*, which, realistic but stylish, were not for the million but undoubtedly for the fifty or possibly the hundred thousand. Writing of a little production called *Derrière La Façade*, he claimed that there were 'more brains, elegance, wit and charm in a hundred feet of this film than in ten thousand feet sent over by Hollywood.' (Which is not surprising since the cast numbered Elvire Popesco of the witty eyebrows, Erich von Stroheim and those peerless players Jules Berry, Gaby Morlay and Gabrielle Dorziat.) *La Bête Humaine*, a version true to Zola, impressed him with its genuine passion and a scene of a railwaymen's ball which was a piece of mob characterisation the French do so brilliantly. Sacha Guitry's *Ils Etaient Neuf Célibataires*, where Sacha made of his own part no more than a witty footnote, evoked the *cri du coeur*: 'How sick one gets of the film's eternal wisecracking! And how delightful it is to move once again in a world of well-bred wit!'

Could the cinema produce anyone to rival Irving and the others whom Agate worshipped? Yes – one man, the German Emil Jannings, who, in *The Blue Angel* and other films, had a sheer power, a massivity which called to mind Richter's handling of Wagner. Then there were two women. Greta Garbo, even when daring enough to challenge Sarah Bernhardt in a version of *La Dame aux Camélias* mutilated by Hollywood, emerged, for him, 'ensky'd and sainted' as among the most heavenly of Northern lights. Even in her early days, he said, she had that indefinable something which draws your eye to one unbroken filly in the field and keeps you from looking at all the others. She was superb moper, magnificent along Duse's lines but also capable of making successful raids into the Bernhardt country. Her lack of warm humanity – she could on occasion be as alluring as an iceberg – was complemented by Marlene Dietrich in a film like *Morocco*. At Marlene's début in *The Blue Angel* Agate hailed her as the only serious competitor to Garbo, a capable, fascinating and lovely actress who, despite the varying quality of her later films, never ceased to enchant with an extraordinary loveliness as inviolate as the rose. But this was strictly an enchantment and therefore had nothing to do with actuality and all the unloveliness which attends real love.

In 1941 Caroline Lejeune flung down a challenge: what were the seven best films to be snowbound with for a whole winter? Agate loved this sort of thing – 'List, list, oh list,' as the Ghost said in *Hamlet* anent other things – and he was for ever making lists of the world's best courtisanes, the ten greatest novels, the eight greatest actors, the fifteen most incompetent British film directors. The first film on his list was *Broken Blossoms*, on account of the ache and beauty Richard Barthelmess put into his acting, and of Lillian

Gish, who in those days closely resembled the young Sarah Bernhardt, the hair falling down the sides of her pinched, woebegone face, the countenance wistfully expressive. Next came *The Four Horsemen of The Apocalypse* which had the one and only Rudolph Valentino. Charlie Chaplin could not be left out, so *The Gold Rush* qualified automatically. *The Blue Angel* came fourth because of Jannings's dramatic power and the gorgeous sexuality of La Dietrich, first, among film actresses, in the line of Helen and Sappho. To ignore the gangster film would be like dropping Restoration comedy from a list of the best in English drama, and *Scarface* therefore was included for the sake of Paul Muni's fine acting and George Raft's unforgettable dying. If Agate had had to live with any one film it would be *Pépé le Moko* in the original French version: 'The moment when the fat man, seeking shelter behind the mechanical piano, accidentally sets it playing, is in my view the most dramatically effective thing the cinema has given us since Jannings's cock crow.' And as his seventh and final choice he simply had, although he hated agreeing with Caroline Lejeune, to vote for *Un Carnet de Bal*.

Chapter Eight

NO LETTERS IN THE GRAVE

'What worries me when I am ill is not dying but the idea of ceasing to work. Dr Johnson said: "An odd thought strikes me: we shall receive no letters in the grave." An odd thought strikes me: we shall keep no diaries.'

James Agate

i
BUSINESS AS USUAL

'What! No blazing star appear? No monsters born? No whale thrown up?' Not being Swift, I shall merely announce the publication this morning of *Ego 6*.

JAMES AGATE

From September 1940 to January 1941 he vegetated unwillingly in Oxford. He spoke at the Union, dined at High Tables when he would sooner be supping at low, and was ready to give all Oxford in exchange for some dingy little pub in Victoria. The tedium lifted for a while as he took in hand a local repertory production of *Hedda Gabler*, coached the promising young actress Pamela Brown in the title part, and abused the townsfolk of Oxford for not appreciating so talented a band of players. It fell again when his landlady sternly ruled 'No visitors' and prevented him from entertaining a caller such as Leo Pavia. He admitted to himself that he could have the dingy little pub in Victoria straightaway if only he'd the courage to go back to London. But he hadn't. He was, he thought, a more contemptible figure than he'd ever been.

In October his Brother Edward died during an operation

for an unsuspected disease. 'This poor remnant of humanity, this fluttering scarecrow on a couple of peasticks,' as Edward described himself, was buried in the family grave at a Unitarian church in Manchester. As the coffin lurched down into the hole a siren wailed. Agate thought of Macbeth's 'Nothing can touch him further'. Edward had made for himself a way of living, austere, uncompromising, and was not to be turned from it. Half Thersites, half Mr Dick, he died worth four shillings and ninepence. When Agate looked through his papers afterward he came across an unposted letter to Jock. It contained one of those quotations from seventeenth-century divines with which Edward used to repay small loans: 'When our Saviour was reared up aloft on the Cross that same hanging was very painful unto Him. But where He did hang here but for a time, if *thou* amend not thy life, thou shalt hang in the gibbet of hell for evermore.'

Early next year Agate could abide Oxford no longer and returned to London with its air-raids and moaning sirens, its black-outs and bomb ruins. Almost immediately he parted company with Jock Dent after a final row. While Agate was away in Oxford Jock had tasted freedom from the battered typewriter on which he was forced to work. Furthermore, long-suffering and frugal though he was, he could no longer exist on the pittance Agate jealously doled out to him. Taking as his excuse the outbreak of war Agate had tried to reduce the sum still further, although he himself still had his contracts with *The Sunday Times* and *The Daily Express*. 'He was with me fourteen years, four months and some odd days,' Agate recorded bleakly in *Ego 5*. They remained on good terms, and when Jock published his first collection of essays, *Preludes and Studies*, his old master gave it a warm review. Some time later Jock looked in to announce that he had been called up for the Navy – unless he refused to go. In which case, said Agate, they'd put him in prison. Dr Johnson would have been delighted, replied Jock. 'He'd have said: "Here is a man who, rather than be a sailor, had had contrivance enough to get himself into a jail!"'*

* 'No man will be a sailor who has contrivance enough to get himself into a jail; for being in a ship is being in a jail, with the chance of being drowned.' Dr Johnson

The pace at the Villa Volpone maintained its hectic rhythm. He made up volumes of his articles from *The Daily Express* and *John o'London's Weekly*, called them *Express and Admirable* and *Thursdays and Fridays*, and sent them off to the press. Why was it, he thought, that when anthologists chose niceish bits of prose from contemporary writers his own stuff was never included? As a defensive measure he threw together a self-selected anthology, unblushingly titled it *Here's Richness!*, and charmed Osbert Sitwell into writing a preface. It sold out before publication and a new impression had to be put in hand.

Jock's place was taken by Leo Pavia, at whose hands typing became witty, inventive and, in inessentials, wildly inaccurate. Leo moaned that he was deaf and could not hear what Agate dictated. He lamented that his handwriting was illegible. Agate suggested he make it legible. 'What's the good? I'm too blind to read it anyhow!' snapped Leo. He was garrulous, had no tact, and veered crazily between moods of ecstasy and despair. He coughed, sneezed, spat on the floor. Agate kept a book to hand which, after long practice, he was able to hurl accurately at him in moments of rage. His linen was dubious, his clothes were frayed and his hats greasy. Agate one day rashly took him to the Savoy for lunch with a distinguished guest. He looked at the suit Leo wore, slipped a pound note into his hand and tactfully suggested that he wouldn't like the people or the food and would be happier lunching elsewhere. Which, cheerfully, Leo did. One of Agate's New Year Resolutions for 1942 was to put up with the permanent irritation of Leo for the sake of the perpetual delight he gave him. Having driven him half frantic Leo would then go to the piano and play Beethoven more Beethovenishly than any virtuoso, sing in a cracked voice the *tuttis* to the concertos and improvise his own cadenzas. When at his angriest with him Agate would think of Verlaine, whom he resembled in his love of sensuous beauty. After all, the author of *Mes Prisons* would not have been an ideal secretary, either.

In a London where no lamp shone after dark, where the night was shattered by terrifying explosions and where, next morning, you could never be sure that the houses in your road would still be there, Agate worked as doggedly as he ever had. He loathed inaction. He could work, he boasted, until he dropped, and he shied at any idea of resting. Going to bed at night was, for him, literally 'the death of each day's life'. In the summer of 1942 he collapsed. He imagined Macbeth's witches dancing round his bed, and he held parley with hags and monsters who were not there. His doctor diagnosed overwork and prescribed regular meals, early bed, no cigars, and not more whisky than would sustain a fly. The papers he wrote for gave him a holiday, and, reluctantly, he set off for Bournemouth with George Felton Mathew. It was no good. He just could not do nothing, and before long he was fiddling with review copies again. Messengers from civilisation called on him. John Gielgud reported how, when a touring company bringing art to the masses played *Dear Brutus* at a Canadian soldiers' camp, the audience marched out saying 'Jesus, they're crackers!' Mark Hambourg came down to play the Beethoven C minor concerto and revealed to an approving Agate that the composer had written on the manuscript 'Not for women'.

A week of Bournemouth was enough. While he was away he had told Leo to forward on any correspondence that looked non-worrying All that arrived was a demand from the Inland Revenue for instant payment of £166 and a bill for fourteen shillings' worth of milk consumed at Bognor in 1940. When he got back to the Villa Volpone he found a huge pile of letters which would have made pleasant reading. 'I thought I'd save them for you,' said Leo innocently.

He reached his sixty-fifty birthday in the Autumn of that year. Jock sent a telegram, one of his ex-houseboys made a long-distance telephone call from Cornwall, and Leo gave him the vocal score of *Tristan and Isolde*. He felt restless. The Villa Volpone was too far out and taxis around wartime Swiss Cottage were scarce. In Grape Street, a narrow canyon that skulks between New Oxford Street and Shaftesbury Avenue, he found a flat of seven rooms on a first floor. At one side of the street towers the back of the old Shaftesbury Theatre, and from the other the dismal bulk of Queen Alexandra Mansions casts its shadow. Piccadilly Circus was only ten minutes away and all the main theatres clustered nearby. He took a lease on Queen Alexandra Mansions at £250 a year. Since he had vowed never again to live in a flat and move out of it at the same time, he also rented a suite at Kensington Palace Mansions for three weeks at eighteen guineas a week. This, he reasoned à la Balzac, would be an economy in the long run.

He took possession at the Mansion of Queen Alexandra in March, 1943. It was to be his last London home, a high-ceilinged mansion flat with enormous rooms. In the entrance hall he established a Musée Sarah Bernhardt consisting of two immense photographs and some smaller ones, an autograph letter, and a tiny picture of Rachel to keep Sarah in her place. Later he added a marble female bust sculpted by Sarah and an inkstand she designed, this time in the shape of her own head, which she had given to Mrs Patrick Campbell. Somehow, up a twisted stair, the removal firm manoeuvred the old Agate family piano. On his own in the cavernous flat he practised for an hour, something he had not done since he was a boy, and his flailing fingers attacked with vigour and a joyful cascade of wrong notes the well-remembered tunes of Mendelssohn. Afterwards he cooked his own lunch, a pork chop, the first time in twenty years, having turned up his cookery book under the letter P for pork, and C for chop, but finding neither and managing very well to produce a good semblance of the real thing which he crowned with a chunk of elderly cheese.

Noël Coward and Gladys Calthrop visited the new flat. Gladys fell in love with the balcony and decided to use it in her next set of designs. Noël said he would write a new comedy round it. Afterwards, at the Ivy, they were joined by the actor Michael Shepley. Talk turned to an intellectual actor, who, said Shepley, couldn't act. 'The worst thing about him is the way he whinnies.' Agate interrupted: 'I think you mean he "neighs". Only mares whinny.' 'Splendid!' cried Noël clapping his hands. 'You've given me the title for my new comedy: *Only Mares Whinny!*'

Queen Alexandra Mansions was popular with theatricals. In the flat above dwelt the sharp-tongued Alan Melville, dramatist and revue writer. He had, like Agate, his own quaint little ways. His fetish involved raincoats, and at dead of night he would go out naked except for a flapping Burberry. This did not inhibit him from directing barbs of malice at the supposed unspeakable debaucheries of his neighbour below. Agate once wrote an article which he took a lot of trouble to make as witty as possible. When it appeared in print he fumed to see that it ended in the middle of a page and was followed without a break by another article which began: 'The wittiest man in London, Mr Alan Melville, lives immediately over the flat occupied by Mr James Agate.'

The new flat pleased him. Its hall was forty feet long and had the advantage that whenever a scene developed with Leo he would be able to quote Pinero's *His House in Order*: 'Shall we choose another topic – or would you prefer to walk?' What most charmed him was his freedom there: since 1921 he had always had a servant, but now he was free of dependants except for a houseboy or three. He had never been good with servants, preferring to treat them as equals whereas they wanted to be treated as hirelings. In their place he was attended by a Cockney lad, once a removal man, whom he christened 'Smike' on account of his starveling appearance and simple mind. 'Smike' repaid him, as the Dickensian original did Nicholas Nickleby, with admiring devotion. Often late at night, on returned from the Savage Club, Agate would play his old gramophone records of *Siegfried's Journey* followed by the Funeral March and the *Meistersinger* overture. Old Ludwig had the right notion, he thought to himself. The perfect way to listen to music was late at night with no audience but oneself and a houseboy to put the records on. Around two o'clock he had arrived at the Richard Strauss section in his record cabinet. Towards three he was saying: 'Always remember that in the theatre the clotted cream of pure sound is better than the vinegary lees of sour intellectuality.' 'Righto,' said 'Smike', 'I won't forget. Now what about me putting away the whisky and you going to bed?'

Other faces came to brighten the gloomy depths of Queen Alexandra Mansions. Jack Naughton, who made the morning tea and polished the furniture, brought with him Joseph, a young evacuee from Gibraltar, black-haired and with darkly handsome Italo-Spanish looks. Joseph's command of English was not then as good as it later became. 'Are you queer?' people asked him in this new and bewildering household. 'No, thank you,' he replied, touched by their solicitude about his health, 'I feel perfectly fine.' 'Do you like chicken?' they would enquire at a point when the conversation had touched on everything but food. 'But of course I do,' he answered, a little puzzled.

Odd characters flitted through the place and objects of value disappeared mysteriously, though Agate, through fear of blackmail, made no complaint. One morning he was discovered tightly bound and gagged in a chair, having languished there all night after an experiment in bondage. Complaisant Guardsmen went on trooping in and out, and he commissioned a well-known theatrical photographer to make nude pictures of them which he hung on the rambling walls of his flat.

The caretaker and his wife at Queen Alexandra Mansions were a pleasant couple. Agate took tea with them up on the roof looking out over tall chimney pots and the buildings of Long Acre. Their two sons joined them, an elder boy in Army uniform and the younger, Peter, an invalid unfit for military service. Peter had diabetes and tuberculosis, and, looking no more than fifteen years old, was in fact twenty-three. Agate admired his pluck, for, like Mark Tapley, he kept up an air of unalterable jollity. Soon Agate came to have an affection for this brave little Cockney and to worry over the diseases that were gnawing away at him. One day Peter was taken to hospital at Colindale and had a sudden collapse there. At five in the morning his parents woke Agate and asked if he could find a car to take them to the hospital. He rang up a night service and in just over a quarter of an hour they arrived at Peter's bedside, ten minutes before he died. It was the day of his birthday. Agate wept, for he had loved the boy with paternal fondness, and in his will he directed that he himself be buried next to Peter's grave.

He no longer bothered very much about his personal appearance and subordinated everything to his work, the constant treadmill of articles, speeches and broadcasts round which his life for years had been structured. In his time he was something of a dandy, a connoisseur of shirts and matching socks, an expert in the cut of a suit and the nap of a bowler. Now he wore the same shirt two days running and underlinen that verged on a positively Johnsonian state. His wardrobe was reduced to a pair of summer suits and check trousers much bagged and worn. He grudged every minute spent away from his writing desk and stopped taking baths because they demanded too much time. Instead, he doused himself all over with talcum powder and left the bedroom in a haze looking as if a snowstorm had suddenly descended upon it. Even going to the lavatory wasted precious seconds, and it was so much easier to grab one of his silver horse trophies from the mantelpiece and to relieve himself in it. Sybil Thorndike called once and was struck by the imposing row of engraved cups with their history of races won and triumphs carried off. One of them, aslop with brackish liquor, she reached out to pick up and inspect more closely. Jack Naughton hastily came forward and moved it to safety. 'Not that one, Madam,' he improvised, 'it hasn't been dusted.'

ii
THE MOST UNKINDEST CUT

> 'The web of our life is a mingled yarn, good and ill together: our virtues would be proud, if our faults whipped them not; and our crimes would despair, if they were not cherished by our virtues.'
>
> *All's Well That Ends Well*, ACT IV, SC. III

In 1943 also he fêted his twenty years on *The Sunday Times*. Even after so long a period of time the proprietor Lord Kemsley was still somewhat puzzled by his unconventional employee and, shrewd in business, innocent in worldly matters, had never been entirely sure that Agate was a wholly respectable citizen who cherished the sanctity of family life.

He brought Lady Kemsley with him on a tour of the new flat in Queen Alexandra Mansions – where the pictures of Guardsmen had been discreetly removed for the time being and the silver trophies attended to – and afterwards was entertained with the editor, W. W. Hadley, at the Ivy. Later on there was a formal luncheon in Kemsley House where he presented both Agate and Ernest Newman with gold watches in recognition of their long service. Agate was so pleased with his watch that after the ceremony he telephoned a Jewish friend and asked if he would like to know the time. The friend said he thought the joke in bad taste and hung up. It was 6.50 in the evening. Agate asked Leo the reason for this unaccustomed brusqueness. 'He thought you were pulling his leg,' explained Leo. 'The Day of Atonement starts in ten minutes!'

Agate looked back over his twenty years with *The Sunday Times* and reflected on the changes he had seen in the theatre. During that period Shaw wrote his best play. Sean O'Casey flamed in the Dublin sky with two blazing masterpieces after which his genius seemed for the moment to burn itself out. Noël Coward emerged as the successor to Wilde and Maugham. With *Dangerous Corner* and *Eden End* J. B. Priestley looked like becoming a dramatist of the first rank but then lost his way in the slough of metaphysics and sociology. There had been three considerable performers: John Gielgud, the legitimate successor to Forbes-Robertson; Charles Laughton, a born actor who drifted into the cinema; and Edith Evans, the nearest approach to a great actress. Unfortunately the producer (or director, as he is called today) had tightened his unholy grip. What was a producer, asked Agate? A person engaged by the management to conceal the inability of actors to act. No actor-manager of the old school would have brooked a producer's impertinent fussing. All an actor who could really play Macbeth wanted in the way of a producer was a stage-manager to see that the ghost of Banquo popped up at the right moment. On the lighter stage audiences had witnessed the arrival of the singer without a voice. For this the microphone was responsible.

Such opinions would seem to justify those who were

irritated by Agate's constant harking back to the great actors of yesterday and who mocked him as a reactionary. It is possible that if Irving or Bernhardt returned today they would be dismissed as grotesques. For the audiences of their time, however, they were the supreme examples of their art, and, with a simple modulation, a look, a gesture, a smile or a sigh they could, like Garrick or John Gielgud, thrill those who saw and heard them. Audiences change as much as styles in acting. By measuring the actors of his time against the performances he had seen in youth Agate was trying to place things in the wider perspective of theatrical history. His remarks on Ellen Terry set out what he thought was the duty of the drama critic: 'I will even say that so long as those who never saw Ellen Terry can read what was written about her by those who were artists in another sphere her spirit is not wholly gone. There is a sonnet of Shakespeare which puts this point of view perfectly. It is the sonnet which ends:

> But thy eternal summer shall not fade,
> Nor lose possession of that fair thou owest,
> Nor shall death brag thou wander'st in his shade,
> When in eternal lines to time thou growest;
>   So long as men can breathe, or eyes can see,
>   So long lives this, and this gives life to thee.

In their humble sphere this is the responsibility and the privilege of the dramatic critics – to see to it that the memory of the great player does not perish utterly.'

His definition of a good play was simple. 'A play which doesn't make you yawn or fidget is a good play relative to you. A play at which only a numskull would yawn or fidget is a good play absolutely.' What were the rules of drama criticism? 'Only two that matter. One. Decide what the playwright was trying to do and pronounce how well or ill he has done it. Two. Decide whether the well-done thing was worth doing at all.'

He was, as Jock Dent said, a warrior chief of his craft and kept going to the very end. Others could not sustain the pace – Ken Tynan, on whom his mantle largely fell, got off to a spectacular beginning but, in a relatively short space of time, started to flag. Agate never lost his vigour. Whatever he had to write about, a book, a play, a film, he used as an occasion to unburden his large and overflowing mind. The collections of essays and criticisms are there to prove it, and if they are a valuable mine for the historian they are also a source of pleasure to the general reader, whom they can by turn stimulate, annoy, enchant or infuriate. Agate was boastful and vainglorious. He loved, as we all do, praise. But if anyone lauded his style the critic in him rose to the surface. As he frankly confessed: 'By hopping about from one bit of gusto to another like a kangaroo I give the illusion of good writing. But that's only because it doesn't bore you. Of what really makes writing – the bone and muscles under the skin of the prose – I know nothing whatever, no more than I did twenty years ago.'

It is a fair judgment, and all the more telling in that he made it himself. The rhythm of his writing is unequal and his ear for cadence often defective. By his own admission, then, he does not belong in the class of Hazlitt, whom he venerated. Against this may be put the sheer readability of his style. He is always readable, as lively as Shaw and as witty as Beerbohm. But where Beerbohm tended to disdain actors and actresses, 'mimes' as he called them, Agate was fascinated by them and sought to analyse their techniques, to define the way in which they achieved their effects. As a critic of acting alone he deserves a place alongside Shaw and Beerbohm. He brought to his criticism a solid range of background knowledge. This included nineteenth-century French literature, Dickens, the drama criticisms of his famous predecessors, Hackney horses, golf and cricket. He could play the piano – badly, but well enough to appraise the performance of a virtuoso – and although his enjoyment of music did not go much beyond Wagner and early Strauss, in art he was able to appreciate Goerg and Picasso. As Dr Johnson said, it is better to know a thing than not know it, and the critic of wide background knowledge is more fully equipped to do his job than the narrow specialist.

Agate's interest in acting was nourished by the tendency to dramatise his own personality. Though not with quite such determined artistry as, for example, Evelyn Waugh, he constructed for himself an image which he projected tirelessly. The bowler hat, the bright check overcoat, the monocle and the chunky walking stick were 'props' essential to a character who, at dinner in the Ivy, in the bar of the Savage Club, in theatre foyers, would sacrifice everything for a witty repartee and who insisted having the last word with the finality of a third-act curtain. In the picture which emerges of him from the *Ego* volumes – a character, he wrote, 'who looked like a farmer, dressed like a bookmaker, ate like a Parisian, and drank like a Hollander' – he heads a cast of inimitable characters whose epigrams and adventures are described in the light of what he slyly called 'the higher truth', that is to say, with the aid of discreet embroidery which elaborates an incident or a situation and presents it as the author felt it should have happened. The success of the *Ego*'s in their time was so great that reprints were called for and also three volumes of *A Shorter Ego*. They are the perfect bedside books. You pick one up to check a point, and, before you realize what is happening, you are bewitched into reading on, and on, and on. Agate will be remembered as a critic, and also as a diarist of a very special sort whose journals are certainly more entertaining than those of Kilvert or Parson Woodforde.

He loved his work and he loved encouraging talent. In 1944, while staying with a friend in Brighton, he met 'a boy of twenty, Don Sinden'. After a morning spent in cutting 10,000 words out of *Ego 6* and reading Hazlitt, he was persuaded to give the boy an interview and to advise him on whether he should take up the stage or remain with his craft of cabinet-making. 'Stick to your fretwork, young man!' was Agate's first reaction. Then, as they played a Shakespeare scene together, he began to note the young man's resemblance to Henry Ainley, his resonant voice, his height and his attractive head. 'Did you ever *speak* to Irving?' Sinden asked. 'Certainly not,' Agate snapped. '*Greatness* is not to be spoken to – I don't know how you can sit there speaking to *me* like that!' He ended by advising him, yes, to go on the stage, and the later career of Donald Sinden shows that his opinion was justified.

A year later he spoke at a Sixth Form Conference and explained why English musical comedies were so awful: 'Because the English like it so. As a nation we admire any playwright, composer, actor, clown, who has no talent and is modest about it.' His chairman was a schoolboy called K. P. Tynan who showed him a 'prose poem' which brought in the names of Gautier, Montesquieu, Heredia, de Sade, Huysmans, Moore, Verlaine, Rimbaud, Proust, Apollinaire, Mallarmé and Flaubert – with Balzac, Voltaire, Meredith and Marlowe dragged in as well. 'Tell me, boy,' enquired Agate, 'are you a homosexual?' Tynan, who should by all appearance have been so but was not, replied in the negative. That interesting question having been settled, Agate set about nurturing what, despite the precocious flummery, he perceived as a genuine talent. 'Absent thee from quotation a while,' he begged, and despatched Ken Tynan to a performance of *Othello* with Frederick Valk as the Moor and Wolfit as Iago. What Tynan wrote about it made him remark: 'Anybody reading this in a hundred years' time should know what these two actors had been like in these two great rôles. And that, and nothing else, in my view is dramatic criticism. In other words, here is a great dramatic critic in the making.'

The General Election of 1945 which ousted Churchill and replaced him with Mr Attlee appalled Agate, who did not normally bother about politics. He immediately telephoned the head waiter at the Ivy and said: 'Listen to me carefully, Paul. I am quite willing that in future you address me as "comrade" or "fellow-worker", and chuck the food at me in the manner of Socialists to their kind. But that doesn't start until tomorrow morning. Tonight I am bringing two friends with the intention that we may eat our last meal as gentlemen. There will be a magnum of champagne and the best food your restaurant can provide. You, Paul, will behave with your wonted obsequiousness. The *sommelier*, the table waiter, and the *commis* waiter will smirk and cringe in the usual way. From tomorrow you will get no tips. Tonight you will all be tipped royally.' 'Bien, m'sieu,' said Paul.

That evening Agate arrived and was escorted with much deference to his table. There he found the magnum standing in its bucket, and three plates each laid with two small slices of spam.* Who, he wondered to himself, would have thought a head waiter to have so much wit in him?

Intimations of mortality assailed him. He reached his sixty-eighth birthday a few weeks after the end of the war and tried to forget the encroaching years in contemplation of the presents he received: a snake-wood walking stick with a tortoise-shell handle from one of his protégés, two tickets for a Beecham concert from Jock, a copy of Adelaide Ristori's memoirs from Leo, a bottle of whisky from the actress Coral Browne. Gwen Chenhalls, widow of his former accountant and his closest woman friend, gave him socks, a handkerchief and half a pound of sausages, items which, especially the last, were luxuries in those austere days.

He thought it time to make his will and spent a melancholy afternoon at Grays Inn with Stanley Rubinstein looking through what he had to bequeath. There did not seem to be a great deal. His Sarah Bernhardt collection was earmarked for Sister May, his gold watch and some furniture for his surviving brothers Gustave and Harry. Jock was to have all his theatre books and George Felton Mathew the remainder of his library. To Leo he gave three months' salary, and to the Savage Club his walking-sticks that had belonged to Charlie Chaplin and George Robey. 'Smike' was not forgotten: he was left all Agate's clothes, a silver cup of his choice and a sum of money. As the unwilling testator raised his head and looked out of Rubinstein's window he saw a funeral hearse pass by. He felt a sense of great relief, almost jollity, at the thought that he wasn't in it.

Despite his conviction that the world he had known was 'finished', despite his foreboding that there would be no more cakes and ale in the post-war Beveridge society to which he was now condemned, his *joie de vivre* remained unchecked. He read Cyril Connolly's *The Unquiet Grave* and was shocked by its atmosphere of anxiety and Baudelairean remorse. The author reminded him of Gilbert's Bunthorne, the ever-so

* An austerity form of meat loaf issued during the 1939–45 war to eke out official rations.

delicate aesthete in *Patience*. There was some exquisite writing in the book, but a depressing lack of humour. What the author needed was a box of Bunthorne's pills, or some useful exercise like wheeling crippled airmen round the Park. Life was to be lived, seized by the throat and shaken until it had disgorged all its joys and excitements – not muffled in anguish and drowned with tears.

Living meant working, and Bertie Van Thal's suggestion that he issue his collected film criticisms was taken up with enthusiasm. One Sunday afternoon was enough for him to cream off the best of a thousand articles and write a preface to what became *Around Cinemas*. Bertie now had his own publishing firm, and, over the next few years, put out a number of interesting titles. Among them were a second volume of *Around Cinemas*, a selection of Agate's essays called *Thus To Revisit*, ('Thus to reprint', commented Jock drily), and May's admirable study of Sarah Bernhardt. Unfortunately the books Bertie published were too good – or rather, he neglected to include in his lists the popular rubbish needed to sustain his quality output. He had, moreover, started his firm at the worst possible time, immediately after the war, when paper was short and money scarce. Soon the imprint of Home & Van Thal went under, though not before it had produced quite a few memorable books. Bertie did not repine, nor did he indulge in useless regret, for his bland, almost somnolent exterior hid a character of steel. How otherwise could he have handled Agate? Both publisher and author were on excellent terms and even invented a crazy Franco-German lingo in which they telephoned arrangements for lunch at the Ivy:-

Bertie. Bonjour, jeune homme. Lunchen sie?
J. A. Danke sehr. Beaucoup plaisir. Où?
Bertie Au Lierre.
J. A. Entendu. Um wieviel heure?
Bertie Two sharp!

Soon after Agate's birthday Leo fell ill. He refused, grumpily, to rest, and went on typing out articles full of glorious misprints. At last he gave up, retired amid snuffling protests to bed, and died in his sleep on the 26 September, 1945. His drawl, his screech, his Viennese courtesies were never to be heard again in Queen Alexandra Mansions, and no more were he and Agate to stage those high-pitched squabbles that reminded one observer of a Hinge and Bracket before their time. The wizened little body was cremated while through the open door of the chapel came autumn sunshine and the twitter of a few late birds. The organ played the adagio from the 'Pathétique' Sonata, there was a reading of 'Fear no more the heat o' the sun,' and the music ended with the slow movement from the *Emperor* concerto – Beethoven and Shakespeare, as Leo had said he always wanted. 'Smike' broke his holiday to bring a posy and to join Agate, George Mathew and the few other mourners in the pew. *The Times* published Agate's affectionate tribute to his old friend in the same issue as, by coincidence, an obituary of Bartok, the composer Leo most hated.

Agate missed Leo horribly and thought of him every day, of their bickerings, of their arguments, of Leo's unbearable habits . . . and then of his fun, his wit, the measure of genius that made him an adorable companion. A little cheerfulness broke through when he was elected President of the Hackney Horse Society, an honour he had coveted since youth. He invited to luncheon in his flat one of those hearty, horsey Brigadiers associated with that world. As they came out into Grape Street he remembered he had left his walking-stick behind. 'Get through to my man and tell him to bring my stick,' he rumbled at the hall porter. Within earshot of the bristling Brigadier the porter picked up the house phone and trilled: 'Is that you, Emma? She's forgotten her wand again!'

In the hot summer of 1946 he went for the last time on a journey to France. The Cannes Film Festival, originally planned for 1939 but postponed because of the war, had opened at last, and Monsieur Agate, *collaborateur distingué au Sunday Times*, was invited to attend. He set off with an actor crony, Wilfred Rouse, who proved to be an excellent travelling companion fully aware that a ten-shilling tip saved a pound's worth of discomfort. (The pound was then worth four hundred and seventy-two francs, an amount which, even before

General de Gaulle subtracted the two inflationary zeroes, was substantial.) On the train from Calais to Paris Agate gulped with nostalgia at the horse-drawn carts in the fields, the coquetry of the villas, the sudden glimpses of magnificent châteaux, the succulence of the dining-car meals which could not possibly be anything but French. At Amiens he remembered that he had last seen the town in 1915 and enjoyed a wonderful shave there. He went to bed in Paris thinking of the Calais porter who carried their luggage, the most Michaelangelesque ruffian he had ever seen and one fit to make Lady Wishfort dream.

Next day they entrained for Cannes. At Avignon the screech of Willie Rouse's crazy voice singing Massenet's *Ah, fuyez, douce image!* failed to stifle a sombre remembrance of things past, for here, in Provence, he had spent the sun-filled years of the Great War, and here he had married his pretty French girl and here divorced. In Marseille, though, the mood vanished, and by the time they reached Cannes he recovered his usual pugnacious form to do battle with Festival officials who had bungled the hotel arrangements. Throughout the oven-like heat he preserved collar, tie and bowler, obstinately refusing to give way to Southern *dolce far niente*. On the second night, in a dive called the Zanzi-Bar, he entertained the company until two o'clock – *patronne* and nondescript husband, two tarts, an obvious gigolo, a flower-seller who looked like Marie Lloyd and a young man who might have been Yvonne Printemps' brother – with some of his best stories told in a wealth of slang which, he afterwards realized, must have been very out-of-date, being chiefly culled from Zola. Next morning Wilfred told him he had engaged Yvonne Printemps' brother as secretary at twenty pounds a week and that the boy was on his way round to sign the contract.

That afternoon he went to the Villa Sardou in Le Cannet where Rachel died. For years he had dreamed of such a visit. There he saw the marble bed, the drawing-room with decanters and glasses used by Rachel, the long dark drawing-room with the firmament depicted on its ceiling, the stained glass windows, the fireplace in the shape of a marble tree trunk and the whole room still black with smoke. An old lady of great age showed the visitors round. 'There is Rachel's deathbed,' she said. 'Please do not touch it!' Outside, an extraordinary jumble of terraces and balconies and towers suggested a baroque version of Tower Bridge with a hint of Mr Wemmick's castle in *Bleak House*.

The Film Festival staggered on in a welter of inefficiency. A Mexican film of lunar idiocy took up one whole evening in an almost empty hall, and at midnight the projectionist started showing Hitchcock's new picture *Notorious* with reels in the wrong order. Agate fled to the Zanzi-Bar where a furious political argument boiled up. Suddenly the barman rapped on the counter. 'Ladies and gentlemen, I have sad news to report. Raimu died this evening.' The dispute was submerged in general grief.

The next five days were spent waiting for a homeward-bound aeroplane. Often it was announced, and as often it was cancelled after hour-long waits at the airport. 'Wilfred,' said Agate in his best Lady Bracknell tones, 'we have already missed five, if not six, 'planes. To miss any more might expose us to comment on the runway.' The heat now was so intense that he paddled cautiously in the sea and gave up wearing a collar, replacing it with a light scarf which made him resemble an elderly Sid Field – or, as a friend called him, 'Slasher Guitry'.

The aeroplane finally arrived but went no further than Paris, where, having no more money left, he sat in the doorway of his little hotel and treated himself to the free entertainment of what he called the 'Jean Gabinerie' of the French street. It was Monday and everything was closed. He happened to see his actor friend Eric Portman who gave him a glass of champagne, and Harold Nicolson who also treated him kindly and made him feel less like an orphan of the storm. The French government, or at least that department concerned with the Film Festival, eventually produced air tickets. Wilfred, too, produced a thousand francs which Agate did not know he had, and they lunched thankfully on ham sandwiches and champagne. The plane landed at Croydon, and the first words he saw breathed the spirit of England,

Home, Beauty and Dr Johnson. They were 'Barclay Perkins, Ltd.'

What heaven, he thought, to be back in foggy Holborn where a man could work undistracted by the enervating sunshine and heat of Provence. He was, moreover, lucky indeed to have a job at all. Some twelve months previously he had been obliged to leave, precipitately and without his trousers, a male brothel near Gray's Inn Road on the occasion of a police raid. This was the sort of scrape in which he often found himself, and it wouldn't have mattered had not news of the escapade somehow reached *The Sunday Times*. Lord Kemsley was appalled. He probably believed, with King George V, that men like that shot themselves, and he resolved to sack Agate. In his place, he said, he would appoint Harold Hobson, then Agate's deputy. 'Hobson's all right,' Kemsley declared. 'Hobson has a daughter. Let's have Hobson.' It was pointed out to the irate Lord that Agate was without a doubt the head of his profession and that, in any case, many great men had been homosexuals. Kemsley simmered. In the end, with reluctance, he let himself be persuaded, and Agate was safe.

Another incident soon afterwards helped to ensure Hobson's succession. Agate fell ill and notified the editor, W. W. Hadley, that he had asked a friend to write his Sunday article for him. Normally a mild man, Hadley exploded to Hobson: 'This is intolerable. I have rung James and told him that he can have as much time off as he wants, but his successor will be chosen, not by him, but by me.' Agate saw clearly how the land lay. From then on his attitude toward Hobson was deferential. He made flattering mentions of him in his articles, and puzzled Hobson, who did not then know what had gone on behind the scenes, with his obsequious behaviour. They met frequently for lunch at the Ivy, and Agate would ask him, anxiously, who he thought was the greatest living drama critic, hoping that Hobson would name the critic of *The Sunday Times*. He told Hobson how he longed for the recognition of a knighthood, not so much for himself as for the honour of his profession, since at that time every other branch of the theatre had been so distinguished and only the drama critics were ignored. As the champagne flowed he grew confidential. The size and colour of his testicles, he observed to Hobson, had in recent years given him concern. They were, he claimed, as large as billiard balls and had taken on a shade of bright orange. What could be the reason? he wondered.

Agate's uncharacteristic humility sprang from his fear that Hobson had it in his power to ruin him and that his friendship must be secured at all costs. He need not have worried, for Hobson was, and is, a Christian and a man of honour. Nonetheless, terrified of the danger in which he stood, Agate committed a brutal act of treachery. It had always been understood that Jock Dent would succeed him at *The Sunday Times*. Agate had told everybody this and encouraged Jock to think so himself. Yet he now wrote a letter to his old friend Sydney Carroll, an influential adviser to Lord Kemsley, in which he stated firmly that he wanted to be succeeded by Harold Hobson. Jock was left high and dry. The letter did Jock great harm and was to change entirely the course of his career. Illness, and the desperate urge for survival, drove Agate to betray the friend whom he had loved most dearly of all.

iii
THE VASTY HALL OF DEATH

'Tell me, James, will your *Ego 9* be Choral?'

LEO PAVIA

'Mr Agate,' said a Tax Inspector once, 'with all the money you have made you ought to leave nine rows of houses.' 'Mr Inspector,' Agate replied, 'with all the money I have spent I am going to leave nine volumes of Ego.'

Early in 1946 he had written about a quarter of *Ego 9*. He decided to complete it so that it could be published on his seventieth birthday in September, 1947. It would, he informed his friends, be the last of the series. The machine was running down, and he felt that to end with a ninth volume would round off the work and leave it as a satisfactory whole. At the end of the year he made his annual word count and found that it came out at 264,000. Turning up past records he was able to estimate that between 1921 and 1946 he had achieved a total of well over seven million words. 'Whaur's your Balzac and Bennett noo? he crowed, adding, self-defensively, 'In the scales of quantity, not quality, idiot!'

His old extravagance flourished. Taxis were kept waiting for hours, bottles of champagne and cigars were consumed by the dozen, writs and tax demands piled up in forgotten corners. At the age of sixty-eight he became infatuated with a dashing G.I., butch, clean-cut, irresistible in his dapper uniform, who on returning to the USA sent him food parcels that were eagerly devoured by the austerity-oppressed inmates of Queen Alexandra Mansions. In the theatre he 'discovered' the short-lived comedian Sid Field and evoked Dan Leno, Grock and Charlie Chaplin in his attempt to define the talent of this gifted Cockney. Having launched Ken Tynan he next concerned himself with the young writer Peter Forster, who announced that he intended to follow Agate on *The Sunday Times*. After military service, Agate promised, he would find him a job as a fledgling critic.

His asthma was so bad now that he found it difficult to walk more than a few yards, and the sound of his strangled wheezing, like that of some animal in torment, made passers-by look round in astonishment. He did not dare broadcast 'live' for fear that the excitement might bring on a heart attack. Stairs were beyond him, and he could only mount them on all-fours. Early in 1947 his doctor sent him to bed for a fortnight. A male nurse arrived, fresh from a job in a lunatic asylum. 'You'll be the first patient in five years I've been able to turn my back on,' he said. 'Don't be too sure!' croaked Agate from under the blankets.

By March he was allowed out for 'a sort of bath-chair existence on foot.' The saintly Gwen Chenhalls took him for drives in her car and gave him a kill-or-cure luncheon: anchovies, lobster salad, treacle tart and coffee laced with brandy. She brought two glass ornaments from the dining-room, put them on the kitchen table at which he sat and announced: 'Claridges!' He had never thought much of women: they were good only as nurses, cooks, laundresses, typists and governesses. A woman barrister was ridiculous, a woman doctor absurd, a woman composer ludicrous. Gwen made him revise his opinion. She was the ideal ministering angel, not too sympathetic and therefore bracing.

Every day Gwen made lunch for him at Queen Alexandra Mansions. The newspapers for which he wrote sent generous presents to the invalid, and from his publisher came bottles of champagne. Francis L. Sullivan, an actor of enormous girth who specialised in portraying sinister Gestapo officers and Jaggers-type lawyers, called to see him, his pockets bulging with eggs and grapes. *Ego 8* was published and a review by Elizabeth Bowen perked him up: 'I think Mr Agate should stand out as the prominent man who has talked least nonsense about the atomic bomb.'

In April he started writing for *The Sunday Times* again with a pungent essay on Rachel à-propos of an inferior novel by March Cost. Those seven hundred words caught the essence of a player whose legend had haunted him all his life. Less than six months ago he had stood by the bed on which she died, and the atmosphere of the room, where the furniture remained untouched, was with him still.

On Whit-Monday he looked forward to the fifteenth birthday of his *Ego* diary. When he began it in 1932 he had already known the best minds on the *Manchester Guardian* and in Fleet Street. He had spent forty-five years looking at great acting and hearing great music. Of Balzac and Maupassant he had read every word, and of Zola nearly all. He was about to make acquaintance with his hundredth golf-course and had exhibited harness ponies at half the horse shows in England. At the age of fifty-five he possessed the vigour of a young man able to work fourteen hours a day. Four of those hours a day over fifteen years had been devoted to *Ego*, and that was the equivalent of two and a half years working round the clock. His motive was not entirely vanity: might it not also be a desire to repay some of the delight the world had given him? By the 2 June he would have finished it.

A few days afterward he invited Jock to lunch. 'The Ivy at

one, and not a minute later,' he commanded. 'I have to see a film at two.' As always he was late, and Jock, thrifty with his time, occupied the wait by drafting an article. It was an obituary of Agate which the *Manchester Guardian* had asked him to prepare, for, like vultures scenting death, newspapers look ahead and are rarely caught out. As he wrote the last words of his piece Agate appeared, grey-faced, at the door. 'Fifty minutes late, I know, but it takes me a time to dress,' he said. 'What are you writing there, Jock – *my obituary, I suppose*?'

Jock, without denying it, shuffled his papers away and the meal was ordered. When the soup arrived Agate said: 'Come, boy – as one journalist to another – let me read what you think of me!' It was an agitating moment, for Jock knew that, with Agate's fear of death, he might then and there have had his fatal heart attack. He handed over the article and ate his soup with a trembling hand. The obituary, fair and generous, brought a beam to Agate's Rowlandson face. When he came to the list of his enthusiasms which Jock had mentioned he entreated him to include golf. He gave the paper back and remarked: 'I'm proud, Jock, to have that written about me, and you've written it well!' He changed the subject and it was never referred to again.

On the 2 June, as planned, he made his last entry in *Ego 9*. The Inland Revenue were still badgering him for £940 within a week and threatening to take away everything in his flat except the bed he lay on. He did not worry. Something would turn up, it always did, and all that mattered was to complete his diary. He quoted Montaigne: 'The deadest deaths are the best.' His whole body cried out for sleep, but the incessant pain of asthma and dropsy kept him in wakeful agony. He could not read because of the fatigue and did not play the gramophone much because the noise hurt, but he could sit and nurse the records, hearing them, as it were, in his head. People telephoned, sent him fruit and tried to amuse him with jokes. His room was as full of flowers as Sarah Bernhardt's *loge* on a first night. He had a vast amount to be thankful for, and he was determined not to grouse.

One day, in spite of the hot weather, he felt cold, icy cold, and he begged Joseph the Gibraltarian to climb into his bed. They lay there, motionless, the older man shivering and squeezed up close to the young body in the attempt to warm his chilled limbs. Yet his blood still ran feebly, he quivered and shook, and it seemed as if his flesh was at last beginning to give up the struggle.

Exactly a fortnight after his lunch with Jock – it was Friday, the 6 June – he was alone in the flat. Joseph and the houseboy had gone to see a film, and, longing for human contact, he rang up George Felton Mathew. George arrived late in the evening and Agate opened the door to him wearing the crumpled shirt he always put on for bed. They talked a little, and then Agate lumbered back along the passage to his bedroom and, he hoped, sleep. '*Dear* George!' he whispered.

A few minutes later George went to join him. Something was obstructing the bedroom door, and when he finally managed to push it open he found Agate's body lying on the floor, his shirt rucked up, his mouth in a ghastly rictus. His heart must have given way round about eleven o'clock.

George rang Agate's solicitor, who told him he must stay in the flat and sleep there overnight to guard against pilfering. The body was heaved up on the bed, and Joseph returned to see Agate on his back, his blank eyes staring at the ceiling. Someone hammered noisily at the front door. George opened it and there stood 'Smike', who with tears pouring down his cheeks wailed: 'Let me in! I must see 'im. I want to kiss 'im!' The news quickly spread and other callers insisted on entering, among them a barrow boy who claimed acquaintance. Despite the vigilant presence of George, Joseph and the houseboy, at some time during the night Agate's gold watch vanished.

'The Hazlitt of our time,' said the *Manchester Guardian* headline announcing his death. *The Times*, as usual hedging its bets with cautious dexterity, observed: 'Immensely prolific, he often wrote entertainingly on a broomstick and illuminatingly on a masterpiece, and it may be that a residue of his work will have lasting value.' Of the *Ego* books it added: 'What is most engaging in these volumes is the vividly emergent picture of a man boyishly enchanted with the astonishing romance of his professional career.' *The Sunday Times* carried a tribute by Harold Hobson – 'I read him always with admiration and envious despair' – and homage from Lilian Braithwaite, C. B. Cochran, Noël Coward, Ernest Newman and Dilys Powell. J. B. Priestley, with whom Agate clashed violently on many occasions, remarked: 'We always suspected we had an affection for the man; and now, too late, we know.' The *Daily Express* printed an obituary which Agate himself had written for the file, at Arthur Christiansen's prompting, some years ago. It ended: 'But the subject is inexhaustible, like the man himself. His death eclipses the gaiety of newspapers. His enemies will miss him.'

The public-spirited George Bishop, who over the years had developed into a past-master of such occasions, organised a memorial service with the aid of the producer Charles La Trobe. He arranged a time and place, and telephoned the news to the Haymarket Theatre where La Trobe was then working on *The Heiress*. The call was taken by the stage door keeper, an institution only a little less venerable than the theatre itself, he being close on his ninetieth birthday and renowned for the Surrealistic quality of the messages he passed on. The note he gave to La Trobe read: 'Mr A. Gate will be at Sir Martin Fields at 11.30 and would like you to join him.'

And so on the 9 June, 1947, the service was held at St Martin-in-the-Fields off Trafalgar Square. Agate's old Savage friend Mark Hambourg played two Chopin preludes, Olive Groves sang 'I Know That My Redeemer Liveth', and there was music also by Elgar and Beethoven. Franklyn Dyall and Leslie Banks read lessons and passages from Bunyan and Shakespeare. The intermittent stillness was broken by half-stifled sobs from the girls who typed Agate's manuscripts.

He had asked to be buried next to Peter, the caretaker's son at Queen Alexandra Mansions, but a problem arose. Peter's grave lay in the 'cheap' section of Hendon Cemetery, and Agate's family objected. A compromise suggested itself: Agate's tomb was placed in the 'expensive' section as near as possible to the boundary which divided it from the 'cheap'.

The highest-paid journalist of his time was found to have

left the modest sum of £2,522.17s. 1d. Probate figures, as everyone knows, partake of the ideal rather than the factual, and in Agate's case the bulk of the money derived from an insurance policy which his solicitor, despite protests, had taken out for him some years ago. Even so, immediate debts swallowed everything up, and the legatees were fortunate to have anything at all. Did the Savage Club ever receive his marble statuette of Sarah Bernhardt? Did it get the canes of Charlie Chaplin and George Robey, and did 'the Nation', as he phrased it in his will, become the recipient of Hogarth's walking stick? George Mathew, the inheritor of his non-theatrical library and Sheraton book-case, was obliged to pay for them. Neither did he benefit from the hundred pounds left him in gratitude 'for many years of devotion on his part.' Forty years later Agate's medical bill and numerous other debts remain unsettled. The Inland Revenue, which is alone of all creditors immortal, still pounces on the tiny royalties that dribble in from time to time.

Jock survived until 1978 and left an even smaller amount than Agate. After the *Manchester Guardian* he became drama critic for fifteen years on *The News Chronicle*, and when that newspaper crashed in 1960 he worked as a writer at large. Editors knew him as a reliable contributor who would always turn in a thoughtful article, well phrased and neatly expressed. It would be untrue to say that he did not fulfil Agate's high hopes of him, for he lacked his old master's overpowering ambition. In any case, Agate's final betrayal had robbed him of the glittering prizes. 'It served me right in some ways,' he used to say, wryly. He bore no malice, for his admiration of Agate the writer outweighed any resentment he might have felt at being so harshly treated. When Anthony Curtis visited him in his last illness and asked about the notorious incident, he simply replied without bitterness: 'Och, it was my own fault. I stayed with him far too long.' And perhaps his final verdict on Agate best sums it all up: 'No great shakes as a man but always, and even now, very great shakes as a witty and influential critic.'

THE WORKS OF JAMES AGATE

Theatre Criticism

Buzz, Buzz! Collins, 1918
Alarums and Excursions, Grant Richards, 1922
At Half Past Eight, Jonathan Cape, 1923
The Contemporary Theatre, 1923. Chapman and Hall, 1924
The Contemporary Theatre, 1924. Chapman and Hall, 1925
The Contemporary Theatre, 1925. Chapman and Hall, 1926
A Short View of The English Stage, 1900–1926. Herbert Jenkins, 1926
Playgoing. Jarrolds, 1927
The Contemporary Theatre, 1926. Chapman and Hall, 1927
Their Hour Upon The Stage. Mandarin Press, Cambridge, 1930
My Theatre Talks. Arthur Barker, 1933
First Nights. Ivor Nicholson and Watson, 1934
More First Nights. Gollancz, 1937
The Amazing Theatre. Harrap, 1939
Brief Chronicles. Jonathan Cape, 1943
Red Letter Nights. Jonathan Cape, 1944
Immoment Toys. Jonathan Cape, 1945
The Contemporary Theatre, 1944 and 1945. Harrap, 1946
Oscar Wilde and The Theatre. Curtain Press, 1947.

Film Criticism

Around Cinemas. Home and Van Thal, 1946
Around Cinemas, Second Series. Home and Van Thal, 1948

General Essays

(including theatre also)
L. of C. Constable, 1917
Fantasies and Impromptus. Collins, 1923
On An English Screen. John Lane The Bodley Head, 1924

White Horse and Red Lion. Collins, 1924
Agate's Folly. Chapman and Hall, 1925
The Common Touch. Chapman and Hall, 1926
Kingdoms For Horses. Gollancz, 1936
Bad Manners. John Mills, 1938
Express and Admirable. Hutchinson, 1941
Thursdays and Fridays. Hutchinson, 1941
Noblesse Oblige. Home and Van Thal, 1944
Thus To Revisit. Home and Van Thal, 1947

Autobiography
Ego. Hamish Hamilton, 1935
Ego 2. Gollancz, 1936
Ego 3. Harrap, 1938
Ego 4. Harrap, 1940
Ego 5. Harrap, 1942
Ego 6. Harrap, 1944
Ego 7. Harrap, 1945
Ego 8. Harrap, 1947
Ego 9. Harrap, 1948
A Shorter Ego. Volume One. Harrap, 1946
A Shorter Ego. Volume Two. Harrap, 1946
A Shorter Ego. Volume Three. Harrap, 1949

Self-Selected Anthologies
Essays of Today and Yesterday. James Agate. Harrap, 1926
Here's Richness! Foreword by Sir Osbert Sitwell. Harrap, 1942

Posthumous Anthologies
James Agate. An Anthology. Edited by Herbert Van Thal with an introduction by Alan Dent. Rupert Hart-Davis, 1961.
The Selective Ego. Edited by Tim Beaumont. Harrap, 1976.

Anthologies
The English Dramatic Critics, 1660–1932. Arthur Barker, 1932
Speak For England. Hutchinson, 1939

These Were Actors. Extracts from a Newspaper Cutting Book, 1811–1833. Hutchinson, 1943
Those Were The Nights. Hutchinson, 1947
Words I Have Lived With. A Personal Choice. Hutchinson, 1949

Biography
Rachel. Gerald Howe, 1928

Novels
Responsibility. Grant Richards, 1919/Hutchinson, 1943
Blessed Are The Rich. Leonard Parsons, 1924/Hutchinson, 1944
Gemel In London. Chapman and Hall, 1928/Hutchinson, 1945

Play
Blessed Are The Rich. Unpublished. 1928

BIBLIOGRAPHY

Albaret, Céleste. Monsieur Proust. Souvenirs recueillis par Georges Belmont. Robert Laffont, 1973

Bax, Clifford. Some I Knew Well. Phoenix House, 1951

Bennett, Arnold. Journals, 1896–1928. Cassell, 1932–1934

Bennett, Arnold. The Evening Standard Years. Books and Persons 1926–1931. Edited and introduced by Andrew Mylett. Chatto and Windus, 1974

Bishop, George. My Betters. Heinemann, 1957

Cardus, Neville. Autobiography. Collins, 1975

Cardus, Neville. Conversations With Cardus. Edited by Robin Daniels. Gollancz, 1976

Curtis, Anthony. James Agate Centenary: radio programme, BBC Radio 4. Producer John Theocharis. September, 1977

Curtis, Anthony. Alan Dent. Obituary appreciation. The Sunday Telegraph, 24 December, 1978

Dent, Alan. Preludes and Studies. Macmillan, 1942

Dent, Alan. James Agate's Ego. Stage and Screen, Summer, 1947

Dent, Alan. Nocturnes and Rhapsodies. Hamish Hamilton, 1950

Dent, Alan. Mrs Patrick Campbell. Museum Press, 1961

Dent, Alan. My Covent Garden. J. M. Dent, 1973

Devlin, Diana. A Speaking Part. Lewis Casson And The Theatre of His Time. Hodder and Stoughton, 1982

Douglas, Lord Alfred. Bernard Shaw and Alfred Douglas: A Correspondence. Edited by Mary Hyde. John Murray, 1982

Hart-Davis, Rupert. Hugh Walpole. Macmillan, 1952

Harwood, Ronald. Sir Donald Wolfit. Secker and Warburg, 1971

Hobson, Harold; Knightley, Philip; Russell, Leonard. The

Pearl of Days. An Intimate Memoir of The Sunday Times. Hamish Hamilton, 1972
Hobson, Harold. Indirect Journey. Weidenfeld and Nicolson, 1978
Lanchester, Elsa. Elsa Lanchester By Herself. Michael Joseph, 1983
Lucas, Audrey. E. V. Lucas. A Portrait. Methuen, 1939
MacQueen Pope, W. The Footlights Flickered. Herbert Jenkins, 1959
Melville, Alan. Merely Melville. Hodder and Stoughton, 1970
Nichols, Beverley. The Sweet and Twenties. Weidenfeld and Nicolson, 1958
Nichols, Beverley. The Unforgiving Minute. W. H. Allen, 1978
Pound, Reginald. Running Commentary. Rockliffe, 1946
Proust, Marcel. A la recherche du temps perdu. Vol 3: Le Temps Retrouvé. Gallimard/Pléiade, 1954
Sinden, Donald. A Touch of The Memoirs. Hodder and Stoughton, 1982
Swinnerton, Frank. Arnold Bennett. A Last Word. Heinemann, 1978
Van Thal, Herbert. The Tops of the Mulberry Trees. Allen and Unwin, 1971
Wilson, A. E. Theatre Guyed. The Baedeker of Thespia. Methuen, 1935
Wilson, A. E. Playgoer's Pilgrimage. Stanley Paul, 1948

INDEX